Managing Clinical Supervision

ETHICAL PRACTICE AND LEGAL RISK MANAGEMENT

Managing Clinical Supervision

ETHICAL PRACTICE AND LEGAL RISK MANAGEMENT

JANET ELIZABETH FALVEY, PhD, NCC

University of New Hampshire

with assistance in legal research from
TIMOTHY E. BRAY, MA

BROOKS/COLE

THOMSON LEARNING

Australia ◆ Canada ◆ Mexico ◆ Singapore ◆ Spain ◆ United Kingdom ◆ United States

BROOKS/COLE

THOMSON LEARNING

Acquisitions Editor: *Julie Martinez*
Marketing Team: *Caroline Concilla, Megan Hansen*
Editorial Assistant: *Cat Broz*
Project Editor: *Kim Svetich-Will*
Production Service: *Scratchgravel Publishing Services*
Manuscript Editor: *Frank Hubert*

Permissions Editor: *Sue Ewing*
Interior Design: *Anne Draus*
Cover Design: *Russ Stanton*
Art Editor: *Vernon Boes*
Print Buyer: *Nancy Panziera*
Compositor: *Scratchgravel Publishing Services*
Printing and Binding: *Webcom, Ltd*

For more information about this or any other Brooks/Cole product, contact:
BROOKS/COLE
511 Forest Lodge Road
Pacific Grove, CA 93950 USA
www.brookscole.com
1-800-423-0563 (Thomson Learning Academic Resource Center)

Printed in Canada

10   9   8   7   6   5   4   3   2   1

Library of Congress Cataloging-in-Publication Data
Falvey, Janet Elizabeth.
    Managing clincial supervision : ethical practice and legal risk management / Janet Elizabeth Falvey ; with assistance in legal research from Timothy E. Bray.
        p. cm.
    Includes bibliographical references and index.
    ISBN 0-534-53074-5 (alk. paper)
    1. Medicine—Study and teaching—Supervision. 2. Medical personnel—In-service training. 3. Mentoring in medicine. 4. Clinical competence. I. Title.

R834 .F34 2001
610'.71'55—dc21
                                                                        00-066740

Dedication

To mentors and colleagues for their support and challenge
throughout my clinical career

To two decades of supervisees for their fundamental trust
in the benefit of our reflective processes

To Rick and Jeni for their patience and affection
in standing my watches during creation of this text

Contents

Tables

Figures

Legal Case Analyses

Preface

How I conduct supervision has changed considerably over the past decade. The growing professionalism and empirical base supporting supervision as a clinical specialty have certainly aided my understanding of developmental processes of both supervisors and myself. Clinical work that led colleagues and me to develop the Focused Risk Management Supervision System (FoRMSS) (Falvey, Caldwell, & Cohen, 2002) alerted me to the need for a thoughtful, organized and accountable approach to overseeing the work of trainees and junior colleagues. I now think about, plan for, and document what occurs in the supervisory process to a much greater degree.

While supervision remains an important and rewarding collegial activity, it no longer can be relegated to a relatively unstructured discussion of those cases that our supervisees choose to present. I have become more sensitized to the numerous ethical and legal responsibilities supervisors have to oversee supervisees' work in ways that consistently ensure client welfare, promote supervisees' professional development, implement institutional policies, and protect the safety of the general public. Given that many of us supervise or are supervised by members of related disciplines, I have become convinced of the need for an interdisciplinary approach to supervision. Finally, through my work with field supervisors training graduate students, I am increasingly concerned about the clinical and managerial risks supervisors incur in overseeing the treatment of clients with whom they seldom have direct contact.

These realities became poignant in 1995, when my multidisciplinary peer supervision group began to discuss a particularly difficult case. This client had a history of dissatisfaction with helping professionals and had filed an ethics complaint against a former therapist. While advising our colleague, we became increasingly concerned with risk management—not only hers in managing the case clinically, but our own potential liability in consulting with her. That concern led to a review of the supervision, legal, and ethical literature and to the development of a supervision organizer and risk management tool for clinical supervisors (Falvey et al., 2002).

That incident also became a prime motivation for this book. In their mission to enhance the professional development of their supervisees, supervisors are also responsible for adherence to the ethical codes, standards of conduct, legal statutes, and licensing regulations of each discipline represented in the supervision dyad or group. How can busy professionals succinctly organize and review these documents? How can we minimize our exposure to possible legal or ethical violations arising from our supervisory roles? Accountability, coupled with the need for efficient time management in high-stress environments, warrants the need for a compendium of resources to enhance the professional vigilance of supervisors. This book was thus conceived not as a review of how to *do* supervision, but rather as a guide to how supervisors from mental health disciplines can *manage* it in a responsible manner.

Similar to most clinicians, I highly value the case approach to clinical learning. This book is therefore organized around vignettes from an evolving therapy case. Maria's case involves several counselors from different disciplines as well as several clinical supervisors. Because supervision of this and many other cases occurs in a variety of remedial and developmental contexts, the terms *counseling, therapy,* and *psychotherapy* are used alternately throughout the book. Discussion of the vignettes highlights the existing standards of care for supervisors and identifies foreseeable risks that should guide these supervisors' decision-making processes. Where distinctions exist in accountability among ethical codes and supervisor standards across disciplines, they are noted. Landmark court decisions that currently or potentially affect supervisor liability are summarized from a legal perspective. Recommendations and risk management issues are presented at the end of each chapter as a quick reference for supervisors. The full texts of current supervisor ethical codes, standards of practice, and (where existing) supervisory guidelines for psychiatrists, psychologists, counselors, social workers, marriage and family therapists, and pastoral counselors are included as appendixes.

This book represents a concentrated examination of many issues that concern me and other clinical supervisors in the current context of our work. It could not have been accomplished without innumerable hours of collaboration with colleagues Carol Cohen and Christine Caldwell and without careful legal research by Timothy Bray, a candidate for Juris Doctor at Northeastern University School of Law. The patience and support of our families, and the validation and invaluable feedback from participants at our various workshops, have made the process truly enjoyable.

I hope that this text and the accompanying manual, *Documentation in Supervision: The Focused Risk Management Supervision System (FoRMSS),* will serve as pragmatic resources for advanced graduate students, faculty and internship site supervisors, and community supervisors across many settings and disciplines that provide counseling and mental health services to the public.

While our work at its best is least visible (Alonso, 1985), our impact as professional mentors and gatekeepers is profound. Using the guides available, let's examine more closely the context of clinical supervision.

I would like to acknowledge the following professionals for their thoughtful review and valuable comments: Penny Dahlen, University of Wyoming; Joan Gibson, State University of New York, Oswego; Bob Hayes, Borderline Productions; Samuel Knapp, Pennsylvania Psychological Association; Russ Miars, Portland State University; Susan Neufeldt, University of California, Santa Barbara; Kathy O'Byrne, California State University, Fullerton; Colin Ward, Winona State University; and Richard E. Watts, Baylor University.

Janet Elizabeth Falvey

Managing Clinical Supervision

ETHICAL PRACTICE AND LEGAL RISK MANAGEMENT

SUPERVISION AS CLINICAL MENTORSHIP

It's been a long day. Clients, staff meetings, supervising a trainee, listening to a colleague's crisis, hassles with the administration. The ride home is a chance to decompress, to sort out a collage of responses left over from these encounters. Thoughts diverge and feelings emerge as I process the afternoon. Will Mary follow up on my recommendation for a physical exam? I need to monitor this closely, as she reports headaches that are increasing in frequency and intensity. I'm worried about her impulse control when she feels this stressed—could she become more self-abusive? Does Brian's anxiety mask depression over the loss of his dad? His drinking concerns me, especially those weekend binges. I plan to confront this next week, but tend to become angry in the face of his denials. . . . I need to remember to talk to Sherry about this case; she's great with substance abuse issues. How are we ever going to reduce the 2-week waiting list with the new cutbacks and Jeremy leaving? I doubt they'll ever hire someone at the salary they're advertising. . . . That'll mean even more work for us. Which reminds me, Julie still isn't taking the initiative to organize that eating disorders group we discussed. Those clients need rapid intervention; we have to get that up and running. She has great facilitating skills, but may need more support from me to build her confidence. Maybe I should talk with her faculty supervisor about this. . . .

Sound familiar? It's not just about a busy schedule—each of these musings concerns clients' welfare, potentially even their lives. And my concerns are not simply the altruistic caring of a colleague, friend, or acquaintance. As a mental health professional, I have ethically and legally defined responsibilities—a duty of care—that demand careful consideration when interacting with clients, supervisees, colleagues, employers, and society at large. While not a guarantee against poor outcomes, that duty reflects the standard by which my actions are ultimately judged. This book was developed to assist supervisors in understanding that duty of care and its relationship to their professional practice.

OVERSIGHT OF CLINICAL PRACTICE

The practice and art (though now we are pointedly reminded to call it a business) of psychotherapy are paradoxically profound and mundane. Regardless of one's personal motivation to enter this field, our clinical work influences the lives of others—sometimes in extremely powerful, direct, and immediate ways (Pope & Vasquez, 1998). We address the essence of what it means to be human on a daily basis. Because we are as human as our clients and supervisees, clinicians bring their own instincts, sense of reality, and personal needs to bear on clinical decisions (Steinman, Richardson, & McEnroe, 1998). Formal training, supervision, and the wisdom that comes with experience hone these variables in favor of therapeutic competence. However, status as a mental health professional is increasingly accompanied by socially sanctioned templates for analyzing and responding to complex clinical situations. These templates include ethical codes, standards of practice, and legal mandates. They collectively represent the duty of care to which we are held accountable by our respective professions and by the public. They demand our attention.

Paying attention to this broader context of our work is difficult. It requires thoughtful, creative, and conscientious efforts to address competing demands, multiple perspectives, evolving situations, and the prospect of uncertain consequences (Pope & Vasquez, 1998). For the clinical supervisor, it calls for sensitivity to the various consumers of his or her advice: supervisees, clients, administrators, and community. Paying attention involves taking time before and between clients, staff meetings, and case supervision to think about the potential consequences of our decisions. My earlier homebound reflections suggest that responses to those clinical and supervisory challenges be framed with informed consent, confidentiality, reporting statutes, scope of practice, and supervisory parameters in mind. Paying attention is also predicated on maintaining a working familiarity with the relevant templates of our profession and with those of the professionals we supervise. Personal quality control minimizes judgment errors that can lead to clinical transgressions and professional liability.

Ethical standards and legal mandates are often viewed by practitioners as dry and abstract doctrines, but in fact, they are always evolving. They serve as heuristic decision guides based on colleagues' clinical dilemmas and their outcomes. They are derived from careful review of the particulars of professional practice issues placed within the larger context of social responsibility (Bennett, Bryant, VandenBos, & Greenwood, 1990). Rather than codifying clear-cut solutions, they clarify acceptable codes of conduct to manage the tensions embodied in helping relationships, where power, temptation, vulnerability, and impulsivity can undermine even the most altruistic intentions.

The chapters that follow examine professional standards, legal decisions, and ethical codes related to clinical supervision. Because supervision often occurs across disciplines, where both supervisor and supervisee are held to the standards of each other's profession, guidelines for the major mental health disciplines are presented and contrasted. Chapters are organized to provide succinct summaries of a supervisor's responsibilities and to highlight effective risk management practices. This book is thus not about how to *do* supervision, but rather how to *manage* it effectively.

Illustrations from an evolving therapy case will be presented to highlight the complexity of competent supervisory management. The Focused Risk Management Supervision System (FoRMSS) (Falvey, Caldwell, & Cohen, 2002) is introduced as a comprehensive format for supervisors to monitor and document their professional activities. This system "represents a new standard for supervision record keeping and benefits the entire therapy system by keeping supervision focused on its multiple levels from a variety of angles" (Bernard & Goodyear, 1998, p. 219). Although discussions of common supervisory responsibilities and dilemmas in the following chapters cannot substitute for one's careful reflection on the factors involved in specific circumstances, they do consolidate current ethical and legal guidelines to facilitate supervisory decision making.

ANCIENT ART, EMERGING SPECIALTY

Natural healers of the mind, soul, and heart have been consulted in all cultures throughout human existence. Over the past century, these roles have become formalized in many countries through the evolution of professional guilds in psychiatry, psychology, social work, mental health and school counseling, marriage and family therapy, and other specialty areas. The current practice of counseling and psychotherapy has been increasingly restricted to practitioners of these professions, for which considerable training and formal credentialing are required.

Psychotherapy is not a trade that can be acquired solely in the classroom. We start by seeking knowledge from books, theories, and professors. From them, we gain access to the history, evolution, norms, and science of the helping professions. But it is our clinical supervisors and struggling clients who ultimately become the most notable mentors in the art and craft of our trade. Learning to be therapeutic takes time—time that is paid for, step by step, through trial and error and feedback from clients and supervisors. Who among us doesn't recall anguishing over clinical dilemmas during our apprenticeships? Whether in our first internship or as fully licensed professionals, we have all experienced the sobering weight of making clinical decisions when the rules and outcomes are uncertain and our client's welfare hangs in the balance. Supervisors are generally our first line of defense against succumbing to the myriad of personal, clinical, ethical, and legal challenges inherent in psychotherapy practice.

All mental health disciplines view supervision as a core aspect of clinical training, requiring from 1 to 5 years of supervised practice to attain eligibility for professional credentialing (Rich, 1993; Sumerall et al., 1998). Although described as an anachronism in contemporary culture due to its reliance on oral tradition and the intimate one-to-one passing on of clinical knowledge (Jacobs, David, & Meyer, 1995), supervision remains an integral requirement of preprofessional internships and many clinical positions. It has, in the words of one writer, attained a "cultural presence" in the mental health field (Hess, 1998).

Supervision spans the history of many arts, trades, and professions. It is the fundamental way that people initiate others who seek to be trained in their field of expertise. Modern supervision emerged from guilds formed during the Middle Ages in European cities, where skilled workers in a trade banded together to control working conditions and foster business (Schroeder, 1995). It was customary for these guilds to accept a certain number of apprentices each year, usually for a 3-year training period. Master craftspeople were required to treat apprentices as their own offspring and guide them to adulthood (Carroll, 1999). The apprentice in return ran errands, opened and closed the shop, and worked faithfully to learn the master's trade. At the end of this training period, apprentices demonstrated their skill through a final piece of work—a masterpiece—to be accepted into the guild.

Guilds were very powerful in protecting members' rights and the products of their trade. Over time, they forced lords to share their wealth through charters granting them free access to roads and bridges and exemption from taxes—in effect, becoming the first middle classes. Even today, we experience the power of mental health guilds in the United States. They shape the educational and credentialing requirements of new members. They establish ethical codes and standards to guide clinical practice. They lobby in government venues to influence public policy and expand member access to client populations. In the current climate of managed care, they are politically active in protecting consumer rights and obtaining third-party reimbursement for their respective members.

Clinical supervisors are the gatekeepers of these mental health guilds (Adelson, 1995; Welfel, 1998a). They have been likened to professional parents whose social mandate is to understand timeless truths, communicate them to the present generation of psychotherapists, and enlarge upon them for the future (Alonso, 1985). Supervisors guide the internship experiences of all mental health trainees. They establish the baseline for competent and ethical practice in professional settings. They provide pivotal references to students in clinical training programs, to applicants for licensure, and to practitioners seeking employment or promotion. Some states mandate the presence of clinical supervisors on site during service delivery (Koocher & Keith-Spiegel, 1998). Ethics boards and legal doctrines hold supervisors ultimately responsible for the welfare of their supervisees' clients (Corey, Corey, & Callanan, 1998; Hassenfield, 1987; Pope & Vasquez, 1998).

ASSUMED VERSUS ASSESSED COMPETENCE

Yet despite their singularly important charge, clinical supervisors are seldom trained and infrequently credentialed for this role by their disciplines (Watkins, 1997b). Historically considered an extension of clinical practice, supervisory methods were often extrapolated from major theories of counseling and psychotherapy. In fact, expertise as a clinician was frequently the sole rationale for promotion to supervisory roles (Borders & Leddick, 1987; Falvey, 1987). Without formal training, supervisors relied heavily on recall of their own (similarly untrained) supervisors as models when mentoring their junior colleagues. This led to characteristic training errors perpetuated across generations of clinicians (Alonso, 1985; Powell, 1993; Welch, 1999):

◆ confusing supervision with case management and thus focusing disproportionately on the client's needs at the expense of supervisee development
◆ relying on one's clinical skills in supervision, thereby assuming the stance of counselor with supervisees
◆ adopting a laissez-faire attitude in which supervision occurs on a sporadic basis and is relegated to quasi-casual conversations about cases
◆ using supervisory power to inappropriately require the supervisee to adhere to one's own theory of psychotherapy

Unfortunately, every clinician currently in the field can probably name at least one supervisor who fits the foregoing descriptions. Although there are now numerous models and a research base supporting supervisory practice as a clinical specialty, many practitioners continue to receive and deliver supervision through this bootstrapping approach.

Sparked by expanded internship requirements, training program accreditation standards, and increasing accountability demands, numerous supervision models and empirical studies emerged during the 1980s (Bernard & Goodyear, 1998; Ellis, Ladany, Krengel, & Schult, 1996). In particular, the developmental and social role models of supervision heralded a growing awareness of the need for supervisory training and practice guidelines (Holloway, 1999). Although there still remains a paucity of theory and research on the training of supervisors, since the late 1980s, many disciplines have developed specific criteria for supervisory practice.

The professions that account for the largest proportion of clinical supervisors have, ironically, been the slowest to establish standards. The American Psychiatric Association (ApA) has yet to develop supervisor guidelines, even though it is recognized as a major venue for clinical teaching (Rodenhauser, 1995; Whitman & Jacobs, 1998). The American Psychological Association (APA) similarly does not credential supervisors, despite several surveys revealing that over half of licensed psychologists conduct clinical supervision on a regular basis (Norcross, Prochaska, & Farber, 1993; Osipow & Fitzgerald, 1986). The Association of State and Provincial Psychology Boards (ASPPB), which advises state credentialing bodies on various practice issues in psychology, published their first "Supervision Guidelines" for psychologists supervising doctoral and nondoctoral clinicians in 1998 (Appendix A).

Other disciplines have made more substantial contributions to the emergence of clinical supervision as a specialty area. The American Association for Marriage and Family Therapy (AAMFT) was the first to formalize supervisor training, developing standards as early as 1971 and establishing an "approved supervisor" designation in 1983. They regularly update their "Responsibilities and Guidelines for AAMFT Approved Supervisors and Supervisors-in-Training" (Appendix F). The American Association of Pastoral Counselors (AAPC) has for decades included two membership levels (fellow and diplomate) that conduct supervisory activities as stipulated in the "AAPC Supervision Standards" (Appendix G). The American Counseling Association (ACA) adopted the "ACES Standards for Counseling Supervisors" in 1989 (Appendix B), and the Association for Counselor Education and Supervision (ACES) published their first "Ethical Guidelines for Counseling Supervisors" in 1993 (Appendix C). This was followed a year later by the National Association of Social Workers (NASW) "Guidelines for Clinical Social Work Supervision" (Appendix E). The National Board for Certified Counselors (NBCC) published "Standards for the Ethical Practice of Supervision" in 1998 (Appendix D).

Recognition of supervision as a specialty through professional certification is emerging as well. Several states (Alabama, South Carolina, Texas) currently license counseling or clinical supervisors (Borders & Cashwell, 1992; Guest & Dooley, 1999). The following professional organizations offer national credentialing as a clinical supervisor:

NBCC APPROVED CLINICAL SUPERVISOR

National Board for Certified Counselors, Inc.
3 Terrace Way, Suite D
Greensboro, NC 27403-3660
(336) 547-0607 (phone) (336) 547-0017 (fax)

AAMFT APPROVED SUPERVISOR

> The American Association for Marriage and Family Therapy
> 1133 15th Street, NW, Suite 300
> Washington, DC 20005-2710
> (202) 452-0109 (phone) (202) 223-2329 (fax)

AAPC CERTIFIED SUPERVISOR

> American Association of Pastoral Counselors
> 9504A Lee Highway
> Fairfax, VA 22031-2303
> (703) 385-6967 (phone) (703) 352-7725 (fax)

BUT ARTISTS DON'T GET SUED!

A work of art may fall short of its creator's aspirations. It may fail to move its audience. It may disappoint or even revolt the beholder. But the artist does not bear responsibility for the effects his or her efforts have on other individuals. As supervisors, however, we create a training environment within which multiple audiences are affected. Our insights and recommendations promote (or hinder) client welfare, facilitate (or impede) supervisee growth, maintain (or undermine) institutional integrity, and enhance (or jeopardize) the stature of our profession. Although our work at its best entails artistry, our practice is not art. It is grounded in biopsychosocial and behavioral sciences. Thus, we do bear responsibility for our actions and their consequences.

The practice of psychotherapy has become more focused, more empirically supported, and more frequently used by the mainstream of society since the 1970s. It has also become subject to increasing regulation and litigation. Supervisors of paraprofessionals, trainees, or even seasoned clinicians are now recognized by the public as no longer merely master to the apprentice but as overseers of client welfare. Responsibility for our actions and their consequences is now ultimately decided in a court of law. Thus, supervisors need to pay close attention to areas of ethical or legal exposure (Stromberg et al., 1988).

Law is complex, sometimes contradictory, always confusing. Not unlike mental health disciplines, it has its own mysterious jargon. While deciphering the language may be difficult, the knowledge of legal pitfalls and prevention strategies is essential to practitioners and supervisors.

The law is reactive, not proactive. Cases that appear in this book, and indeed all cases, involve rulings on an injury or harm to someone that has already occurred. Because of this, lawyers often talk about what you cannot do rather than what you can do. Even the U.S. Constitution is written such that we are told what the government (federal and state) cannot do. However, from the body of existing case law, we can begin to piece together certain patterns and practices—what supervisors *can* do—that will result in the reduction of legal exposure. That is the essence of risk management.

The chapters that follow attempt to present relevant case law in ways that are meaningful to the practice of supervision. It is important to note that nothing in this book is to be construed as giving legal advice. That is best done by an attorney in your geographic area who is familiar with mental health laws.

Aspects of liability discussed in these chapters will ideally challenge supervisors to examine their practices. Clinical supervision has historically been informal and casual. However, as supervisors, we have legal and ethical responsibilities not only to our supervisees, but directly to their clients as well. This is something the courts have not taken lightly. The intersection of law and mental health is unquestionably growing.

The musings of the therapist/supervisor at the beginning of this chapter illustrate the delicate balance we all seek between our clinical practice and risk management. We are well trained to process cases based on clinical issues. But we may spend less time thinking about what those issues may trigger. By looking to the disciplines' ethical codes and professional standards, reviewing current research, and considering legal precedents, the following chapters will familiarize supervisors with those triggers and their successful management.

Professional and Legal Mandates for Accountability

Psychotherapy supervisors have long enjoyed a quiet distinction and respect in the mental health field (Alonso, 1985). They are regarded by trainees and colleagues as clinical experts. To the extent that many have distinguished themselves as highly effective practitioners, this accolade is accurate. Supervisors assume an invaluable role in mentoring future generations of professionals.

However, they also serve as teachers, advisers, consultants, counselors, mentors, evaluators, and even coaches to their junior colleagues (Bernard & Goodyear, 1998; Brashears, 1995; Hess, 1998; Holloway & Carroll, 1999; Welfel, 1998a; Whitman & Jacobs, 1998). For these roles, supervisors are seldom formally trained. This renders them vulnerable to ethical complaints by supervisees and/or their clients. The information or advice supervisors provide in these roles may leave them open to charges of practicing outside their scope of competence due to a lack of formal training.

Paralleling the schism between psychotherapy research and practice is a disturbing disjunction between clinical practice and supervision. Although many disciplines recently established supervisor standards and training criteria, the majority of supervisors remain unable to specify supervisory models, theories, or research that inform their practice (Freeman & McHenry, 1996; Rodolfa et al., 1998). Graduate training programs and internship sites seldom require or even offer formal supervision training (Borders, Cashwell, & Rotter, 1995; Navin, Beamish, & Johanson, 1995; Watkins, 1995). Practical applications of existing theoretical models to guide supervisory practice remain largely absent from the literature (Itzhaky & Itzhaky, 1996; Rich, 1993). Even where these guides do exist, they may be ignored. "It is not common practice for supervisors to consult with one another, review the literature on supervision independently, or attend courses on supervision" (Rodenhauser, 1997, p. 539). Thus, despite the increasing sophistication of our knowledge base, the majority of supervisors rely solely on clinical training to inform their supervisory practice.

Given that mental health practitioners often prefer to rely on "practice knowledge" derived from clinical cases to teach and learn the skills of their discipline, this book has adopted that format. The following clinical case evolves throughout the remaining chapters as a context for discussing professional issues, ethical codes, practice standards, case law, and risk management for supervisors. Although not an actual case, circumstances presented in these vignettes reflect a composite of experiences and challenges commonly encountered by supervisors in private practice, community agency, school guidance, and graduate training environments.

THE CASE OF MARIA

Maria Ritter, a 36-year-old divorced Latina mother of two, has requested counseling at Lakeland Mental Health Center (LMHC) for self-reported depression. After intake, she was assigned to Georgia Doyle, MA, for weekly psychotherapy. Georgia has been employed at LMHC for the past 18 months and is completing postgraduate requirements to become a licensed mental health counselor. She is supervised by Jeremy Marcas, LCSW, a senior therapist on staff who has worked at LMHC for 7 years. Renee Johnson, PhD, is a licensed psychologist and the Clinical Director of Adult Outpatient Services in which both Jeremy and Georgia work. She provides administrative supervision to these therapists and clinical supervision to Jeremy.

Based on her reported 5-month history of tearfulness, apathy, sleep disturbance (early morning awakening), low self-esteem, and vague suicidal ideation, Maria was diagnosed with a major depressive episode. She also reports parenting difficulties in raising her two children Carrie (age 15) and Carlos (age 12). She has received financial assistance but little parenting support from ex-husband Ringo since their divorce 3 years ago. Maria has physical and legal custody of the children, while their father has visitation with them at his local apartment on weekends. Carrie recently began refusing to go to her dad's, citing that he is "too strict."

Carlos has a reported history of "minor behavioral infractions" since fourth grade, which appear to be escalating since he entered the middle school last year. He recently got into trouble again, receiving a 2-day suspension for writing graffiti on a bathroom wall. This was his third behavioral incident this year, and his return to school was contingent upon a family visit from the home-school coordinator. Maria found this humiliating and fears it proves her inadequacy as a mother. She wishes to return with her family to Mexico, where "children respect their elders more." However, this is not feasible given her financial situation and family ties in this area.

Daughter Carrie is reportedly popular with peers and active in school sports, pressuring her mother "endlessly" to allow her more freedom and later curfews. She is dating an 18-year-old high school dropout whom both her parents disapprove of. Carrie has been meeting with school counseling intern Paul Maynor for the past 2 months at Maria's request. Paul helped Carrie and her mother develop "house rules" that are easing the tension between them to some degree. Maria worries that her daughter is growing up too fast. She reports that Carrie is sometimes disrespectful at home. She feels overwhelmed and unable to cope with these parenting issues.

Significant family history includes being the third of four children from an intact family that moved to the United States from Mexico when Maria was 8. She describes her parents as "loving but strict." The family experienced some acculturation difficulty (father underemployed, older siblings had academic and social adjustment problems). However, Maria's language skills were excellent and she made friends easily. She reported successful completion of high school at age 18. She met Ringo 1 year later at her dispatcher job. He was from Cuba, already a success in his small business (restaurant supply), and approved by her parents. They married when Maria was 20 and he was 23. The marriage lasted 12 years and ended when Ringo left Maria for another woman whom he continues to date.

Maria attends Catholic church and relies heavily on her support system, which includes two siblings living nearby and several friends in whom she confides. Her employer, a local bank where she is a teller, has been flexible in allowing her to arrange work hours around the children's school schedules. Maria's parents, who live in a neighboring state, call regularly but are critical of her divorce and parenting decisions.

Maria's suicidal risk was assessed as low at this time, as she is very committed to her children, has an adequate support network, and denies substance abuse or self-destructive behaviors. She was started on Elavil 2 weeks ago after evaluation by a staff psychiatrist. Maria's HMO has authorized 10 therapy sessions, after which a utilization review will be required before additional sessions may be allowed.

Initial therapy is focused on improving Maria's affect, monitoring her compliance with and response to the medication, and cognitive-behavioral strategies to enhance her coping skills and self-esteem. Maria signed releases for Georgia to communicate with both Carrie's guidance counselor and Carlos's home-school coordinator. Georgia has scheduled weekly therapy sessions, informed Maria of her treatment approach and supervisory relationship, and given her contact numbers to assure 24-hour emergency coverage.

SUPERVISORY MANAGEMENT OF MARIA'S CASE

Maria would typically be assigned a case number and clinical folder by the agency upon intake. Her informed consent for services as well as Georgia's intake evaluation, treatment plan, progress notes, and all contacts regarding the case are maintained in this record.

Medications and med checks, information releases, and insurance billing information are also retained in the clinical record. Financial records may also be included, although many agencies now maintain them on computer. As Georgia's supervisor, Jeremy Marcas would periodically review this chart to ensure that records are complete and to monitor treatment progress.

As clinical director, Dr. Johnson requires Jeremy to maintain a separate file for each staff member he supervises. This ensures that clinical, administrative, and risk management issues are appropriately handled in supervision. Portions of this file, organized using the Focused Risk Management Supervision System (FoRMSS) (Falvey, Caldwell, & Cohen, 2002), will be reproduced in the chapters that follow to illustrate how supervision of this case can be succinctly documented. Dr. Johnson would periodically review this file in the course of her supervision of Jeremy.

Georgia completes a portion of the FoRMSS Case Overview (Figure 2.1) in preparation for her first supervision session regarding Maria. Briefer than the intake evaluation in Maria's clinical record, this summary enables Georgia and her supervisor to review salient aspects of her presenting circumstances and psychosocial history in relation to her symptom picture. It facilitates their discussion about possible diagnoses and contributing factors (e.g., medical status, cultural stressors). It also highlights priority issues that will require immediate consideration in treatment planning.

From a supervisor's perspective, Maria's profile presents several priority concerns that warrant immediate supervisory discussion:

◆ a potential for suicide risk to increase as her depression lifts
◆ the need to rule out organic contributors to vegetative signs
◆ adequate staff training in Latino cultural norms to treat and supervise this case competently
◆ the need to further assess familial or psychosocial stressors
◆ evaluation of adequate parenting practices in both households
◆ consultation with the school regarding the severity of Carlos's behavioral disruptions

Designed as a comprehensive documentation system, the structured format of FoRMSS alerts Jeremy to identify and address these issues systematically in the initial supervision session regarding Maria. Based on their discussion, he and Georgia develop an initial treatment plan for this case (Figure 2.2). Risk management considerations in overseeing Georgia's therapy with Maria are noted, and both parties sign the document signifying their agreement with the proposed treatment of this case.

While subsequent supervisory sessions will update Georgia's clinical progress with Maria and other clients in her caseload, Jeremy and other supervising professionals included in these vignettes have additional responsibilities. These generally include the following administrative tasks as well as overview of the clinical relationship:

ADMINISTRATIVE TASKS

◆ supervisee selection and case assignment
◆ training program liaison

FIGURE 2.1   FoRMSS Case Overview

FoRMSS CASE OVERVIEW

Client ID: <u>Maria L. Ritter</u>   Date of Intake: <u>3/18/02</u>   Age: <u>36</u>   Gender: <u>F</u>

Occupation/Job: <u>bank teller</u>   Education/Grade: <u>high school</u>

Cultural/Minority ID: <u>Mexican</u>   Religious Affiliation: <u>Catholic (practicing)</u>

Relationship Status: <u>divorced</u>   No. & Ages of Children: <u>daughter (15), son (12)</u>

Referred by: <u>self (acc. by concerned friend)</u>   Reason for Referral: <u>depressed, parenting stress</u>

Major Presenting Issues

1. <u>depressed (5 mo.) - sleep dist., tearful, apathy, low SE, vague suicidal ideation</u>

2. <u>parenting stress - children "uncooperative" and disrespectful</u>

3. <u>son's behavioral problems at school</u>

4. <u>poor communication with ex-husband re. parenting issues</u>

Significant History

1. <u>3rd of 4 sibs - raised in Mexico until family relocated to U.S. (age 8)</u>

2. <u>married age 20 - Cuban immigrant, family approved, 2 children by marriage</u>

3. <u>divorced age 32 - family critical of parenting; lack of co-parenting with ex</u>

4. <u>successful employment history since age 27 (bank teller); supportive employer</u>

Current Living Circumstances   ☑ stable   ☐ at risk   ☐ crisis

Explain: <u>nuclear family nearby; adequate financial resources (incl. child support)</u>

<u>   wish to return to Mexico to minimize cultural stress re. parenting</u>

Health Status   ☐ excellent   ☐ good   ☑ fair   ☐ poor

Explain: <u>need to rule out organic cause for vegetative signs & depressed mood</u>

<u>   denies any history of substance abuse (personal or familial)</u>

Current Support System   ☐ excellent   ☑ good   ☐ fair   ☐ poor

Explain: <u>parents nearby but critical of Maria; sister supportive; several close</u>

<u>female friends; lack of communication with ex-husband (describes as "hot-headed")</u>

Diagnostic Impression (DSM-IV)

Axis I (current disorders) _____

Axis II (Personality Disorders/MR) _____

Axis III (current medical conditions) _____

Axis IV (psychosocial/env. problems) _____

Axis V (GAF: level of functioning) _____

Treatment Goals

1. _____

2. _____

3. _____

4. _____

PRIORITY ISSUES

	Yes	?	No		Yes	?	No		Yes	?	No
Suicide Risk	☐	☑	☐	Substance Abuse	☐	☐	☑	Unstable Living Situation	☐	☐	☑
Homicide Risk	☐	☐	☑	Mental Status	☐	☑	☐	Economic Issues	☐	☐	☑
Abuse/Neglect	☐	☑	☐	Medical Condition	☐	☑	☐	cultural stress	☑	☐	☐

FIGURE 2.2   FoRMSS Treatment Planning and Risk Management

INITIAL SUPERVISION RISK MANAGEMENT

Frequency of Case Review _weekly - monitor suicidal risk & vegetative signs_

Legal Considerations _none known_

Ethical Considerations _familiarity with cultural/acculturation issues_

Supervisory Needs _assess cultural awareness; possible family TX history_

Treatment Constraints _HMO - 10 sessions_

Case Documentation: Informed Consent for treatment ☑ Client Rights ☑ 3rd Party Information ☑
 Informed Consent for supervision ☑ Intake Evaluation ☑ ___ ☐
 Confidentiality ☑ Treatment Plan ☐ ___ ☐

INITIAL TREATMENT PLAN

Initiate medication evaluation and refer for updated physical exam (last in '98)

assess parenting skills (both parents if possible)

cog-beh strategies to improve mood and coping skills

family session to assess problem areas & facilitate co-parenting

Jeremy Marcas, LCSW   SOCIAL WORKER   10/2/00
Supervisor Signature/Degree   Title   Date

Georgia Doyle, MA   staff counselor   10/2/00
Supervisee Signature/Degree   Title   Date

Source: From *Documentation in Supervision: The Focused Risk Management Supervision System (FoRMSS)*, by J. E. Falvey, C. F. Caldwell, and C. R. Cohen. Copyright © 2002 Wadsworth Group.

- ◆ providing supervisee orientation to policies and emergency procedures at the site
- ◆ monitoring supervisee compliance with ethical codes as well as state and federal statutes governing clinical practice
- ◆ conducting formative and summative evaluations of the supervisee
- ◆ ensuring adequate documentation of clinical and supervisory sessions as well as important decision processes in treatment

CLINICAL AND SUPERVISORY OVERSIGHT

- ◆ monitoring supervisor and supervisee competence
- ◆ assuring informed consent in treatment and in supervision
- ◆ maintaining confidentiality and adhering to its limits
- ◆ protecting client welfare
- ◆ promoting the supervisee's professional development
- ◆ avoiding dual relationships in treatment and in supervision
- ◆ implementing legal mandates to warn, protect, and/or report

There are seldom firm directives specifying exactly how these responsibilities are to be carried out. Within the various disciplines, research and clinical experience continually inform psychotherapy practice. The larger society also regulates and monitors mental health professions in the interest of the public. In this arena, supervisors are held to a "standard of care" or "standard of practice" benchmark. This essentially means that our professional activities must be consistent with what other similarly trained professionals would do under similar circumstances. This standard is continually evolving and is influenced by many sources: professional association ethical standards; certifying body ethical codes; state licensing laws, rules, and interpretations; institutional and organizational policies; insurance industry and other reimbursing or funding expectations; federal, state, and local statutes; and case law (Bertram & Wheeler, 1995; Knapp & VandeCreek, 1997a). As we shall see, clinical supervisors need to maintain regularly updated working knowledge of these standards as they are implemented in their particular state or jurisdiction.

A BRIEF LEGAL PRIMER FOR MENTAL HEALTH PROFESSIONALS

Laws strive to balance the wishes of a society against the liberties of its members (Meyer, Landis, & Hays, 1988). As professionals, clinical supervisors have a duty to ensure the welfare of individual clients and supervisees while also protecting the wishes of the larger community. We are responsible for our own actions (direct liability) as well as the actions of our supervisees (vicarious liability). It behooves supervisors to inform themselves about how the law intersects with their practice. Throughout this book and in the various court cases presented, there are legal concepts and language that bear some definition. While outlined in general here, supervisors are encouraged to review these legal doctrines with a mental health attorney familiar with their state statutes.

Negligence/Malpractice

Doing what is right is no guarantee against misfortune. However, knowledge of how the courts define accountability in clinical supervision can assist greatly in risk management. Responsible behavior is clearly a necessary, if not a sufficient, condition for legal conduct (Hopkins & Anderson, 1990; Huber, 1994; Munson, 1993; Swenson, 1997).

Malpractice is professional negligence (Pozgar, 1996). To establish that a supervisor has acted negligently, there are four legal criteria that must be shown by a preponderance of the evidence:

◆ *Duty:* Duty can be established by a relationship or by statutory law. It refers to the fiduciary responsibility to care for the welfare of another person(s) over which a supervisor has direct control and knows, or should know, of their actions.
◆ *Breach:* Breach is based on a violation of the preceding duty, where specific actions or inactions occurred that were both foreseeable and unreasonable given that fiduciary responsibility.

◆ *Causation:* The breach of duty was a direct and/or proximate cause of injuries incurred by a client or patient.
◆ *Damage:* Demonstrable physical, financial, or emotional injury (including pain and suffering) must have occurred as a result of the foregoing three criteria.

A fiduciary duty must first be established for malpractice to occur. In legal terms, this is defined as

> a relationship requiring the highest duty of care and arising between parties usually in one of four situations: (1) when one person places trust in the faithful integrity of another, who as a result gains superiority or influence over the first; (2) when one person assumes control and responsibility over another; (3) when one person has a duty to act for or give advice to another on matters falling within the scope of the relationship; or (4) when there is a specific relationship that has traditionally been recognized as involving fiduciary duties. . . . (Garner, 1999, pp. 256–257)

The New Hampshire Supreme Court recently clarified that a fiduciary relationship is a comprehensive term and liability exists "wherever influence has been acquired and abused or confidence has been reposed and betrayed" (*Schneider v. Plymouth State College*, 1999).

Breach of a duty depends on a number of things, the two most important being the *standard of care* (essential to prove professional malpractice) and *foreseeability.* Standard of care represents what a reasonably prudent professional would do in the same situation. Defining the acceptable standard of care in mental health service delivery can be difficult due to a lack of "best practices" in many contexts. The second factor, foreseeability, is the degree to which the breach of duty could have been reasonably anticipated given the circumstances. The intertwining nature of these concepts has been described by a court as follows:

> We emphasize that in determining whether harm was foreseeable, the psychotherapist is not held to a standard of omniscience, but merely to "that degree of care and skill which is exercised by the average practitioner in the class to which he belongs, acting in the same or similar circumstances." (*Shuster v. Altenberg,* 1988).

Supervisory malpractice involves lawsuits filed by a supervisee or client against a supervisor for allegedly violating professional practice standards. Most state laws define malpractice as professional conduct and skill that fall below the standard established for similar professionals in good standing under similar circumstances (Swenson, 1997). These standards may vary across states and disciplines.

Failure to supervise adequately has been cited as a small but growing complaint in mental health malpractice suits (Sherry, 1991). For example, the American Psychological Association Insurance Trust (APAIT) reported that, between 1976 and 1991, civil lawsuits against psychologists claiming failure to supervise properly accounted for 2% of all claims filed (Pope & Vasquez, 1998). Stromberg and Dellinger (1993) cited failure to adequately supervise students or assistants as one of the ten most common causes of malpractice, and Meyer et al. (1988) cautioned that "while the major therapeutic professions as a whole are rarely affected by malpractice or other professional liability actions, there is a clear trend toward increasing litigation" (p. 12). Dickson (1995) surveyed legal actions against psychiatrists, psychologists, social workers, and pastoral counselors and concluded that "while outside of the field of medicine there are relatively few reported malpractice cases . . . this low number may be misleading since many malpractice and liability actions are settled prior to court or go unreported" (p. 521).

Direct versus Vicarious Liability

Malpractice can be direct or vicarious. Direct liability is based on erroneous actions or omissions of the supervisor. Harrar, VandeCreek, and Knapp (1990) summarized major sources of direct liability:

◆ dereliction in carrying out supervisory responsibility for the planning, course, and outcome of a supervisee's work
◆ giving a supervisee inappropriate advice about treatment that the supervisee implements to the client's detriment
◆ failure to listen carefully to a supervisee's comments about a client and therefore failing to comprehend the client's needs
◆ assigning tasks to supervisees whom the supervisor knew, or should have known, to be inadequately trained to execute them

Vicarious liability is based on the concept of *respondeat superior. Black's Law Dictionary* (Garner, 1999) defines respondeat superior as the common-law doctrine holding an employer or principal liable for their employee's or agent's actions committed during the scope of his or her employment. This applies to all employers and thus is potentially more applicable to administrative than clinical supervisors. Respondeat superior holds supervisors liable for the actions of supervisees because (a) they are in a position of responsibility and authority and (b) they stand to profit from the actions of their supervisees (Harrar et al., 1990). Three conditions must be met for vicarious liability:

◆ Supervisees must voluntarily agree to work under the direction and control of the supervisor and act in ways that benefit the supervisor.

◆ Supervisees must be acting within the defined scope of tasks permitted by the supervisor.
◆ The supervisor must have the power to control and direct the supervisee's work.

The following legal clarification by the Supreme Court of North Dakota helps illuminate how respondeat superior and other doctrines intersect: "It is 'negligent supervision' when the employer fails to exercise ordinary care in supervising the employment relationship, so as to prevent the foreseeable misconduct of an employee from causing harm to other employees or third persons" (*Nelson v. Gillette,* 1997). A key element of this doctrine is in defining what constitutes the "scope of employment" of the supervisee. Legal cases in the following chapters demonstrate conflicting determinations of what that scope of employment entails.

Courts have thus far not spoken on the liability of professionals in educational roles such as school counselors, school psychologists, and graduate training faculty in supervising trainees. They seem to recognize the need for discretion regarding treatment decisions lest supervisors' work be unduly constrained by the threat of liability (McCarthy & Sorenson, 1993). However, Guest and Dooley (1999) predict that liability for counseling and clinical supervisors in these settings might increase as supervision becomes a well-defined specialty area: "malpractice litigation against supervisors by their supervisees may emerge as a new area of risk management in counseling" (p. 276).

Confidentiality versus Privilege

This is a particularly confusing and often misunderstood area of mental health law. Confidentiality is often equated with total protection of client or supervisee communication, when in reality it offers much less protection from disclosure than does privilege:

> The concept of confidentiality must be distinguished from the law of privilege. An evidentiary privilege is a law that permits a person to prevent a court from requiring revelation of relational communications. Confidentiality refers to a duty, frequently an ethical limitation imposed by a profession not to disclose relational communications. (*Shuman & Weiner,* 1982)

Lawyers and physicians have traditionally enjoyed privileged communications with their clients and patients. It wasn't until 1996 that the U.S. Supreme Court expressly endorsed privileged communications for all psychotherapists in federal cases. In *Jaffee v. Redmond,* the court held that confidential communications between a client and a licensed therapist in the course of diagnosis or treatment are privileged and protected from compelled disclosure. The court also conceded that this privilege does not prevail under all circumstances

(*Jaffee v. Redmond,* 1996). All 50 states as well as the District of Columbia currently have enacted into law some form of psychotherapist privilege.

State legislatures, rather than mental health disciplines, retain the ability to define who is a psychotherapist. This definition varies notably across states. Privilege statutes have not been extended to include professionals who are not licensed or certified and in some states do not even include credentialed professionals from specific disciplines (e.g., mental health counselors, marriage and family therapists, substance abuse counselors). Privilege also varies depending on the nature of the supervisory relationship. The Indiana Supreme Court, for example, wrestled with this issue in a case involving an adolescent seen at a mental health center by a social worker supervised by a psychiatrist. This court wrote:

> The question is whether patient communications to a counselor who is supervised by a psychiatrist falls within the doctor–patient privilege. We hold that a counselor who aids the psychiatrist is covered by the privilege. By contrast, a counselor who is in fact the caregiver and acts largely independently is not an adjunct to the psychiatrist and thus is not covered by the privilege. (*In the matter of C.P.,* 1990)

In a separate case, a registered nurse supervised by a licensed psychologist was found to be an agent of that psychologist and thus protected by his privilege (*Kalenevitch v. Finger,* 1991). The courts thus consider the nature and degree of control exercised by a supervisor central to the determination of privilege.

Several other recent cases addressed the issue of privilege when the therapist is a licensed psychologist. The New Jersey Supreme Court established a three-part test required to pierce attorney–patient privilege, also extending to mental health professionals in that jurisdiction (*In re Kozlov,* 1979):

◆ There must be a legitimate need for the evidence.
◆ Evidence must be relevant and material to the issue before the court.
◆ The information cannot be secured through any less intrusive source.

In *Kinsella v. Kinsella* (1997), the court addressed whether privilege could be invoked by spouses to prevent disclosure by their respective psychologists of treatment records in a bitter divorce and child custody dispute. The following exceptions to psychotherapist–client privilege were outlined in this court's ruling:

◆ where a party waives privilege by placing his or her emotional and mental state at issue
◆ where the privilege may be required to yield to defendant's right to present exculpatory evidence in a criminal proceeding
◆ where piercing of the privilege is recognized in the best interests of the children (*Kinsella v. Kinsella,* 1997)

Criteria for waiving client privilege are not for psychotherapists to assess unilaterally, but rather with the advice and counsel of the courts. Therapists can be found liable for breach of confidentiality unless a court rules that their testimony is required: "If a psychologist fails to raise the privilege of the patient and makes disclosure of confidential information without a determination by the court that disclosure is required, the psychologist has breached a duty owed to the patient" (*Runyon v. Smith,* 1999). Thus, confidentiality and privilege interact in legally complex ways.

Therefore, it is prudent for supervisors to consult with an attorney to determine the status of their supervisees or interns regarding confidentiality and privilege. In some cases, an unlicensed intern or therapist (e.g., Georgia) receiving direct clinical supervision could be subsumed under the privilege entitled to the licensed supervisor (e.g., Jeremy). As we shall see, this may become important should legal intervention ensue.

The U.S. Court System

Laws that affect mental health professionals have four sources. They may originate from the U.S. or state constitutions, from state statutes written by legislatures, from regulations established to administer those statutes, or from existing precedents established by accumulating case law (Swenson, 1997). Trial courts apply existing laws to the facts of specific cases, while appeals courts interpret the existing laws. Appeals courts may overrule the findings of lower courts and create new laws through their published opinions (Meyer et al., 1988; Swenson, 1997).

Courts settle disputes through criminal and civil law. In criminal cases, the legal dispute is between the government and an individual. Defendants face possible fines, incarceration, and/or loss of licenses or occupational options (e.g., running for public office). The burden of proof is on the government to demonstrate "beyond a reasonable doubt" that the defendant committed the alleged crime(s). In civil cases, the legal dispute is between individuals. Defendants face financial losses and/or restrictions on their conduct. The burden of proof in civil cases is less stringent than for criminal cases; merely a "preponderance of evidence" is necessary to convict.

An area of law that has evolved considerably over the last 30 years is mental health law (Malley & Reilly, 1999; Swenson, 1997). In these cases, the legal dispute is usually between the government and/or affected parties and individuals with mental illness. Defendants face required mental health treatment and possible involuntary confinement. The burden of proof requires "clear and convincing evidence" of mental disability (Swenson, 1997).

Many state statutes relevant to mental health practice have incorporated the various disciplines' codes of ethics into their wording. In this way, legal and ethical issues have become increasingly intertwined. Because mental health professionals possess special education and training, they receive certain privileges (e.g., licensure) that carry a more stringent duty of care than that of the average citizen. They are thus held to a high standard of competence in the courts.

State Regulatory Boards

States establish special administrative laws and regulations to govern the practice of licensed, certified, or registered professions. These regulations are enforced by boards that have the force of law. State boards have the authority to set entry standards, define the scope of practice, hold hearings to investigate complaints, and apply sanctions (Koocher & Keith-Spiegel, 1998). Boards can also set accreditation standards for universities and professional schools that train mental health professionals (Swenson, 1997). Codification of the ethical codes of various professional associations into state law increasingly equates unethical behavior with illegal conduct. Violation of state regulations can lead to a number of disciplinary actions, including letters of reprimand, censure, stipulated resignation, rehabilitation through continuing education or supervision, or revocation of one's license to practice in that state.

Supervision has come to the attention of state boards. An Association of State and Provincial Psychology Boards (ASPPB) summary of disciplinary actions taken by state licensing boards against psychologists between 1983 and 1998 reported that inadequate or improper supervision ranked fifth in frequency among violations (Reaves, 1998). A recent survey of 284 licensed psychologists found that the largest category of complaints (22.6%) filed with one state licensing board dealt with supervision issues, including supervisory relationships and supervisors' overview of their supervisees' clinical performance (Montgomery, Cupit, & Wimberley, 1999). As noted earlier, supervisor liability for the conduct of supervisees is tempered by factors such as the extent of a supervisor's power over the subordinate, the aspect of counseling in which the negligence occurred, circumstances surrounding the actions by supervisee and supervisor, motivation of the supervisee, and the foreseeability of a supervisee's misconduct (Welfel, 1998b).

All psychotherapists need to be informed of their state's statutes regulating clinical practice. Supervisors, in addition, need to be cognizant of statutes regulating the professional practice of their supervisees who may represent different disciplines. These regulations, coupled with case law and ethical codes, "extensively regulate the who and how of psychological practice" (Swenson, 1997, p. 145).

Professional Association Ethics Committees

All professional associations have ethics committees that establish ethical standards and investigate charges of unethical conduct brought by clients, supervisees, students, employees, or colleagues of a member professional. Punitive action by these committees may include suspension of membership, censure in the organization's publications, referral to legal process, limiting practice, or requiring additional training or supervision. The most severe punishment is limited to revoking one's professional membership in the association (Swenson, 1997). Given that many employers, managed-care panels, insurance carriers, and referral organizations require professional association membership, this action could in effect restrict one's access to professional practice.

A large number of cases processed by state ethics committees are subsequent to other complaints brought against a professional. These may include actions taken by state licensing boards, felony convictions, expulsion from state associations, and professional malpractice (American Psychological Association, 1997). It is important to remember that membership in voluntary professional associations, while incurring certain contractual obligations on the part of the professional, does not override state statutes.

As this discussion has emphasized, the supervisor's task becomes highly complex when one considers the many levels of professionalism required to provide clinically, ethically, and legally competent supervision of a supervisee's work. We will follow Maria's case and review a number of legal decisions in the following chapters to illustrate how intertwined the legal, ethical, and professional parameters of clinical practice have become.

Supervisor Competence

As the prelude to examining a variety of professional, legal, and ethical concerns regarding supervisory competence, let's return to our case and summarize the supervision background of four hypothetical supervisors. Their credentials reflect a composite of the profiles of a majority of supervisors surveyed in several recent studies (Borders, Cashwell, & Rotter, 1995; McCarthy, Kulakowski, & Kenfield, 1994; Navin, Beamish, & Johanson, 1995; Rodolfa et al., 1998; Sutton & Page, 1994).

Supervisor Resumés

Jeremy Marcas, LCSW, who supervises counselor Georgia Doyle, received his MSW in 1988 and was licensed in 1991. He worked in a psychiatric inpatient facility for 2 years and has been employed as a staff social worker at the Lakeland Mental Health Center (LMHC) for the past 7 years. He received weekly supervision from two clinical social workers during his graduate internships and has received regular supervision from a licensed social worker (4 years) and a licensed psychologist (5 years) since graduation. Jeremy was promoted to a supervisory position 2 years ago based on his excellent clinical skills and performance evaluations. He has had no formal supervision training, although he did attend a weekend workshop on clinical supervision last year.

Renee Johnson, PhD, clinical director of the adult outpatient services in which both Georgia and Jeremy are employed, received her doctorate in clinical psychology in 1994. She completed a postdoctoral internship at a community mental health center in 1995 and was licensed in 1997. She received weekly supervision from licensed psychologists and a psychiatrist during her predoctoral and postdoctoral internships, and during the subsequent 2 years she accrued hours toward licensure. Renee has worked at this agency since becoming licensed. She was hired as director of adult outpatient services based on a successful interview and outstanding references from her academic institution and three clinical supervisors. Renee had one course on clinical supervision in her doctoral program. She has attended various management seminars and meets with other directors monthly to review supervisory and program management issues. She has a staff of seven therapists at LMHC for whom she provides administrative and clinical supervision.

Edith Smith, MEd, is guidance director at the middle school where Paul Maynor is interning. She is a certified school counselor with 13 years of experience in this public school. She was supervised by a certified school counselor and a licensed psychologist on her graduate program's faculty during her 1-year internship but has received no supervision since graduating in 1988. She became guidance director in 1995 and has accepted interns from two local universities over the past 4 years. Edith meets with each intern's faculty supervisor at least once per semester to review their progress and submits a formal evaluation at the end of each semester for all interns. She has not received formal training in supervision but meets periodically with campus faculty and other intern supervisors to discuss professional issues and emerging knowledge in supervision.

Chris Olan, PhD, intern Paul Maynor's graduate program faculty supervisor, received his doctorate in counseling psychology in 1987. It included a supervised 1-year internship at a university counseling center. He was hired as tenure-track faculty in a graduate counselor education program in 1988 and received tenure in 1994. Chris teaches courses in counseling theory, assessment, and group counseling, as well as several internship seminars. He also maintains a small private practice in the community. In 1997, he became the internship coordinator for his program, overseeing student placement and liaison with internship field site supervisors. Chris completed a supervision course in his doctoral studies and has participated in a peer supervision group in the community for the past 10 years. He periodically attends workshops on supervision at regional and national counselor education conferences.

What is immediately evident about these supervisors is that their training as counselors, therapists, administrators, and/or educators is considerably more extensive than is their supervisory training. At most, one course in supervision was completed at the preprofessional level, and none received formal supervised training in clinical supervision after graduating. Even though these professionals entered their respective disciplines after the proliferation of supervision theories and models during the 1980s, their supervisory assignments appear to be grounded in traditional assumptions (a) that a trained therapist is a good supervisor (Holloway & Neufeldt, 1995) and (b) that having been supervised qualifies one to supervise others (Alonso, 1985). Hoffman (1994) has referred to this lack of supervisory training as the mental health profession's "dirty little secret."

While this may be the norm, it is certainly not an ethically or legally defensible position. We are held to a standard of competence in our professional activities. As Table 3.1 reveals, ethical codes of each mental health discipline affirm that competence is a basic requirement for professional practice. But what constitutes competence among various disciplines with such diverse

TABLE 3.1   Ethical Mandates for Professional Competence

The American Association for Marriage and Family Therapy
Code of Ethics
Standard 3.6: Marriage and family therapists do not diagnose, treat, or advise on problems outside the recognized boundaries of their competence.

American Association of Pastoral Counselors
Code of Ethics
Standard I.F: As members of AAPC we covenant to accept the following foundational premises . . . To diagnose or provide treatment only for those problems or issues that are within the reasonable boundaries of our competence.

American Counseling Association
Code of Ethics and Standards of Practice
Standard C.2.a: Counselors practice only within the boundaries of their competence, based on their education, training, supervised experience, state and national professional credentials, and appropriate professional experience.

American Psychiatric Association
Principles of Medical Ethics
Section 1: A physician shall be dedicated to providing competent medical service with compassion and respect for human dignity.

American Psychological Association
Ethical Principles of Psychologists and Code of Conduct
Standard 1.04a: Psychologists provide services, teach, and conduct research only within the boundaries of their competence, based on their education, training, supervised experience, or appropriate professional experience.

National Association of Social Workers
Code of Ethics
Standard 1.04: Social workers should provide services and represent themselves as competent only within the boundaries of their education, training, license, certification, consultation received, supervised experience, or other relevant professional experience.

National Organization for Human Service Education
Ethical Standards of Human Service Professionals
Statement 26: Human service professionals know the limit and scope of their professional knowledge and offer services only within their knowledge and skill base.

---

theories and approaches? Several professional associations (i.e., APA, ACA, NASW) define competence as requiring (a) formal education, (b) professional training, and (c) carefully supervised experience. The legal standard of competent practice within a discipline is matching the performance of an average fellow professional in good standing under similar circumstances (Swenson, 1997). Competent practice thus requires a synergistic melding of knowledge, skills, and judgment that enables one to know what to do, how to do it, and when to do it (Haas & Malouf, 1995). Can the aforementioned supervisors presume to acquire this level of competence on the basis of unsupervised supervision experience or one academic course?

REGULATORY STANDARDS AND CLINICAL PRACTICES

All states and the District of Columbia have formal mechanisms to regulate the practice of counseling and psychotherapy. National accrediting bodies govern the content of most graduate programs that train these professionals. Supervised clinical internships for trainees are stipulated in the graduate curricula of all disciplines. Upon graduation, professionals must receive from one to several years of additional supervised experience to become eligible for state licensure or certification. There are thus well-defined, consistent, and recognized sequences of training that precede credentialing as a mental health counselor or psychotherapist across disciplines.

Supervision is a required component of this sequence. It has evolved beyond the informal master–apprentice relationship and is now recognized as a key mechanism by which (a) emerging professionals acquire and improve upon their skills, (b) quality control is exercised, and (c) quality service is assured (Sumerall et al., 1998; Vasquez, 1992; Watkins, 1997a). It is often cited as the most important component in one's professional training (Goodyear & Bernard, 1999; Jacobs, David, & Meyer, 1995; Kadushin, 1992; Watkins, 1997a).

But who are the supervisors? As our vignette illustrates, they are typically professionals with graduate degrees and clinical credentials. Some state credentialing boards specify additional qualifications, and three states (Alabama, South Carolina, and Texas) currently license supervisors (Guest & Dooley, 1999). Disney and Stephens (1994) predict that there will eventually be uniform national specialty standards for supervisors. But for the most part, supervisors still have no training beyond a preprofessional course or occasional workshop.

Few credentialing boards to date recognize a need for specialized training of clinical supervisors (Borders & Cashwell, 1992). Neufeldt (1999) observed, "Although professional organizations and state licensing boards sometimes specify a necessary amount of post-licensure practice experience for supervisors, they seldom require training focused on the task of guiding less-experienced professional therapists" (p. 22). In instances where regulating agencies do specify qualifications, those credentials (typically licensure and years of clinical experience) do not empirically correlate with supervisory competence. For example, Koocher and Keith-Spiegal (1998) found little evidence for a relationship between level of professional degree and supervisor competence. Similarly, Rodolfa et al. (1998) found that increased experience did not ensure more competent supervision among licensed psychologists. Both studies concluded that formal supervision training is the crucial variable in the acquisition of supervisory skills.

Supervision is not a rare activity. Surveys have found that over 50% of psychiatrists and psychologists (Norcross, Prochaska, & Farber, 1993; Osipow & Fitzgerald, 1986; Rodenhauser, 1996; Vasquez, 1992) and 24–30% of social workers (Gibelman & Schervish, 1997; Munson, 1993) regularly spend time supervising other professionals. Although estimates for other disciplines are not available, one would expect a significant percentage among marriage and family therapists, who must be supervised by American Association for Marriage and Family Therapy (AAMFT) approved supervisors to attain clinical membership. Many mental health counselors and school counselors are supervised by other disciplines and thus may represent smaller percentages.

Although graduates of clinical and counseling disciplines typically seek initial positions in direct service provision, it is likely that at some point in their careers many will assume supervisory roles such as program or guidance director (Borders & Leddick, 1987; Falvey, 1987). These managerial positions offer attractive career options for therapists who would otherwise be limited to line staff positions. They are generally accompanied by higher salaries as well as opportunities to serve as change agents within institutions (Falvey, 1987). Less tangible but nonetheless significant benefits of supervisory positions also include providing an alternative to the stress of direct service and achieving professional stature as a mentor to the next generation of practitioners (Alonso, 1995; Munson, 1993; Shanfield, Matthews, & Hetherly, 1993).

What formal preparation *should* accompany this professional activity? Rodenhauser (1997) asserts that standards for supervisor competence have not been developed, but the record suggests otherwise. A number of disciplines have promulgated standards or guidelines for supervisors (Table 3.2). These suggest that coursework or other formal training in supervision theory and methods, as well as a period of supervised supervision of others, should be prerequisites for supervisory practice. Those disciplines that offer specialty credentials in supervision concur. They require candidates for supervisor credentialing to document these training experiences as summarized here.

NBCC Approved Clinical Supervisor

- ◆ clinical experience: 5 years postgraduate counseling experience
- ◆ supervision coursework: two semesters or 30 workshop hours
- ◆ supervision experience: 100 postgraduate hours
- ◆ supervision of supervision: 20 hours
- ◆ written professional disclosure statement
- ◆ statement of compliance with the NBCC code of ethics

AAMFT Approved Supervisor (Standard Track)

- ◆ clinical experience: 3,000 postgraduate hours
- ◆ supervision coursework: one semester graduate course
- ◆ supervision experience: 180 postgraduate hours
- ◆ supervision of supervision: 36 hours
- ◆ written supervision philosophy statement
- ◆ supervisory case study
- ◆ statement of professional ethics and conduct

TABLE 3.2   Standards for Clinical Supervisor Competence

The American Association for Marriage and Family Therapy
*Responsibilities and Guidelines for AAMFT Approved Supervisors
and Supervisors-in-Training*
AAMFT Approved Supervisors are dedicated professionals who have obtained the
educational, experiential and supervisory training required for the competent supervision
of marriage and family therapists and trainees . . .

Association for Counselor Education and Supervision
Standards for Counseling Supervisors
The Education and Training of Supervisors: Counseling supervision is a distinct field of
preparation and practice. Knowledge and competencies necessary for effective performance are acquired through a sequence of training and experience which ordinarily
includes the following: graduate training in counseling . . . successful supervised employment as a professional counselor . . . credentialing . . . graduate training in counseling
supervision including didactic courses, seminars, laboratory courses, and supervised
practica. . . .

Ethical Guidelines for Counseling Supervisors
Guideline 2.01: Supervisors should have had training in supervision prior to initiating their
role as supervisors.
Guideline 3.02: Supervisors should teach courses and/or supervise clinical work only in
areas where they are fully competent and experienced.

Association of State and Provincial Psychology Boards
Supervision Guidelines
Guideline II.A: Supervisors have adequate training, knowledge and skill to render
competently any psychological service that their supervisee undertakes . . . The supervisor
has had at least three (3) years of post licensure experience and has had training and/or
experience in supervision.

ASPPB Code of Conduct
Rule A.1: The psychologist shall limit practice and supervision to the areas of competence
in which proficiency has been gained through education, training, and experience.

National Association of Social Workers
Guidelines for Clinical Social Work Supervision
To be a qualified clinical social work supervisor, a social worker should . . . have undertaken formalized training and participated in ongoing professional development in the
practice of supervision (that is, course content, workshops, and continuing education
programs that clearly address methods of providing clinical supervision including the study
of current professional literature on supervision) . . . have experience and expertise with
the supervisee's client population . . . possess appropriate supervisory skills. . . .

National Board for Certified Counselors
Standards for the Ethical Practice of Clinical Supervision
Standard 11: Clinical supervisors shall refrain from offering supervision outside of their
area(s) of competence.

AAPC Certified Supervisor (Diplomate Level)

- religious body endorsement
- demonstrated achievement in three professional areas
- supervision coursework: 30 hours graduate coursework
- supervision experience: 150 hours (at least 30 hours each supervisee)
- supervision of supervision: 50 hours
- written supervisory theory paper
- supervisory work sample
- evidence of compliance with the AAPC code of ethics

There do exist, then, remarkably consistent standards for what constitutes adequate preparation as a supervisor in all disciplines except psychiatry. The courts may use these criteria collectively to determine the professional standard of supervisory practice. The problem is that there are few courses or supervised experiences to allow professionals to fulfill these standards. For example, the American Psychological Association's (APA) accreditation standards for doctoral-level psychology programs do not require supervisory training (Knapp & VandeCreek, 1997a). APA does not allow masters-level students to provide supervised supervision of other students. Most masters-level counseling programs do not have supervision courses or training experiences available in their curriculum (Bernard & Goodyear, 1998). The Council for the Accreditation of Counseling and Related Programs (CACREP) does not include masters-level supervision courses in its graduate training guidelines. Research has cited the pervasive lack of formal supervisory training among social workers (Schindler & Talen, 1996), school psychologists (Crespi & Lopez, 1998), psychiatrists (Rodenhauser, 1997), psychologists (McCarthy et al., 1994), community counselors (Freeman & McHenry, 1996), and across multidisciplinary samples of field-based supervisors (Hoffman, 1994; Navin et al., 1995).

Guest and Dooley (1999) observed that "courses in clinical supervision are required only of doctoral level professionals. In practice, numbers of master's level professionals serve as supervisors in agencies without having even a workshop in clinical supervision practice" (p. 276). Bonney (1994) equated this initiation into supervisory roles with learning to practice psychotherapy by being a client and subsequently modeling the therapist's behavior. The occasional weekend workshop cannot be expected to compensate for this lack of thoughtful, reflective training.

Enforcing the Mandate to "Do No Harm"

Some training programs are criticized for subscribing to a "germ theory" of psychotherapy education, where skill is presumed to be acquired through exposure or osmosis (Norcross & Beutler, 1998). Such programs are characterized by the absence of specifically targeted skills training and systematic feedback. This theory also seems to predominate in preparing supervisors, where the majority have only their own supervised experience to guide their supervisory practice (Handelsman, 1986; Watkins, 1997b). One author has argued that the natural evolution of supervisors from line staff positions is actually preferable to formal training: "the patient would benefit much more from his therapist's supervisor if she had been allowed to develop the art of supervision gradually, as her own expertise and knowledge as a practitioner increased, rather than in a rushed once and for all qualifying course" (Bramley, 1996, p. 182). However, this tradition leaves us vulnerable to ethical complaints as well as legal charges of practicing beyond our scope of competence or outside the bounds of the standard of practice. Let's look at several examples.

Many ethical violations as well as legal malpractice claims among mental health professionals involve dual relationships, particularly sexual relationships, with clients. When state ethics committees find such violations, they may take a variety of actions, among which is to require the offending clinician to receive close supervision of his or her clinical practice for an extended period of time. One such case, handled by the American Psychological Association Insurance Trust, was summarized in Bennett, Bryant, VandenBos, and Greenwood (1990):

> The offending psychologist (Dr. K) was required to practice under direct supervision of a psychologist selected by the committee (Dr. A) for a 2-year period. For the first year all was satisfactory. Dr. A then had a family illness that required leaving town for one month. Not particularly concerned about Dr. K's being able to function without active supervision, Dr. A arranged for a colleague to serve as Dr. K's emergency contact, and gave Dr. K the number.
>
> Dr. K never contacted the colleague. Some weeks after Dr. A returned to town, several clients filed suit against Dr. K for sexually inappropriate incidents that occurred during Dr. A's absence. The suit subsequently was extended to include Dr. A, charging failure to supervise properly. They ultimately settled out of court. (p. 10)

Despite being specifically selected by the ethics committee, did Dr. A have adequate supervisory training to understand the potential legal and ethical consequences of the supervisory decisions involved? Given the foregoing discussion, it seems unlikely. In a study of similar ethical violations among psychiatrists, Frick, McCartney, and Lazarus (1995) reported that *none* among ten psychiatrists selected by the American Psychiatric Association's Ethics Committee to supervise sexually exploitative psychiatric practitioners had any formal training in ethics supervision, and only one was even informed of the charges and findings against the psychiatrist being supervised!

Even if not censured by an ethics committee, all mental health professionals are responsible for recognizing personal impairment and seeking consultation or supervision if they become unable to provide competent services to clients. Table 3.3 highlights ethical guidelines that mandate this careful

TABLE 3.3 Ethical Guidelines for Supervision of Impaired Professionals

---

American Association for Marriage and Family Therapy
Standard 3.2: Marriage and family therapists seek appropriate professional assistance for
their personal problems or conflicts that may impair work performance or clinical
judgment.

American Counseling Association
Standard C.2.g: Counselors refrain from offering or accepting professional services when
their physical, mental or emotional problems are likely to harm a client or others. They are
alert to the signs of impairment, seek assistance for problems, and, if necessary, limit,
suspend, or terminate their professional responsibilities.

American Psychiatric Association
Section 2.4: Special consideration should be given to those psychiatrists who, because of
mental illness, jeopardize the welfare of their patients and their own reputations and
practices. It is ethical, even encouraged, for another psychiatrist to intercede in such
situations.

American Psychological Association
Standard 1.13: When psychologists become aware of personal problems that may interfere
with their performing work-related duties adequately, they take appropriate measures,
such as obtaining professional consultation or assistance, and determine whether they
should limit, suspend, or terminate their work-related duties.

National Association of Social Workers
Standard 4.05(b): Social workers whose personal problems, psychosocial distress, legal
problems, substance abuse, or mental health difficulties interfere with their professional
judgment and performance should immediately seek consultation and take appropriate
remedial action by seeking professional help, making adjustments in workload, terminat-
ing practice, or taking any other steps necessary to protect clients and others.

National Organization for Human Service Education
Statement 27: Human service professionals seek appropriate consultation and supervision
to assist in decision-making when there are legal, ethical or other dilemmas.

---

self-monitoring. Haas and Hall (1991) distinguish among three primary
sources of substandard performance, offering resolutions for each:

1. Incompetence: unable to perform certain necessary tasks or not having
   skills required to conduct certain activities. Resolution involves providing
   training, information, and/or supervision in performing those specific
   activities.
2. Unethical judgment: choosing to act in such a way (through ignorance or
   conscious decision) that serves the client, profession, or society poorly.
   Resolution includes providing legal and ethical information and close
   supervision of the professional's activities.
3. Professional impairment: deficits in professional functioning that are
   judged to be symptoms of some underlying trouble (e.g., substance
   abuse, situational crises, organic impairment, psychopathology). Resolution includes limiting professional activities during the period of impairment and providing close supervision of the professional's activities.

A dramatic example of potential impairment among even the most highly credentialed professionals is presented in the case of *Gilmore v. Board of Psychologist Examiners* (Case 3.1). In this case, an ethics complaint by a client, resulting in the revocation of a psychologist's license, was appealed to the courts in Oregon. Their decision clearly affirms this mandate. Dr. Gilmore was an experienced educator, author, and clinician possessing the highest credential (Diplomate in Counseling Psychology) in her discipline and had served as chair of the Board of Psychologist Examiners that ultimately revoked her license. She clearly knew, or should have known, the ethical and professional standards governing clinical practice in her state. The Oregon Court of Appeals upheld revocation of her license, noting "if a practitioner's personal interests intrude into the relationship, the practitioner is obligated to re-create objectivity through a third party" (*Gilmore v. Board of Psychologists Examiners*, 1986). The court additionally stipulated that when this therapist became aware of her sexual attraction to these clients, she had three rational choices: to avoid the relationships, to seek professional help, or to refer the clients to other therapists. Thus, Dr. Gilmore's failure to seek supervision was an important consideration in the outcome of this case.

A final example draws an important distinction between the legal consequences of aspirational and mandatory standards of conduct. A psychologist appealed the revocation of his license by the North Carolina state ethics board based on its evidentiary hearing of various complaints regarding his professional conduct. The court of appeals, in *White v. North Carolina State Board of Examiners of Practicing Psychologists* (1990), ruled that while the preamble to the Ethical Principles of Psychologists was too vague to be used as a basis for disciplinary action, the ethical principles themselves are specific enough "that a reasonably intelligent psychologist would understand that the conduct in question is forbidden." This ruling may serve as a precedent for other disciplines and reflects how ethics and law intersect in defining competent practice.

BLUEPRINTS FOR SUPERVISOR COMPETENCE

Despite the lack of training offered by most academic institutions and field settings, various theory-based as well as atheoretical supervision approaches and training models have emerged since the 1980s. These guides offer succinct outlines of important supervisory tasks and responsibilities. Although extensive review of these models is beyond the scope of this book, texts by Bernard and Goodyear (1998), Bradley and Ladany (2001), Holloway and Carroll (1999), Munson (1993), Powell (1993), and Watkins (1997a) provide thorough discussions of a number of supervisor training models. Several approaches are outlined here briefly to highlight representative competencies expected of clinical supervisors.

Gilmore v. Board of Psychologist Examiners
725 P.2d 400 (Or. Ct. App. 1986) *Oregon Court of Appeals*

FACTS

This was an appeal by Dr. Susan Gilmore from an order of the Board of Psychologist Examiners revoking her license to practice psychology. Dr. Gilmore had been a psychology professor, practitioner, and author for 12 years when two of her clients complained to the board of unethical treatment. It was alleged that Dr. Gilmore had sexual relations with these two clients. After an investigation in which she claimed treatment had ended before having the relationships, the board found that she had engaged in unprofessional and unethical practices and revoked her license. Along with the charges of sexual impropriety, the board also found that Dr. Gilmore failed to obtain supervision when she knew, or should have known, that her personal life was interfering with her practice. This was a violation of the Ethical Principles of Psychologists.

HOLDING OF THE COURT

The court found that the Board of Psychologist Examiners had given Dr. Gilmore adequate due process rights and that the revocation of her license was warranted based on her violation of ethical rules proscribed by the state licensing statute.

IMPLICATIONS

In the strange world of licensing, we have a unique opportunity to witness a confluence between the law, ethics, and practice. Many states incorporate ethics into their rules of professional practice that practitioners must follow to keep their license or certification. The law in this case was based primarily on ethical standards and a standard of practice. These standards included having the practitioner seek professional assistance (i.e., supervision) when personal problems emerge and are intended to help determine if the practitioner can effectively continue to work with clients or how to continue in his or her current capacity more effectively. As a result of these principles being incorporated into the law, it became the jurisdiction of a government administrative agency and ultimately a court of law. The court can address the constitutionality of a licensing statute, as well as review the procedure and process of the administrative agency.

   This case suggests several important risk management practices for therapists. First, be familiar with your state's licensing/certification laws and your discipline's ethical standards. Second, consider the need for supervision. Third, the charges of unethical and unprofessional conduct, which resulted in Dr. Gilmore's license revocation, could be used as a basis for further legal action (e.g., malpractice) by injured clients. While many of us intuitively know that having sex with a client is wrong, there is still an alarmingly high rate of complaints regarding this issue. As more clients sue for malpractice (for sexual victimization in therapy) in order to receive monetary damages, we are all advised to seek clinical supervision or consultation to appropriately handle sexual feelings toward clients or patients.

A training curriculum for supervisors developed by Borders et al. (1991) centered on seven core areas of graduate study: (a) models of supervision; (b) counselor development; (c) supervision methods and techniques; (d) supervisory relationships; (e) ethical, legal, and professional regulatory issues; (f) evaluation; and (g) executive (administrative) skills. For each area, these authors articulated specific learning objectives to foster self-awareness, theoretical and conceptual knowledge, and skills and techniques.

Kerson (1994) proposed a teaching framework for field instructors that encompasses six major tasks of social work supervisors: (a) to create and maintain a trusting learning environment; (b) to orient trainees to setting, clients, community, and learning expectations; (c) to provide consistent formal supervision; (d) to model professional skills, behaviors, and values; (e) to provide ongoing feedback as well as periodic formal evaluations; and (f) to introduce trainees to broader practice issues. Implementation of these tasks is geared toward assisting trainees to develop a professional identity through their field experiences.

Carroll (1999) identified a cluster of generic tasks associated with training in a social-role model of supervision. They include facilitating the supervisory relationship, teaching, counseling, monitoring, evaluation, consulting, and administration. For each task, he outlines sources of training information, readings, discussion points, experiential learning activities, and skills practice assignments.

Neufeldt (1999) developed the first complete training manual for supervising novice counselors and therapists. Her curriculum articulates an ethical framework for supervision, provides numerous strategies for supervising beginning and advanced trainees, and provides a detailed two-semester practicum course outline.

Holloway (1999) developed and refined the Systems Approach to Supervision (SAS) as a framework for supervisory teaching and practice. This model incorporates seven interactive dimensions: (a) the supervisory relationship, (b) supervisor factors, (c) institutional factors, (d) client factors, (e) trainee factors, (f) supervision functions, and (g) supervisory tasks. The SAS model encourages supervisors to view their professional activities as embedded within the character of the supervisory relationship and the context within which it is operating (Holloway, 1999).

A structure for training and assessing supervisor competence has been presented by Getz (1999). This approach includes didactic instruction in seven core areas of supervisory knowledge that were previously identified by Borders et al. (1991). Goals, action steps, and evidence of competence are described for each core area. This approach also includes experiential work in supervised supervision. This author outlines a formal structure for use in training supervisors to organize supervision sessions based on the following format (Getz, 1999):

◆ case history presentation: information about the client and the presenting problem, history of the presenting problem, and previous attempts at problem solution

◆ case conceptualization: client goals, desired outcomes, and counseling approach

◆ supervisee's reaction: information about the supervisee's reactions to the client and the counseling process

◆ request to the supervisor: how the supervisee desires help and what supervision approach is desired

◆ supervisee's presentation of progress on his or her specific goals, accompanied by action steps and evidence

◆ viewing of session videotape by supervisor and supervisee

◆ supervisor's feedback to supervisee

◆ summary: future directions for the case and supervisee's future goals related to counseling skills, case conceptualization skills, emotional and cognitive self-awareness, and professional role

With this approach, supervisors in training are in turn supervised in a peer group setting using a structure that parallels the supervision session. Documentation of supervision activities and development of an informed consent document for supervisees are also addressed (Getz, 1999).

Each of these models outlines major responsibilities of clinical supervisors and can be used as the basis for formal supervision training. Most authors concur that these skills should be taught in a one- or two-semester course, followed by supervised practice of supervision, to acquire and demonstrate competence in this specialty area.

SUMMARY AND RECOMMENDATIONS

Because supervisory relationships are at a minimum triadic, both the supervisee and the client in treatment are consumers of a supervisor's expertise (Kurpius, Gibson, Lewis, & Corbett, 1991). From a legal perspective, society at large is also a consumer of the supervisor's competence when safety issues emerge in treatment. Our four vignette supervisors, although clearly minimally trained for their roles, nonetheless bear ethical and legal responsibility for their supervisory decisions. What guides are available to assist them and us in enhancing supervisory competence?

Adherence to existing supervisor standards (Table 3.2), obtaining formal training, and acquiring specialty supervisor credentials are obvious avenues to demonstrating competence. Bennett et al. (1990) developed a series of risk management "focus lists" to foster increased awareness of ethical and legal obligations associated with various aspects of clinical mental health practice. Regarding competence in the supervision of others, they pose the following general questions:

- Have you learned the skills necessary to supervise, whether those skills relate to reaching and training students or to overseeing the work of an employee?
- If you teach students, supervise interns, or direct other training programs, do you provide those you teach with appropriate and timely support and guidance and a firm grounding in knowledge, skills, and ethics required to provide their future clients with appropriate care?
- Do you instruct those you supervise to adhere to the tenets of the profession that are relevant to them and to perform tasks that they are qualified and legally and ethically certified or licensed to perform?
- Have you established procedures for providing evaluations of employees or students in a timely manner? Have you included provisions for both oral and written evaluations? Do you document even oral evaluations?
- Do you provide accurate references? If you are concerned about a person's reactions to a poor reference, do you consider alternatives such as only confirming dates of employment or study, only providing grades and indicating that the individual needed improvement in a given area, or, if feasible, giving no reference? When in doubt, do you consult a more experienced colleague?
- Do you maintain accurate documentation of performance, including positive and negative aspects, written evaluations, factual observations, work history, reasons for termination, and similar information? Do you include records of references provided? (Bennett et al., 1990, pp. 47–48)

Important aspects of supervisor competence are also implicit in a Supervisee Bill of Rights proposed by Munson (1993). This document establishes a foundation of expectations for social work supervisees and supervisors, stipulating that every clinical supervisee has the right to:

- a supervisor who supervises consistently and at regular intervals
- growth-oriented supervision that respects personal privacy
- supervision that is technically sound and theoretically grounded
- be evaluated on criteria that are made clear in advance and evaluations that are based on actual observation of performance
- a supervisor who is adequately skilled in clinical practice and trained in supervision practice (Munson, 1993)

Finally, definitions of professional competence include the responsibility to maintain a working knowledge of ethical codes that pertain to both supervisor's and supervisee's disciplines and to keep updated on state credentialing regulations and case law.

SUPERVISION CONTRACTS AND POLICIES

CASE UPDATE

Maria reports an improvement in her mood and energy in the third therapy session. She slept through the night "for the first time in months" yesterday, enjoyed an outing to the lake with her children last weekend, and denied any suicidal ideation during the week. She also followed up on Georgia's recommendation for an updated physical exam, which occurred this week. She reports that the exam and blood work were normal. Her physician advised her to get more exercise and prescribed a sedative to help her sleep.

Maria's efforts to spend quality time with each child were not very successful. Carrie was playing sports or out with her boyfriend every afternoon, and she rejected Maria's offer to help her with a homework project. They did attend Sunday church service together, but Carrie "bolted" immediately afterward to visit some friends. Carlos was grounded for the week due to the graffiti incident and remained sullen in his room except for meals and church. Maria reported several angry exchanges with him in which she ended up in tears and he withdrew further. They did go to a picnic at the lake with cousins on Saturday, and both children appeared to have a good time. Maria enjoyed herself also, noting that "it was great to feel like a normal family for a little while."

Maria remains adamant about not wanting a couple's meeting with ex-husband Ringo to discuss the children's behavior. Georgia reiterated her belief in the importance of having the father involved in parenting concerns and explored Maria's resistance further. She is convinced that he will "blow up" and blame her for their problems, and feels that she cannot face his anger anymore. She also expressed a fear that if Ringo hears about the latest school incident, he may try to persuade Carlos to live with him. Maria is certain that would be detrimental to Carlos and tearfully states, "It would kill me to lose him."

Georgia did speak by phone with the home–school coordinator about Carlos. She confirmed that there had been no contact between the school and his father, given that Maria was the custodial parent. She noted that during her home visit,

Maria was cooperative and cordial and that Carlos seemed verbal and responsive both to her and to his mother. Her impression was that Carlos was a likable boy who was acting out his grief over the parents' divorce and his mother's recent emotional unavailability due to her depression. Carrie had not been present during this first home visit.

Georgia reported confusion to her supervisor about how to proceed with the case. She is concerned that, although Maria complains of Ringo's lack of parenting support, she avoids informing him about incidents or concerns regarding the children. Georgia cannot assess whether Maria's fear of Ringo is warranted and feels frustrated by the lack of basic communication between the parents. She hypothesizes that this may be contributing both to Maria's depression and to the oppositional behavior of Carlos and Carrie. She also questions whether there may be a history of undisclosed domestic violence underlying Maria's avoidance behavior.

Georgia and her supervisor, Jeremy, have moved from an initial appraisal into a review of therapeutic progress in Maria's case. It is here that the impact of supervisory structure and institutional scaffolding become keenly evident. What policies guide Jeremy's recommendations to Georgia regarding how to proceed with Maria? How are respective clinical duties of this supervisor, supervisee, and backup staff delineated? What criteria govern consultations, referrals, or crisis management decisions that may emerge as treatment continues? How are supervisory activities documented and followed up?

As reviewed earlier, there are at least three levels of accountability that supervisors are held to: (a) ethical codes and professional standards of their disciplines; (b) state regulations governing professional practice; and (c) local, state, and federal laws. In providing cross-disciplinary supervision as Jeremy (a social worker) is for Georgia (a mental health counselor), it becomes even more complex. Jeremy is responsible for adhering to his discipline's ethical standards in supervising Georgia's work, whereas Georgia is responsible for conducting ethical practice as defined by both her and Jeremy's professions (Knapp & VandeCreek, 1997a). Furthermore, supervisors are accountable for implementing policies of their employers, regulations of the managed-care industry, and requirements of any training institutions that contract their supervision services. That's a lot to keep track of.

It makes good sense for supervisors to have some organized way of accessing this information to guide their decisions. Ethical codes and professional standards establish the basic parameters for policies and procedures that should exist in supervisory settings. We will start with them in discussing policy implications for the vignette characters and our own practices.

Table 4.1 highlights guidelines of major mental health disciplines regarding the structure of supervision. Several of these statements (i.e., ASPPB, NASW, ACA, AAMFT) stipulate that written supervisory agreements or contracts

TABLE 4.1 Supervisory Policies and Procedures

American Association for Marriage and Family Therapy
Responsibilities and Guidelines for AAMFT Approved Supervisors
and Supervisors-in-Training
A contract should be developed for the supervision which delineates fees, hours, time and place of meetings, case responsibility, caseload review, handling of suicidal threats, other dangerous client situations, and so forth.

American Association of Pastoral Counselors
Supervision Standards
Supervision is normally expected to be a regular face-to-face meeting to examine the clinical materials of therapeutic interaction, such as audio or video tapes, process notes, or live observation. . . . The minimum expected frequency is twice a month. . . . Individual supervision may include two trainees. When more than two trainees are present, this is considered group supervision. . . . A [pastoral educator] is normally expected to have an hour of supervision for each four to six hours of counseling provided. . . . A [certified member] is normally expected to have an hour of supervision for each eight to twelve hours of counseling provided.

American Counseling Association
Code of Ethics and Standards of Practice
Standard D.1.b: Counselors establish working agreements with supervisors, colleagues, and subordinates regarding counseling or clinical relationships, confidentiality, adherence to professional standards, distinction between public and private material, maintenance and dissemination of recorded information, workload, and accountability.

Association for Counselor Education and Supervision
Ethical Guidelines for Counseling Supervisors
Guideline 2.03: Supervisors should make their supervisees aware of professional and ethical standards and legal responsibilities of the counseling profession.

Guideline 2.05: Procedures for contacting the supervisor, or an alternative supervisor, to assist in handling crisis situations should be established and communicated to supervisees.

Guideline 2.14: Supervisors should incorporate the principles of informed consent and participation; clarity of requirements, expectations, roles and rules; and due process and appeal into the establishment of policies and procedures of the institution, program, courses, and individual supervisory relationships.

Guideline 3.07: Supervisors should inform supervisees of the goals, policies, theoretical orientations toward counseling, training, and supervision model or approach on which the supervision is based.

Guideline 3.12: Supervisors in university settings should establish and communicate specific policies and procedures regarding field placement of students. The respective roles of the student counselor, the university supervisor, and the field supervisor should be clearly differentiated in areas such as evaluation, requirements, and confidentiality.

(continued on next page)

TABLE 4.1   Supervisory Policies and Procedures *(continued)*

Association of State and Provincial Psychology Boards
Supervision Guidelines
Guideline I.B: The setting must provide the prospective supervisee with a written document specifying the rules and regulations of the program, as well as the roles, goals and objectives expected from both supervisee and supervisor. At the onset of training, the supervisor will be responsible for developing, along with the supervisee, a written individualized training plan that meets the needs of the supervisee and is consistent with the purpose of the setting. . . .

Guideline II.C: The supervisor, or a qualified designee who meets the requirements as a supervisor, provides 24-hour availability to both the supervisee and the supervisee's clients. The psychologist shall have sufficient knowledge of all clients, including face-to-face contact when necessary, in order to plan effective service delivery procedures. The supervisor makes reasonable effort to provide for another qualified supervisor in the case of any interruption of supervision due to such factors as the supervisor's illness, unavailability, or relocation.

National Association of Social Workers
Guidelines for Clinical Social Work Supervision
A written understanding should be signed by both the supervisor and the supervisee (and the agency supervisor or administrator when appropriate) at the beginning of supervision and amended or renegotiated to reflect change. The agreement should clarify the following items: supervisory context, learning plan, format and schedule, supervisor responsibilities, supervisee responsibilities, accountability, evaluation measures, documentation and reporting, conflict resolution, compensation, client notification, duration and termination.

National Board for Certified Counselors
Standards for the Ethical Practice of Clinical Supervision
Standard 3: Clinical supervisors shall inform supervisees about the process of supervision, including supervision goals, case management procedures, and the supervisor's preferred supervision model(s).

Standard 6: Clinical supervisors shall establish procedures with their supervisees for handling crisis situations.

Standard 12: Clinical supervisors shall ensure that supervisees are aware of the current ethical standards related to their professional practice, as well as legal standards that regulate the practice of counseling.

Standard 13: Clinical supervisors shall engage supervisees in an examination of cultural issues that might affect supervision and/or counseling.

---

should be developed. All disciplines identify at least some of the following considerations in structuring supervision:

- ◆ an individualized supervisee training plan
- ◆ description of the schedule, format, and duration of supervision
- ◆ written roles, goals, and objectives of supervision
- ◆ disclosure of a supervisor's training and model of supervision
- ◆ respective responsibilities of the supervisor and supervisee

- client notification of and consent to the supervisory relationship
- formal emergency and crisis management policies
- 24-hour supervisor availability to supervisees and their clients
- communication between academic and field supervisors
- clarification of roles among academic and field supervisors
- policies concerning informed consent and confidentiality of supervision
- supervisor knowledge of all clients in a supervisee's caseload
- supervisory documentation and reporting requirements
- inclusion of legal, ethical, and cultural training in supervision
- limiting the number of supervisees assigned to a supervisor
- limiting the ratio of clients assigned for each supervision hour
- clarification of fees or compensation related to supervision
- formative and summative supervisee evaluation procedures
- disciplinary action and due process rights of supervisees

The remainder of this and the next several chapters will review these standards in light of current practices, recommendations, and legal doctrines. Once again, supervisors are urged to review their own state regulations for possible variations from the following guidelines.

SUPERVISION CONTRACTS: STRUCTURE AND INFORMED CONSENT

Regardless of whether a written contract exists, an implied contract and a corresponding duty of care exist solely on the basis of assuming a supervisory role (Guest & Dooley, 1999). Thus, Jeremy and his employer both assume some responsibility for Georgia's conduct. In *Ray v. County of Delaware* (1997), institutional hiring policies were closely examined as an initial screening of employee competence. They failed, in this case, to reveal any propensity for ethical violations by a social worker who subsequently engaged in sexual relations with a patient. Thus, adequate hiring procedures relieved this agency of liability for negligent hiring. Appropriate policies in the hiring of Georgia should include verifying her training and credentials, contacting references and former employers, conducting a personal interview, and in some settings, performing a background criminal check.

Returning to *Ray v. County of Delaware* (1997), documented evidence of adequate supervision that conformed to standards of the profession protected both the supervisor and employer from charges of negligent supervision of this clinician. By contrast, prior knowledge by the employer and supervisor of an alcohol and drug abuse counselor's criminal history and sexual misconduct while on the job established foreseeability and negligent retention liability in another case (*Porter v. Nemir*, 1995). Jeremy thus has a critical responsibility in his supervision of Georgia's professionalism. As we shall see in the next chapter, failure of a supervisor to take action regarding even *potential* misconduct of a supervisee can result in liability for negligent supervision (*Almonte v. New York Medical College,* 1994; see Case 5.1).

Assuming that Georgia's file provides no indication of past or potential future misconduct, a supervision contract is a valuable training and risk management tool to clarify the expectations and requirements of her supervision. Numerous authors have noted that such contracts help prevent miscommunication, facilitate orientation of the supervisee, minimize covert agendas and abuses of supervisory power, and reduce the legal exposure of all parties (Bernard & Goodyear, 1998; Cohen & Cohen, 1999; Freeman, 1993; Hewson, 1999; Osborn & Davis, 1996; Tanenbaum & Berman, 1990; Watkins, 1997a). Supervisory contracts establish a way of being together in the supervisory relationship. They define parameters of the relationship, which helps reduce supervisee uncertainty and enhance trust (Inskipp & Proctor, 1989). They also serve as a benchmark against which to assess the process of professional development (Hewson, 1999).

Osborn and Davis (1996) outlined five principles supporting the use of supervisory contracts:

1. they clarify methods, goals, and expectations of supervision
2. they encourage professional collaboration between parties
3. they communicate and uphold ethical principles in practice
4. they document services, responsibilities, and accountability
5. they align supervision with counseling and consultation services

Munson (1993) recommends time-limited supervision contracts of 6 months based on an initial "educational diagnosis" of a supervisee's knowledge and experience. McCarthy et al. (1995) identify the following "conflict-prone" topics to include in supervisory contracts to ensure informed consent:

◆ *purpose:* structure and mutual understanding of supervision
◆ *professional disclosure:* supervisor credentials and qualifications
◆ *practical issues:* logistics, fees, contacts, requirements to fulfill academic or licensing demands, professional learning contract
◆ *supervision process:* methods and format of supervision
◆ *evaluation and due process:* criteria, methods, and frequency of evaluations, due process, and complaint procedures
◆ *ethical and legal issues:* policies, regulations, and laws regarding supervisory and therapeutic relationships
◆ *statement of agreement:* signed acknowledgment by all parties that they understand and agree to comply with the contract

Contracts don't need to be lengthy or legalistic. Prest, Schindler-Zimmerman, and Sporakowski (1992) developed the Initial Supervision Session Checklist (Table 4.2) for use in early supervisory sessions. This provides a record of topics covered and forms the basis of a mutual working agreement between the

TABLE 4.2   Initial Supervision Session Checklist (ISSC)

This checklist is designed for use by both supervisor and supervisee during the initial session(s) of the supervisory process. The ISSC will facilitate establishing a clear contract for supervision, maximizing the fit between supervisor and supervisee, and ensuring the attainment of goals established by those involved.

Education, Training and Clinical Experience
Inquire about the following characteristics of the supervisee/supervisor:
____ educational background
____ training experiences
____ setting(s), number of years
____ theoretical orientation
____ clinical competence with various issues, models, techniques, populations, presenting problems, therapy group and family forms
____ sense of mission/purpose in the field
____ educational plans and professional goals of the supervisee

Philosophy of Supervision
Explore the supervisee's/supervisor's philosophy of the supervision process, including:
____ philosophy of therapy and change
____ purpose of supervision

Previous Supervision Experiences
In order to assess the range of a supervisee's competence, the following points should be discussed:
____ previous supervision experiences (e.g., format, setting)
____ strengths and weaknesses as therapist and as supervisee
____ supervisee's competence with stages of therapy process
____ supervisee's level of development in terms of case planning, notes, collateral support and networking
____ supervisory competence with various issues, models, techniques, populations, therapy groups and family forms
____ methods for managing supervisor-supervisee differences

Supervision Goals
In order to establish and evaluate goals of supervision, address the following:
____ goals (personal and professional)
____ process of goal evaluation and time frame (e.g., weekly)
____ requirements for which supervisee is seeking supervision (e.g., licensure, professional certification)
____ requirements to be met by supervision (e.g., total hours, individual or group supervision, direct work samples)

Supervision Style and Techniques
In order to facilitate an optimum fit in terms of supervisory style, address preferred mode(s), including:
____ specific expectations the supervisee/supervisor has of the parties involved (e.g., roles, hierarchy)
____ types of supervision that would facilitate clinical growth of the supervisee
____ preferred supervision style (e.g., didactic, experiential, collegial)
____ parallels between therapy and supervision models

(continued on next page)

TABLE 4.2 Initial Supervision Session Checklist (ISSC) *(continued)*

___ supervision focus (e.g., therapist's development, cases)
___ manner of case review (e.g., crisis management, in-depth focus)
___ modality (e.g., audio, video, verbal report, live observation)

Theoretical Orientation

Recognizing that a good theoretical fit is equally important to the supervisory process, address:

___ models and specific theories in which supervisee and supervisor have been trained, practice, and/or conduct supervision
___ extent to which these models have been used clinically
___ populations, presenting problems and/or family forms with which the models have been most effective
___ interest in learning new approaches
___ integration of theoretical models

Legal/Ethical Considerations

Legal and ethical parameters for the supervision process must be defined. These include:

___ ultimate responsibility for clients discussed in supervision in different contexts (e.g., licensed vs. unlicensed therapist, private practice vs. academic setting)
___ number of cases for which the supervisor will be responsible
___ emergency and back-up procedures (e.g., supervisor accessibility)
___ awareness of professional ethical codes
___ confidentiality regarding the information discussed in supervision
___ confidentiality issues when more than one supervisee is involved
___ specific issues in situations where dual roles exist (e.g., faculty–student boundaries)
___ process for addressing supervisee issues (e.g., burnout, countertransference)

Use of Self in Supervision

Where supervision includes focus on "use of self," discuss the following:

___ utility of "use of self" in supervision
___ supervisee's current family and other relationships
___ discussion of techniques (e.g., genograms, early recollections)
___ conflicts between personal values/beliefs and supervisee goals
___ significant life events that shape supervisee's clinical work

Practical Issues Related to Supervision

The supervision process is a contractual one in which the supervisor provides a service to the supervisee. Practical considerations including the following must be addressed during the initial session:

___ fee and arrangements for payment
___ schedule and duration of meetings
___ place
___ duration of supervision (e.g., semester, number of hours)
___ how time and fees will be split among supervisees
___ format (audio/video, case presentation, individual or group)
___ modality (e.g., experiential, live observation)
___ role of other supervisees
___ supervision session guidelines
___ process for handling conflict among supervision group members
___ process and responsibility for documenting supervision
___ exchange of regular and emergency phone/contact numbers

(continued on next page)

TABLE 4.2   Initial Supervision Session Checklist (ISSC) *(continued)*

Supervisee Workplace

Ecosystemic considerations are important for small private practices to large inpatient units, especially when members are joined from each to create a new supervision system. Discuss the context in which the supervisee works:

____ supervisee's place of employment or practice
____ agency dynamics (e.g., nature of administrative control)
____ agency structure (e.g., hierarchy of supervisory responsibility)
____ agency referral system
____ supervisee's support system

Other Discussion Considerations

What do we need to know about each other that we have not already discussed?

Source: Adapted from "The Initial Supervision Session Checklist (ISSC): A Guide for the MFT Supervision Process," by L. A. Prest, T. Schindler-Zimmerman, and M. J. Sporakowski, 1992, *The Clinical Supervisor, 10,* 117–133. Copyright © 1992, Haworth Press, Inc. Reprinted with permission.

parties. Providing this level of organization also helps reduce the anxiety inherent in supervision: "setting an initial structure, clarifying goals and expectations, and incorporating frequent feedback fosters an atmosphere of openness, flexibility and competency . . . " (Schindler & Talen, 1996, p. 119). Let's examine more closely the content of supervisory contracts in the context of our vignette.

MAKING THE IMPLICIT EXPLICIT: SUPERVISION POLICIES AND FRAMEWORK

How often should Maria's case be reviewed? What follow-up will occur regarding referrals and recommendations? Does Georgia require additional training to treat Maria adequately? Are there cultural, environmental, or financial constraints that may affect her therapy? These are important considerations for Jeremy in supervising this case. The Focused Risk Management Supervision System (FoRMSS) (Falvey, Caldwell, & Cohen, 2002) includes a format for documenting case management aspects of supervision (Figure 4.1). This alerts Jeremy to identify relevant clinical concerns and communicate with Georgia about their presence, impact, or resolution as treatment progresses. Thus, when Georgia has Maria sign a release to consult with her physician about the results of her physical, this is tracked by Jeremy for follow-up discussion. How often they review Maria's case, possible legal or ethical issues that may affect treatment, and Georgia's documentation in Maria's clinical file are other areas that Jeremy is expected to monitor. By explicitly agreeing on these parameters, Georgia and Jeremy operate from a "common frame of reference" (McCarthy et al., 1995) that clarifies and safeguards their supervisory relationship.

A new ethical requirement that has emerged stipulates that clients should give informed consent for their therapists to receive supervision of their case.

FIGURE 4.1   FoRMSS Treatment Referrals and Record Requests

RECOMMENDED REFERRALS

Referral	Dates Discussed in Supervision	Name(s) of Agency/Prof.	Dates Discussed with Client	Release Signed	Client Follow-Up Yes No
Psychiatric Consultation	10/2/01	in - house	10/6/01	☑	☑ ☐
Medical/Physical Evaluation	10/2/01	family MD (Dr. Shorey)	10/6/01	☑	☑ ☐
Substance Abuse Treatment				☐	☐ ☐
Psychological Testing				☐	☐ ☐
Social Services				☐	☐ ☐
Legal Services				☐	☐ ☐
Educational/Special Ed. Services				☐	☐ ☐
Career/Vocational Assessment				☐	☐ ☐
Support/Community Group				☐	☐ ☐
Other				☐	☐ ☐

RECORDS REQUESTED

Records	Dates Discussed in Supervison	Dates Discussed with Client	Release Signed Yes No	Records Received Yes No	Date
Psychiatric			☐ ☐	☐ ☐	
Medical	10/16/01	10/20/01	☑ ☐	☐ ☑	
Substance Abuse Treatment			☐ ☐	☐ ☐	
Counseling/Therapy			☐ ☐	☐ ☐	
Psychological Testing			☐ ☐	☐ ☐	
Social Services			☐ ☐	☐ ☐	
Legal/Court			☐ ☐	☐ ☐	
Education/Special Ed.			☐ ☐	☐ ☐	
Career/Vocational			☐ ☐	☐ ☐	
Other _school guidance_	10/9/01	10/13/01	☑ ☐	☑ ☐	(via phone) 10/15/01

Source: From *Documentation in Supervision: The Focused Risk Management Supervision System (FoRMSS),* by J. E. Falvey, C. F. Caldwell, and C. R. Cohen. Copyright © 2002 Wadsworth Group.

This includes sharing the names and credentials of supervisors, who has access to information about their treatment, and how clients may contact supervisors directly (Neufeldt, 1999; Pope & Vasquez, 1998; Swenson, 1997). For pre-professional interns, this could also require providing the names of faculty supervisors and peers in training seminars who will review their case material. Furthermore, Disney and Stephens (1994) caution that a site's emergency procedures should specify any others who may have access to client records: "If a backup counselor other than the supervisor is used, confidentiality is compromised, and the client must be aware that the supervisee engages in this practice" (p. 49).

Although this may seem burdensome, a counselor's refusal to reveal information about his supervisor probably contributed to filing of the initial complaint by a dissatisfied client in *Steckler v. Ohio State Board of Psychology* (Case 4.1). In this case, the supervisor's license was ultimately revoked for

CASE

4.1

Steckler v. Ohio State Board of Psychology
613 N.E.2d 1070 (Ohio App. 1992)   *Ohio Court of Appeals*

FACTS

A psychologist's license was suspended by the Board of Psychology based on his failure to follow the rules of supervision that governed licensed mental health professionals. The psychologist (Steckler) entered into a verbal consultation agreement with an unlicensed counselor (who had applied for licensure, which had not yet been granted). Steckler assumed the counselor was licensed and therefore thought his role was that of "consultant" and not "supervisor." Steckler's role was to help monitor the counselor's cases, for which he was paid an hourly fee. When the counselor refused to provide Steckler's name to a dissatisfied client, the client filed a complaint with the board.

HOLDING OF THE COURT

The court upheld the board's order of suspension, finding that the psychologist violated the licensing rules governing supervision. The unlicensed counselor was considered an "allied mental health professional," and under Ohio's psychological licensing rules, "full discretion, control, and responsibility for client welfare," *id.* at 1073, rested with the licensed psychologist. Since Steckler never met with, had substantial knowledge of, or provided a diagnosis for this client, he did not maintain full discretion and control and was thus in violation of the rules. In addition, by his signature on the insurance documents, Steckler argued that he provided "immediate personal supervision" over the treatment of the insured client. *Id.* at 1072. The court found this to be false, constituting further evidence of his breach of the rules.

IMPLICATIONS

The most important implication in this case is that, despite what you call your relationship with another professional (i.e., consultant vs. supervisor), the law can call it something else, resulting in dire consequences. The facts didn't add up in this case. Had the counselor been licensed, the relationship would most likely have been characterized as consultation (where there was no requirement for direct control or review of the counselor's cases). However, this would have also eliminated the need for the psychologist to sign insurance forms. It is paramount to maintain up-to-date knowledge of the statutes governing both your and your supervisees' professional activities. If acting in a supervisory capacity, the law has ascribed a greater duty (refer to the legal definition of this concept in Chapter 2) on the part of the supervisor to oversee cases and involve him- or herself in the direct treatment of the client. A familiar theme in this book is highlighted here. Know the duties and responsibilities the law places on you (in your state and within your discipline) as a supervisor. This knowledge will help protect you from getting into situations that lead to increased exposure to liability.

Timothy E. Bray (2000). Reprinted with permission.

breach of the rules governing supervision in his state. He not only failed to provide supervision to the unlicensed counselor regarding the case in question but subsequently signed insurance forms attesting to having done so. This case illustrates how assuming a supervisory role increases the legal responsibility we accept for a colleague's work (Knapp & VandeCreek, 1997a).

Given that Georgia is not yet licensed, Jeremy may have a legal duty similar to Steckler to exercise "full discretion, control and responsibility" for the welfare of her clients. Jeremy and his employer need to consider this in establishing a policy regarding how many supervisees he will oversee and how much supervision is required to monitor their cases adequately. This will vary based on supervisee competence, the time available for supervisory activities, and the nature of the client population (Welfel, 1998a). Guidelines relating to the number of supervisees assigned per supervisor also vary across disciplines and states. State regulatory bodies often set limits of from three to five supervisees per supervisor (Welfel, 1998a). The Association of State and Provincial Psychology Boards (ASPPB) (1998a) limits supervisors to three to four supervisees depending on their credentials, while the National Association of Social Workers (NASW) recommends from two to six supervisees depending on whether supervision is the sole duty of a supervisor (Crespi & Lopez, 1998).

Some professional guidelines also exist for the ratio of clients to supervision time. For example, Moline, Williams, and Austin (1998) report that California requires supervisors to provide 1 hour of individual or 2 hours of group supervision for every 5 hours (premasters) to 10 hours (postmasters) of client contact among marriage, family, and child counseling interns. The American Association of Pastoral Counselors (AAPC) (1999) recommends 1 hour of supervision for every 4 to 6 client contact hours for counselors in training and 1 hour for 8 to 12 client contact hours for certified pastoral counselors. Dr. Johnson, Jeremy's supervisor, is thus well advised to develop and implement policies regarding the frequency and ratio of supervision provided to both unlicensed (e.g., Georgia) and licensed staff clinicians based on their caseload and Jeremy's job description.

FROM A DISTANCE: SUPERVISORY CRISIS MANAGEMENT

If I am responsible for the welfare of someone else, I presumably would want some direct input from or contact with that person. Yet clinical supervisors seldom have any direct knowledge of their supervisee's clients. This presents a serious liability issue when clients become dangerous to self or others or if supervisees behave unethically or illegally in the treatment relationship. For example, what if Maria makes a suicide attempt as her depression lifts? Or what if Georgia refuses to schedule another appointment until her ex-husband is invited to join the treatment? Two related issues emerge for supervisors:

1. How will they know if crises or violations occur?
2. What mechanisms are in place for responding to such crises?

There need to be structures in place for supervisors to become aware of crises that supervisees either may not recognize as such or may choose to withhold from their supervisors. The most obvious of these structures would be for clinical supervisors to have direct contact with clients or actual work samples of their supervisees. While several professional standards recommend these practices (see Table 4.1), surveys reveal that they seldom occur in field settings (Borders, Cashwell, & Rotter, 1995; McCarthy, Kulakowski, & Kenfield, 1994; Navin, Beamish, & Johanson, 1995). Self-report of their clinical work by supervisees remains the predominant method of case review. Who, then, chooses which cases to review—and when?

This is a dilemma that has not been addressed by ethical codes or standards of conduct. It is a leap of faith, as well as legally risky, for the supervisor to expect supervisees to consistently present those cases with which they feel least competent, especially when supervision carries the authority to control a supervisee's promotion, credentialing, or retention. It is thus advisable for supervisors to have a policy for reviewing all cases on a prioritized basis. Knapp and VandeCreek (1996a) caution that supervisors should "not allow the supervisee to select which cases to present during supervisory sessions. Although it is reasonable to assume that the prudent supervisee will give greater focus to problem or troublesome cases, the supervisor should not neglect those cases that the supervisee deems are more routine" (p. 192).

Jeremy uses a log sheet (Figure 4.2) to schedule weekly reviews of Georgia's clinical work. This allows him to track ongoing changes in her caseload, visually scan for cases that need updating, and plan for supervisory sessions. Barring crises, he is able to track and monitor Georgia's cases on a rotating basis.

When crises do occur, there should be written procedures that all staff are trained to follow. *Peck v. Counseling Service of Addison County, Inc.* (Case 4.2) is a landmark case that not only extended the duty-to-warn doctrine to cover threats of serious property damage, but also illustrated the need to formalize crisis policies and communication between supervisors and supervisees. In this case, the Vermont Supreme Court found a counseling agency liable because it "did not have a cross-reference system between its therapists and outside physicians who were treating the medical problems of its patients. Nor did the Counseling Service have any written policy concerning formal intra-staff consultation procedures when a patient presented a serious risk of harm to another" (*Peck v. Counseling Service of Addison County, Inc.*, 1985).

FIGURE 4.2 FoRMSS Log Sheet

FoRMSS LOG SHEET

Date	Duration	No. in Caseload	New Cases (IDs)	Closed Cases (IDs)	Cases Reviewed	Next Review ✓	
9/25/01	1 hr	21	—	SD(#07342)	AC SD RR	10/9/01 ✓ Terminated 10/9/01 ✓	
10/2/01	1 hr	22	MR(#07350)	—	NT LC MR	11/6/01 12/23/01 10/9/01	
10/9/01	1 hr	22	—	—	RR MR AC	10/16/01 (Term) 10/16/01 ✓ 10/16/01 (T) ✓	
10/16/01	1 hr	20	—	RR(#07183) AC(#07332)	RR AC MR	Terminated Terminated 10/23/01 ✓	
10/23/01	1 hr	21	JM(#07371)	—	JM MR LC	11/6/01 11/6/01 11/20/01	
10/30/01	— Vacation — emerg. coverage with L. Doring —						

Source: From *Documentation in Supervision: The Focused Risk Management Supervision System (FoRMSS)*, by J. E. Falvey, C. F. Caldwell, and C. R. Cohen. Copyright © 2002 Wadsworth Group.

Mental health and counseling settings are responsible for having written emergency policies and procedures. These policies should include provisions for qualified consultation or supervision and identify procedures for preserving evidence about decision processes utilized in resolving a crisis (Crawford, 1994; Ellis, 1991). They should address staff safety in areas such as office arrangement, buddy systems, warning devices, incident reports, and restraint techniques (Munson, 1993; Pozgar, 1996). They should "delineate emergency procedures in detail, so that both supervisors and trainees know exactly what to do and when" (Neufeldt, 1999, p. 25). Supervisors share in the responsibility for developing and communicating such policies to their supervisees.

Thus, in our vignette, Georgia should be given numbers to contact Jeremy or his designated backup supervisor 24 hours a day, as well as being trained in agency procedures for handling clinical emergencies such as suicide threats, dangerousness, and child abuse reporting. This promotes her consistent and competent responses under stressful clinical circumstances.

Peck v. Counseling Service of Addison County, Inc.
499 A.2d 422 (Vt. 1985)   *Supreme Court of Vermont*

FACTS

This was a lawsuit brought by John Peck's parents against his therapist and the counseling agency, alleging that the therapist and agency negligently failed to notify them of John's stated intentions to cause property damage. At a session with his outpatient therapist, John expressed intense anger at his father, as they had recently had a fight. At this session, John stated that he was going to burn down his parents' barn. His therapist discussed possible consequences of this act, and John subsequently made a verbal promise not to burn the barn. The therapist, believing John's promise, did not disclose his threats to other staff members or to John's family. The following evening John burned down the barn.

HOLDING OF THE COURT

The court framed this case as one similar to *Tarasoff*, in that it was viewed as a failure to warn a third party of the expressed dangerousness of the client. However, what was different in their analysis was the finding of negligence because the agency did not have a written emergency policy to consult with the external treating psychiatrist and an internal emergency policy to require supervision or consultation when a client presents a serious danger. The court found that the lack of supervision and a formalized process resulted in the uninformed actions of the therapist and constituted failure on the agency's behalf to exercise proper control over its supervisees. The court stated that the therapist was negligent and "did not act as a reasonably prudent counselor, because her good faith belief was based on inadequate information and consultation." *Id*. at 425.

IMPLICATIONS

Emergencies arise every day, in varying degrees, in all types of mental health settings and inevitably to all therapists. Emergencies can be a critical time not only for the client, but for the therapist as well. Crucial decisions are made under pressure. When determining dangerousness, immediate clinical judgment is exercised, which can and often does have potentially disastrous legal consequences. As part of any risk management program, supervision or consultation should always and immediately be sought when a client has expressed violent intentions, or you believe him/her to be dangerous.

There are two important implications of this court decision. First, the court expressly stated that consultation with the treating psychiatrist (or a psychiatrist in general) is paramount. The court recognized that the mental health field conceptualizes pathology through the medical model, and because of this, consultation with a medical doctor is important in an emergency (as physical concerns are often first priority). Second, and most important to our inquiry, is the need for a formalized "in-house" supervision or consultation procedure for therapists to discuss the dangerous and potentially dangerous client. Multiple judgments are more likely than not to result in decisions and actions consistent with the standard of care owed to the client. Even if a therapist's actions are founded on good faith beliefs, if those beliefs are based on information not in accordance with the standard of care, the therapist may be liable for poor outcomes.

Timothy E. Bray (2000). Reprinted with permission.

The time for a clinician to think through difficult issues regarding risk assessment and management is not when a patient makes a threat or misses a follow-up appointment. Rather, general policy choices should be made and reflected upon before the need for them arises in a given case. These policies or guidelines should be committed to writing and should be reviewed by experienced clinicians and lawyers. Staff should be educated in the use of the guidelines, and their compliance should be audited. Finally, forms should be revised to prompt and record the actions contemplated by the policy statement. (Monahan, 1993, p. 247)

SUMMARY AND RECOMMENDATIONS

Within this structural scaffolding, both supervisor and supervisee are informed and protected as they carry out clinical responsibilities. The following chapters elaborate on those responsibilities, which include the selection and screening of supervisees and their clients, liaison with training institutions, overseeing client welfare as well as supervisee professional development, evaluation of supervisee performance, and ensuring appropriate ethical and legal practice.

Osborn and Davis (1996) developed a sample supervision contract. An adaptation of this contract is reprinted here to serve as a model for supervisors and supervisees to construct the parameters of their professional working relationship collaboratively.

SAMPLE SUPERVISION CONTRACT

This contract serves as verification and description of the supervision provided by _name_ ("supervisor"), _credentials, title, institutional affiliation,_ to _name_ ("supervisee"), _credentials, title, institutional affiliation_.

I. Purpose, Goals, and Objectives
  a. Monitor and ensure welfare of clients seen by supervisee
  b. Promote development of supervisee's professional identity and competence
  c. Fulfill requirement for supervisee licensure or certification

II. Context of Services
  a. Weekly individual supervision at _site_ on _day and time_.
  b. _supervision model(s) and case review format(s)_ will be used in supervisory sessions.
  c. Clients of supervisee will give informed consent for supervision of their case, including name and contact number of supervisor.
  d. Supervision will conform to state regulations regarding the supervision of candidates for licensure as _discipline._
  e. Supervisee will have a minimum of 1 hour of supervision for every _#_ client contact hours.

f. All supervisee cases will be reviewed on a rotating basis and in proportion to priority needs of each case.

III. Methods of Evaluation

The *FoRMSS Case Overview, FoRMSS Supervision Record, or FoRMSS Termination Summary* will be used to document content of all supervision sessions. Informal feedback will be provided at the close of each session, and a formal evaluation, using the *Evaluation of Counselor Behaviors—Long Form*, will be conducted every 10 weeks. Supervision notes will be shared with supervisee at the supervisor's discretion or upon request of supervisee. A training schedule (readings, workshops, courses) will be updated following each formal evaluation of the supervisee.

IV. Duties and Responsibilities

The supervisor will:

    a. examine all diagnoses and treatment plans of supervisee

    b. challenge supervisee to justify approach and techniques used

    c. monitor basic attending skills

    d. present and model appropriate clinical interventions

    e. intervene directly if client welfare is at risk

    f. ensure that ethical guidelines and legal statutes are upheld

The supervisee will:

    a. uphold all ethical guidelines and legal statutes of both supervisee's and supervisor's disciplines (copies distributed/available)

    b. be prepared to discuss all client cases using case notes or direct work samples as stipulated by supervisor

    c. discuss diagnoses made as well as approaches and techniques used, and any boundary issues or violations that occur

    d. consult supervisor or designated contact person in emergencies

    e. implement supervisor directives in subsequent client sessions

    f. read, understand, and implement all clinical policies of *site*

V. Procedural Considerations

    a. Supervisee's case notes (including diagnoses and treatment plans) and audiotapes will be reviewed in each session.

    b. Supervisee's professional development will be discussed.

    c. Sessions will address issues of conflict and/or failure of either party to abide by directives outlined in contract. If concerns of either party are not resolved in supervision, *administrative superior at site* will be consulted.

    d. In the event of emergency, supervisee is to contact supervisor. If not available, contact *name, title, and contact information of backup supervisor(s)*.

  e. All crisis or emergency consultations are to be documented by both supervisee and supervisor.

  f. Supervisor will review supervisee's professional development with *identify all site and/or academic training program personnel having access to this information.*

  g. Due process procedures have been distributed to supervisee and discussed as needed.

VI. Supervisor's Scope of Competence

  a. title/date of academic credentials and professional licenses

  b. formal supervisory training and credentials

  c. supervision history (how long, how many supervisees)

  d. current supervisory responsibilities

  e. consultation and supervision of supervision practices

  f. research, publications, and/or presentations on supervision

This contract is subject to revision at any time upon the request of either supervisee or supervisor. Revision of the contract will be made only with consent of the supervisee and approval of the supervisor.

  We agree to uphold the directives specified in this contract to the best of our ability, and to conduct our professional behavior according to the ethical principles of our professional association(s) and the codes of conduct of _____*site*_____ and ____*state regulations*____ .

Supervisor	Title	Date

Supervisee	Title	Date

This contract is in effect from *current date* to *(date of review or termination)*.

Supervisee Selection, Assignment, and Liaison

Case Update

Georgia reports to her supervisor that Maria called the agency in crisis on Monday, and she scheduled an emergency session for the next day. Maria appeared distraught. She was informed by the guidance office that Carrie may have been sexually assaulted on Sunday by her boyfriend after a soccer game they attended. Carrie had revealed this on Monday to Paul Maynor, the counseling intern she was seeing at the school. Paul immediately conferred with his supervisor, Guidance Director Edith Smith, MEd, and with his graduate internship professor, Chris Olan, PhD. Carrie was informed by Paul later that day of the school's need to contact the Division of Children, Youth and Families (DCYF) and her family. She reluctantly consented to have them call her mother but insisted that her father not become involved, as she was "terrified" of his reaction.

Maria subsequently picked Carrie up at school and tried to talk with her about the incident. Carrie was shaken but refused to discuss it. She did agree to go to their family physician, who examined her and found no physical bruises. They met with the DCYF worker who is investigating the incident. She pleaded with her mother not to tell her father, and Maria feels torn about how to respond. Maria wants to bring charges against the 18 year old, but she acknowledged that Carrie's father "might take things into his own hands" if he found out. She kept Carrie out of school Tuesday and struggled in the session with how to handle this.

Maria associated this incident with her own childhood sexual abuse by a relative and acknowledged feeling depressed and angry. She denied suicidal feelings or impulses. She agreed to discuss how to handle this with her sister and will bring Carrie to their scheduled family meeting on Friday.

After meeting with Maria, and with her consent, Georgia phoned the guidance director. Ms. Smith confirmed the alleged incident as reported to her and wanted to assess the family's potential response. She noted that she will be meeting with Paul and Carrie today to further evaluate Carrie's emotional state.

In this supervisory session, Georgia asks Jeremy to help her process a strong personal reaction to the alleged incident (she has an adolescent daughter) and to develop a plan for Maria and the family to address this crisis.

The plot thickens. Georgia is not only working to assist Maria with her major clinical disorder but is now collaborating with other (probably unknown) therapists treating this family. This situation is not uncommon when working with clients who have children in the schools or family members in inpatient or residential facilities. There are now three clinical supervisors and two counselors, representing four different disciplines, directly involved in the case. Each of these parties bears a degree of ethical and legal responsibility for treatment.

Supervisory management of the case was rather straightforward until this juncture. Now, however, coordination is rapidly becoming more complex. Let's examine the various supervisory relationships that affect services to this family. One supervisor (Ms. Smith) has a supervisee (Paul) who is being trained in her discipline of school counseling. They are therefore governed by the same standards of conduct. The other supervisors, Jeremy (social worker) and Dr. Olan (psychologist), supervise individuals from different disciplines. Because they bear ultimate responsibility for treatment, each must assure that Georgia and Paul abide by professional standards of both the supervisee's as well as their own disciplines.

All of these service providers share an ethical and legal mandate to provide competent care. A general rule of law is that unlicensed clinicians are held to the same standard of care to which licensed clinicians in their discipline would be held under similar circumstances (Disney & Stephens, 1994). Supervision is expected to compensate for inexperience. Slovenko (1980) pointedly reminds us that "without the locus of clinical responsibility resting squarely on the supervisor's shoulders, there would be little justification for troubled persons being assigned to partially trained students" (p. 462). Jeremy and Dr. Olan are thus cautioned to familiarize themselves with all relevant codes and statutes pertaining to their supervisees' as well as their own disciplines.

What becomes even more bewildering to consider is that these supervisors, who bear the greatest liability for this case given that both clinicians are unlicensed, are unlikely to have any direct knowledge of Maria or her family. "With few exceptions, a therapy supervisor is posted on what is going on through the reports of the supervisee, he never sees what is done firsthand, he rarely if ever interviews the patient or client" (Slovenko, 1980, p. 460). This anomaly sharply distinguishes clinical supervision from supervision in virtually all other occupations.

Without direct work samples, clinical supervisors must rely heavily on selection criteria, assignment of appropriate clients, and liaison with training institutions to ensure supervisee competence. Let's examine current ethical and legal benchmarks for competent supervision in each of these areas.

PROFESSIONAL APPRENTICESHIP: SELECTING SUPERVISEES

Supervision begins with the initial decision by two or more parties to enter into a clinical training relationship. Supervisors will, of course, interview candidates and review their resumés and references before accepting new supervisees. But this may not be enough. For example, it is important to identify areas of current responsibility for which supervisees have no prior experience; to know whether they have been reprimanded or terminated from previous positions; and in some settings, to conduct background checks to verify their moral character (Knapp & VandeCreek, 1996; Munson, 1993). It is also important to assess the supervisee's appreciation of diverse cultural world-views as they affect clinical values (Cashwell, Looby, & Housley, 1997; Chiaferi & Griffin, 1997; Kerson 1994), therapeutic relationships (Fukuyama, 1994; Hobson & Kanitz, 1996; Stoltenberg, McNeill, & Crethar, 1994), and professional identity (Vasquez, 1992; Welfel, 1998b). If supervisors and their supervisees are from different cultures, this should not be ignored in a "myth of professional sameness" (Helms & Cook, 1999; Leong & Wagner, 1994) that colludes against development of a fully integrated professional identity for the supervisee.

Regarding preprofessional students, field site supervisors and academic training institutions share responsibility for matching trainees to appropriate internship settings (Bernard & Goodyear, 1998; Disney & Stephens, 1994; Knapp & VandeCreek, 1997a). The training institution must also warn field settings of any known risks in accepting a trainee. *Almonte v. New York Medical College* (1994) established this legal duty in a case involving a postgraduate psychiatry resident (Case 5.1). A distinguishing point in this decision was the court's finding that the faculty instructor was considered to have "official authority or control" over the offending resident, which increased the instructor's legal duty to control the resident's conduct.

Although Almonte's instructor served as a training analyst rather than a supervisor per se, faculty members supervising academic seminars related to internships would appear to have similar authority and control over their students. Indeed, Kapp (1984) suggests that, "A health care facility is civilly accountable when a student from an affiliated educational institution negligently injures a patient in the course of a clinical practicum. . . . Likewise, the school in which the student is enrolled may be held vicariously liable" (p. 145). Dr. Olan thus assumes an important clinical and potentially legal role in assuring Paul's competence at his internship site.

A distinction needs to be drawn between clinical supervision and consultation. In situations where supervisees are themselves fully licensed, they assume a larger burden of responsibility for their work. If they consult with peers in the context of this work, those peers are not considered supervisors and thus have not been held liable by the courts for poor clinical outcomes (see Case 5.2).

Almonte v. New York Medical College

851 F.Supp. 34 (D. Conn. 1994) *United States District Court for the District of Connecticut*

FACTS

A postgraduate psychiatric student/resident at New York Medical College had applied to and been accepted at the medical school's Division of Psychoanalytic Training. While in this program, the resident was required to undertake his own psychoanalysis and did so with one of the college's faculty. During his analysis, the resident revealed that he was a pedophile and that he was intending to practice child psychiatry. The college subsequently entered into a training agreement with a hospital, at which the resident began to treat children. The college never informed the hospital of the potential dangers, and a 10-year-old boy was sexually assaulted by the resident.

HOLDING OF THE COURT

Along with its procedural rulings, the court found that the plaintiff (the 10-year-old boy) had given enough facts to support his negligent supervision claim against the medical college and the faculty analyst. The court said that because the college was acting in a supervisory capacity to the resident, it owed a duty to the patients he was treating or was likely to treat. The court first applied a standard similar to *Tarasoff*, saying that a duty to protect a third party is established when there is a specific threat or danger. The legal reference on which the court rested its opinion was that the supervisory relationship created a "special relationship" and that the faculty instructor/analyst had ample indication of danger, given that the resident identified potential victims (combined with the knowledge that he was to be working with children at the hospital).

IMPLICATIONS

Two major implications of this decision are that supervisory institutions have a duty to the supervisee's clients and that this duty is imposed if *reasonable foreseeability* exists (this is determined by either a judge or jury). From this decision, we can extrapolate that a community mental health center, hospital, and even a school could be found liable for supervisory negligence if there is a sufficiently similar supervisory structure (which, in reality, can be said to be the traditional clinical supervisory relationship). In this case, the medical college's instructor/analyst had "official authority" and control over the resident/student as well as clinical influence. While the court discussed this "extra" influence, it indicated that the result would not be substantially different had it not existed. Reasonable foreseeability is a very important doctrine to become familiar with. This concept is further discussed in the *Tarasoff* case later in the book. Possible risk management actions in this case could have included the instructor/analyst at the college informing the hospital of the potential danger to future patients of this resident or taking steps to redirect or remove the resident from practicing with children. Either option would be a reasonable attempt to protect a third party from possible danger and may have reduced the college's liability in the view of this court.

Timothy E. Bray (2000). Reprinted with permission.

CASE

5.2

Hill v. Kokosky, M.D.
463 N.W.2d 265 (Mich. Ct. App. 1990)   *Michigan Court of Appeals*

FACTS

This case was brought as a medical malpractice claim against the medical doctors that the primary physician *consulted* with. The parents of a baby born with many medical problems claimed that, while in the hospital to give birth, their primary obstetrician consulted with physicians not involved in the mother's care and whom they alleged gave negligent advice.

HOLDING OF THE COURT

The court concluded that the primary physician merely solicited colleagues' informal opinions on a particular aspect of a patient's treatment. There was no patient–physician relationship established by the consulting physicians and the treated patient. The consulting physicians never met with the patient, nor did they or the patient consent to their involvement in the course of treatment. This resulted in no duty by the consulting physicians to the patient. Even though the opinions given to the primary physician may have resulted in the injuries to the baby, in the absence of an established relationship, the burden (i.e., duty) remains with the primary physician, who made the decisions based on the alleged erroneous advice.

IMPLICATIONS

It is clear that courts are making distinctions between formal supervision and consultation and informal discussions with colleagues regarding some treatment aspects of cases. However, the line is not so clear when it comes to determining how much information will tip the scales toward the creation of a relationship and duty. Unless specifically delineated by a statute, the courts have the ability to determine if a duty or relationship exists. In this particular case, the consulting physicians had no contact with the patients, there was no formal contract for case review or consent by either the consulting physicians or the patient, and the consulting physicians may not have had any identifying information about the patient as well. It is important to know and perhaps become more consciously aware of the type, amount, and to whom you give clinical advice. If you are meeting with a colleague because she is having a hard time moving forward in treatment with a difficult client and needs advice on how to proceed and additional resources, *dependent on the existing relationship*, your meeting with her may simply be collegial.

Timothy E. Bray (2000). Reprinted with permission.

In *Hill v. Kokosky, M.D.,* (1990) the Michigan Court of Appeals concluded that "the extension of potential malpractice liability to doctors with whom a treating physician has merely conferred . . . would unacceptably inhibit the exchange of information and expertise among physicians." The prudent advice to consult regularly with colleagues regarding difficult clinical cases does not, then, appear to expose licensed professionals to liability for the case under review.

Protecting Consumers: Client Screening and Assignment

Supervisors are responsible for screening potential clients of their supervisees. This starts with decisions made prior to assigning cases (Bernard & Goodyear, 1998; Canter, Bennett, Jones, & Nagy, 1994; Huber, 1994; Knapp & VandeCreek, 1996; Sherry, 1991; Welfel, 1998b; Whitman & Jacobs, 1998):

◆ knowing competencies and limitations of the supervisee
◆ assessing the complexity of potential clients' issues
◆ determining whether the supervisee is adequately trained to assume a case prior to delegating it
◆ ensuring that supervisees do not retain too many clients in their caseloads
◆ protecting supervisees from an overload of difficult-to-treat cases at any one time
◆ supervising only those cases that the supervisor feels personally competent to treat
◆ identifying and resolving learning or character problems that compromise the supervisee's effectiveness
◆ ensuring that sufficient supervision time is available to oversee each case assigned to the supervisee adequately

Table 5.1 highlights guidelines that establish client screening as an ethical and professional standard of care across major mental health disciplines. Common themes across these standards include the need for (a) assessing supervisee skills and (b) restricting activities that supervisees are not adequately trained to perform. These are also common legal mandates.

> The supervisor can be held directly liable if he did not determine the employee's or trainee's competence before assigning responsibilities. . . . The supervisor could also be liable if he determines that someone under his direction is unable to perform his job but takes no action to limit the person's activities. (Weiner & Wettstein, 1993, p. 174)

Despite these unambiguous guidelines, assigning clients based on an awareness of supervisee skills is frequently overlooked. A national survey of counseling supervisors found that only 3% of those supervisors identified client screening as an aspect of their supervisory practice (Freeman & McHenry, 1996). Direct liability can occur if supervisors direct supervisees to perform clinical procedures they are not qualified to perform. How would the supervisor know this without careful assessment of both the supervisee's skills and a potential client's treatment needs?

In our hypothetical case, the FoRMSS Supervisee Profile (Figure 5.1) was completed by Georgia at the start of supervision. It suggests that she has had some experience working with Latina clients prior to this position but little

TABLE 5.1   Supervisory Screening and Oversight

American Association for Marriage and Family Therapy
Responsibilities and Guidelines for AAMFT Approved Supervisors
and Supervisors-in-Training
Supervisors are responsible for an initial screening to evaluate the trainee's knowledge of systems theory, family development, special family issues, gender and cultural issues, systemic approaches and interventions, human development, human sexuality, and ethical responsibilities. . . .

Code of Ethics
Standard 4.2: Marriage and family therapists do not permit students, employees, or supervisees to perform or to hold themselves out as competent to perform professional services beyond their training, level of experience, and competence.

American Association of Pastoral Counselors
Code of Ethics
Standard V.D: We advise our students, supervisees and employees against offering or engaging in, or holding themselves out as competent to engage in, professional services beyond their training, level of experience and competence.

American Counseling Association
Code of Ethics and Standards of Practice
Standard F.1.g: Counselors who supervise the counseling services of others take reasonable measures to ensure that counseling services provided to clients are professional.

Standard F.3.a: Counselors, through ongoing evaluation and appraisal, are aware of the academic and personal limitations that might impede performance. Counselors assist students and supervisees in securing remedial assistance when needed, and dismiss from the training program supervisees who are unable to provide competent service due to academic or personal limitations. . . .

American Psychiatric Association
Principles of Medical Ethics
Section 5.3: When the psychiatrist assumes a collaborative or supervisory role with another mental health worker, he/she must expend sufficient time to assure that proper care is given.

American Psychological Association
Ethical Principles of Psychologists and Code of Conduct
Standard 1.22.a: Psychologists delegate to their employees, supervisees, and research assistants only those responsibilities that such persons can reasonably be expected to perform competently, on the basis of their education, training, or experience, either independently or with the level of supervision being provided.

Standard 1.22.b: Psychologists provide proper training and supervision to their employees or supervisees and take reasonable steps to see that such persons perform services responsibly, competently, and ethically.

Association for Counselor Education and Supervision
Ethical Guidelines for Counseling Supervisors
Guideline 3.09: Supervisors should assess supervisees' skills and experience in order to establish standards for competent professional behavior. Supervisors should restrict supervisees' activities to those that are commensurate with their current level of skills and experiences.

(continued on next page)

TABLE 5.1   Supervisory Screening and Oversight *(continued)*

Association of State and Provincial Psychology Boards
Supervision Guidelines

Guideline I.B: The supervisor is responsible for determining the adequacy of the trainee's preparation for the tasks to be performed.

Guideline II.A: The supervisor has the responsibility to interrupt or terminate the supervisee's activities whenever necessary to ensure adequate training and the protection of the public.

Guideline II.C: The psychologist shall have sufficient knowledge of all clients, including face-to-face contact when necessary, in order to plan effective service delivery procedures.

National Association of Social Workers
Guidelines for Clinical Social Work Supervision

For purposes of risk management, the supervisor should

◆ ensure that the services provided to clients by the supervisee are above minimal standards.

◆ identify practices that might pose a danger to the health and welfare of the supervisee's clients or to the public and take appropriate remedial measures.

National Board for Certified Counselors
Standards for the Ethical Practice of Clinical Supervision

Clinical supervisors shall . . .

Standard 8: Render assistance to any supervisee who is unable to provide competent counseling services to clients.

Standard 9: Intervene in any situation where the supervisee is impaired and the client is at risk.

---

training in family therapy. Supervisor Jeremy will thus want to carefully assess her ability to facilitate the upcoming family meeting with Maria and Carrie. It may be advisable that family sessions be conducted by a different therapist or that Jeremy serves as cotherapist with Georgia in these meetings.

Student trainees place an additional burden on academic training institutions to ensure that services they provide are not substandard. As Case 5.3 establishes, even having clients sign a waiver does not relieve the institution of this duty. In a case involving a dental school that established precedent for other professional training programs, the Georgia Supreme Court affirmed that

> status . . . as primarily a training institution does not allow for an exemption from the duty to exercise reasonable care. The clinic in offering services to the public is engaged in the practice of dentistry. The legislature while allowing such clinics to operate has not exempted them from the standard of care necessary for the protection of the public. (*Emory University v. Porubiansky,* 1981)

While this ruling pertains directly to institutions having on-campus practicum or internship clinics, it follows that liaison with off-campus field sites must be sufficient to ensure adequate care by trainees serving the public.

FIGURE 5.1   FoRMSS Supervisee Profile

FoRMSS SUPERVISEE PROFILE

Supervisee: _Georgia M. Doyle_   Date: _____3/18/02_____

Work Address: _Lakeland Mental Health Center_   Home Address: _552 Main Street, Apt. 5_____

Work Phone: _388-1720_   Home Phone: _388-5129_____

Degrees and Majors: _M.A. - mental health counseling Univ. of Georgia (2000)_____

Licenses and Credentials: _NCC eligible_____

Current Academic Program (if applicable): _____

Malpractice Insurance Carrier: _ACA Insurance Trust (#3145296)_____

Current Position: ___staff counselor - adult outpatient department_____

Job Description: ___intakes; caseload of 17-23 clients; emergency services on____

_____rotating basis (biweekly); staff meetings & supervision (weekly)_

_____

Previous related work/volunteer experience   Resumé on file? ☑ yes ☐ no

Institution   Dates   Primary Responsibilities

Lakeland Comm. Services _8/99-5/00_ _counseling/referrals for pred. Asian/Latino_ pop

Univ. Counseling Center _9/97-5/99_ _intake, brief counseling - trad. college pop._

YMCA camp   _summer 95,96_ _counseling, activities with youth ages 8-17_

Current areas of responsibility in which further training is desired

_intake evaluations (esp. substance abuse, sexual abuse)_____

_family assessments_____

_battered women (reporting, referrals, treatment approaches)_____

Have there ever been any ethical or malpractice complaints brought against the supervisee? ☐ yes ☑ no

If yes, please explain: _____

_____

Supervisee goals for supervison   Supervisory contract completed? ☑ yes ☐ no

• Clinical/counseling skills _intake assessments; brief TX planning; CD interventions;_

_____community referrals/liaison_____

• Legal/ethical knowledge _reporting statutes; confidentiality in couples/family assessments_

_____

• Case management____ _documentation (progress notes, termination summaries)_____

_____

I recognize that I am responsible for following the ethical codes and professional standards of my own as well as my supervisor's discipline. I have read, understand, and agree to abide by these guidelines in my professional conduct. ☑ yes ☐ no

I verify that the above information is accurate to the best of my knowledge.

Georgia Doyle, MA   _3/18/02_
Supervisee's signature   Date signed

I am aware of my responsibilities as supervisor and agree to assume the responsibilities of supervising this clinician.

Jeremy Marcus, LCSW   _3/18/02_
Supervisor's signature   Date signed

Source: From *Documentation in Supervision: The Focused Risk Management Supervision System (FoRMSS),* by J. E. Falvey, C. F. Caldwell, and C. R. Cohen. Copyright © 2002 Wadsworth Group.

CASE

5.3

Emory University v. Porubiansky
282 S.E.2d 903 (Ga. 1981)   *Supreme Court of Georgia*

FACTS

Emory University School of Dentistry had a clinic where low-cost dental services were provided to the public, as it was a training site for new dentists. In return for these services, the university required patients to sign a form waiving their rights to hold the university liable for any malpractice damages. Ms. Porubiansky suffered a broken jaw as a result of a dental procedure that went awry at the hands of a training dentist.

HOLDING OF THE COURT

The court found that a training facility could not disclaim damages due to malpractice using a general release of liability form, as this is solidly against public policy. A major rationale for the court's decision was that the facility's status as a training ground for new professionals did not exempt it from the duty to exercise a reasonable standard of care. The court further reasoned that patients can expect a substantially similar standard of treatment from a trainee as they would receive from a private practitioner.

IMPLICATIONS

Malpractice does not end with the individual directly providing medical, dental, or mental health treatment. A training facility, such as the one discussed in this case, assumes a duty to supervise its trainees adequately. The standard of care that patients should expect is *not* diminished in any way. There is one standard of care for any given field (usually defined by expert testimony at a trial), and it becomes the training facility's responsibility to provide supervisors with the requisite credentials and licensure/certification to ensure that quality treatment is given. This is most certainly applicable to graduate mental health training programs and the schools, clinics, hospitals, and so forth that accept their students as trainees or interns. This can also be applicable to clinics or mental health centers that are training grounds for new professionals as they work toward obtaining their license or certification from the state. Thus, in this context, supervision becomes very important. Competent supervision serves as a constant quality control monitor for those involved in the training of new professionals. Courts do not expect a new therapist to provide the same quality treatment as a seasoned veteran of the field, but the public and client still demand and are entitled to that level of care. The supervisor—with an experienced, watchful eye—can help guide the supervisee through possible malpractice pitfalls and can compensate for the deficiencies that all new therapists experience early in their training.

Timothy E. Bray (2000). Reprinted with permission.

TRAINING PROGRAM LIAISON AND COMMUNICATION

Much has been written about the need for training programs to establish adequate liaison with internship or residency settings in which their students practice (Bernard & Goodyear, 1998; Leonardelli & Gratz, 1985). In this chapter's vignette, Paul appropriately consulted with both his site supervisor and faculty instructor before contacting Maria about her daughter's allegation. But what if he hadn't been able to get in touch with them in such a timely fashion?

There needs to be a mechanism for supervisees to contact their supervisor or a backup professional immediately in the event of clinical crises. This is most usefully included in the supervisory contract, with copies retained by the supervisee, the academic program, and the training institution. The FoRMSS Emergency Contact Information (Figure 5.2) records phone, e-mail, and fax numbers for professionals involved in Paul's supervision, including program directors and faculty coordinators who are responsible for general overview of his training experience.

The "ACES Ethical Guidelines for Counseling Supervisors" (Association for Counselor Education and Supervision, 1993) that pertain to Paul's graduate training program and internship experiences recommend that

- procedures for contacting supervisors and alternates be established (Standard 2.05)
- regular communication between field site and campus supervisors occurs (Standard 3.13)
- there be clear lines of communication between supervisor and supervisees (Standard 3.14)

Clients are also entitled to be informed of the supervisory relationships of their therapist (Disney & Stephens, 1994). In Paul's case, this involved a written document informing Maria of his status as a school counselor trainee, who would supervise his counseling with Carrie (including campus supervisors), how counseling records or session recordings would be used (e.g., individual supervision, peer seminar review), and finally, how she could contact Paul's supervisors with questions or concerns. As a mature minor, Carrie was also advised of these consultative relationships as part of her informed consent to counseling.

In our hypothetical case, Dr. Olan and Ms. Smith should have a written internship agreement that clearly delineates expectations of the high school, the intern, and the university (Disney & Stephens, 1994; Knapp & VandeCreek, 1997a; Munson, 1993; Osborn & Davis, 1996). They should communicate regularly about Paul's progress during his internship at the school. Following this week's events, they would both be well advised to review with Paul his handling of confidentiality and duty-to-warn mandates in relation to school policies, state regulations, and ethical standards.

FIGURE 5.2   FoRMSS Emergency Contact Information

FoRMSS
EMERGENCY CONTACT INFORMATION

SUPERVISOR: ___ Edith R. Smith, M.Ed., NCC ___

Title: ___ Guidance Director ___

Phone: ___ 386-1723 ext. 08 ___   Fax: ___ 386-9792 ___

E-Mail Address: ___ ers@lake.com ___

Work Schedule: ___ M thru F 7:00 A.M.–4:00 P.M. ___

Backup Supervisor: ___ Gail C. Whitner, MSW, ACSW ___

Phone: ___ 386-1723 ext. 10 ___   Fax: ___ 386-9792 ___

SUPERVISEE: ___ Paul E. Maynor, B.A. ___

Title: ___ school counseling intern ___

Phone: ___ 386-1723 ext. 11 ___   Fax: ___ 386-9792 (w)   388-1334 (h) ___

E-Mail Address: ___ pem@lake.com ___

Work Schedule: ___ M & W 7:30 A.M.–3:30 P.M.; F 10:00 A.M.–4:00 P.M. ___

WORK SITE: ___ Lakeland Regional Middle School ___

Address: ___ 85 Central Ave.   Lakeland, IL ___

Program Director: ___ Principal: Richard A. Larson, Ed.D. ___

Phone: ___ 386-1723 ext. 02 ___   Fax: ___ 386-9792 ___

E-Mail Address: ___ larson@lake.com ___

ACADEMIC AFFILIATION*: ___ Lakeland State University ___

Address: ___ Dept. of Counseling and Ed. Psychology ___

___ Carey Hall   Lakeland, IL ___

Faculty Supervisor: ___ Christopher R. Olan, Ph.D. ___

Phone: ___ 388-3029 ext. 513 ___   Fax: ___ 388-1554 ___

E-Mail Address: ___ olan@univ.com ___

Internship Coordinator: ___ Juanita M. Caracas, Ph.D. ___

Phone: ___ 388-3029 ext. 523 ___   Fax: ___ 388-1554 ___

E-Mail Address: ___ jamaca@univ.com ___

*if applicable

Source: From *Documentation in Supervision: The Focused Risk Management Supervision System (FoRMSS),* by J. E. Falvey, C. F. Caldwell, and C. R. Cohen. Copyright © 2002 Wadsworth Group.

SUMMARY AND RECOMMENDATIONS

As is becoming obvious from this discussion, there is a lot to consider when assuming a supervisory role. It is rather astounding that a majority of clinical supervisors continue to undertake this responsibility with no guidelines to inform or document their supervisory practices. This becomes particularly important when supervising unlicensed colleagues or trainees who are often not employees at the supervisor's setting. In these cases, the supervisor assumes considerable legal duty to properly oversee their training.

> This duty goes far beyond simply signing treatment or assessment reports and educating students about their mistakes. It includes making sure clients give competent consent after being fully informed about the professional status of the [trainee], checking that students or other paraprofessionals do not extend themselves beyond their training, and ensuring that the quality of treatment is adequate. (Swenson, 1997, p. 169)

This chapter covered several among a matrix of responsibilities for the clinical supervisor. For programs training new professionals, the identification of appropriate field placements and adequately trained supervisors are important supervisory functions. All supervisors are advised to develop careful protocols for selecting supervisees and monitoring their clinical practice. Regular communication between field supervisors and training institutions or credentialing bodies is considered an integral aspect of supervisory oversight in professional association ethical standards and legal doctrines.

From the preceding discussion, the following recommendations are offered as risk management guidelines for supervisee selection, client screening and assignment, and liaison between field and academic supervisors:

SUPERVISEE SELECTION

- Require resumés and interviews for all prospective supervisees.
- Obtain written professional references and follow up with phone contacts to verify the candidate's competencies, job performance, and ethical/professional character.
- Assess areas of supervised activity for which the candidate has received no prior training or experience. These areas will require close supervision and formal training by the current supervisor.
- Ensure that the training site matches the interests and professional skill level of the candidate.
- Question references and affiliated training programs about any known risks in accepting a candidate for supervision in your setting.

CLIENT SCREENING AND ASSIGNMENT

- The supervisor or other licensed professional should conduct an initial assessment of all clients prior to assignment to supervisees.

◆ Determine whether the supervisee has adequate clinical skills to treat a given client competently. This includes evidence of sensitivity to diversity issues (e.g., acculturation stressors, marginalized populations, institutionalized discrimination) as well as technical expertise.

◆ Monitor supervisee caseloads to ensure that they do not retain too many cases or too many particularly difficult cases to supervise adequately.

◆ Supervise only cases that you yourself are competent to treat.

◆ Document that clients are informed of their therapist's status as a supervisee, including the name and credentials of his or her supervisor.

◆ Ensure that clients have access to contact supervisors directly regarding their therapy experience with the supervisee.

◆ Review with supervisees their initial treatment plans for all clients.

◆ Be prepared to intervene if supervisees become unable to provide competent services to clients.

LIAISON WITH TRAINING PROGRAMS

◆ Develop supervisory agreements with all training programs from which supervisees are selected.

◆ Ensure that all parties have contact information (names, phone/fax numbers, regular and e-mail addresses) to reach one another or backup personnel in the event of clinical emergencies.

◆ Establish mechanisms for regular communication between training programs and field site supervisors regarding each supervisee.

◆ Clarify procedures for sharing of case notes, audio- or videotapes, or other work samples between the training program and field site.

CLINICAL OVERSIGHT: CONSENT AND RELATIONSHIPS

CASE UPDATE

Jeremy co-facilitated the family session Georgia held with Maria and her two children 1 week ago. During the first half hour, only Carrie and her mother were present; then Carlos joined them from his soccer practice. Carrie was able, with support from both therapists, to talk with her mother about the incident with her boyfriend. Maria in turn shared a similar experience she had at Carrie's age. When Carlos joined the session, he expressed his anger at the young man involved in this incident and advocated strongly for "letting dad handle this."

After clarifying each family member's wishes and fears regarding Ringo's presence in their lives, all agreed that it was important that he be more involved in the children's current struggles. They concurred that his temper was frightening. Carlos seems most able to interact with his father without evoking angry exchanges, and he clearly misses Ringo's daily presence in his life. Carrie and Maria both avoid Ringo out of their experience of him as verbally abusive. However, each acknowledged that he is a good parent in other ways and expressed a wish for him to learn to control his anger and "stop being so macho."

Following this discussion, the family worked out a plan for the next week: (a) to have the school guidance office inform Ringo of the incident involving Carrie, (b) to have Carrie and her mother speak with a Sexual Assault Support Services (SASS) advocate this week about their legal options, (c) to have Carrie stay away from her boyfriend and continue weekly meetings with Paul (the guidance intern) to process her reactions to the incident, and (d) to schedule another family meeting in 1 week to which Ringo and Maria's sister will be invited. The focus of this meeting will be to develop a communication system that involves Ringo and extended family members in important events and decisions regarding the children, while setting firm boundaries around expressions of anger or blame in these exchanges.

Georgia and Maria are continuing to meet weekly for individual counseling. In the meeting following this family session, Maria expressed relief at the possibility of getting more help with the children. She remains fearful of Ringo but acknowledged that having her sister and both therapists present will make it easier to talk with him.

Maria and Carrie have an appointment with an SASS advocate in 2 days. She reports that Carrie is talking with her more this week and feels like their sharing in the family session "brought us closer, like we should be."

Maria continues to report improved sleep and eating patterns, with no current suicidal feelings. She does acknowledge rumination over her own past assault in the wake of Carrie's incident and processed this in the current session. She feels conflicted between the submissive role she assumed during that abuse and her wish for Carrie to "fight back" in the current incident. Her own mother had encouraged her to "forget about" her assault by an older cousin at the time but stated, "In America, it's different; maybe I want more for my daughter." She and Georgia also reviewed her expectations of the next family session.

In this supervisory session, Georgia is pleased at the progress Maria and her family appear to be making. However, she feels anxious over her supervisor's involvement in the treatment. While noting that Jeremy's family systems training clearly facilitated the communication during the family meeting, her opening comment of "So, are they like I presented them?" suggested that Georgia needs to process her personal reactions to this supervisor's direct intervention. She also mentioned that she knows Maria's sister casually from their daughters' mutual dance class and wondered if that may complicate her involvement in the family sessions.

Given Georgia's lack of family systems training, it was prudent of Jeremy to co-facilitate the family meeting (assuming, of course, that he is appropriately trained in this approach). His direct intervention (a) helped to ensure competent treatment, (b) offered a training opportunity for Georgia, and (c) provided him with direct observation of the case he is supervising. But it also raises complex questions about clinical oversight and risk management in supervisory relationships.

Probably the most troubling aspect of supervising comes with the recognition that we are ultimately accountable for the welfare of our supervisee's clients—even if we have no direct knowledge of them. Many supervisors fail to recognize the implications of their mandate to oversee a supervisee's clinical work. This chapter covers two of the most commonly violated responsibilities that accompany a supervisor's oversight function: informed consent and dual relationships. Both of these issues are examined as they relate to the supervisor's ethical and legal mandates to protect the rights and welfare of both supervisees and their clients.

Informed Consent

Informed consent provides parties with the information they need to make decisions about their participation in specific activities. In counseling and clinical settings, this information should include the following (Association of State and

Provincial Psychology Boards, 1998b; Roach & Aspen Health Law and Compliance Center, 1998; Welfel, 1998b):

- ◆ qualifications/credentials of the service provider(s)
- ◆ the client's diagnosis (generally in descriptive language)
- ◆ purpose and description of the proposed treatments or interventions
- ◆ clarification of confidentiality rights and limits
- ◆ logistics of treatment (e.g., length, frequency, fees, billing practices)
- ◆ description of the nature and extent of recordkeeping
- ◆ implications of insurance reimbursement (e.g., confidentiality of information)
- ◆ potential risks and benefits of proposed treatments or interventions
- ◆ feasible alternatives to the proposed treatments or interventions
- ◆ options and prognosis if proposed treatment is not acceptable
- ◆ emergency procedures and access information
- ◆ involvement of supervisors or other professionals in treatment
- ◆ client's right to participate in planning interventions or treatment
- ◆ client's right to decline, stop, or register complaints about services

In our vignette, Maria gave informed consent for Georgia to contact the school regarding Carlos, and the school counselor later contacted Maria regarding Carrie. Does there need to be additional communication (and a new release form) for Georgia to consult with the guidance office regarding Carrie's counseling in both settings? How much should Georgia reveal to Ringo in the next family session about her work with Maria? Might her familiarity with Maria's sister constitute a problematic dual relationship in the family work? How will Paul's site supervisor follow up with his campus supervisor regarding developments in his counseling with Carrie and other students? Such questions raise important clinical considerations and underscore the need for professionals to have a clear understanding of their respective legal and ethical responsibilities.

Bernard and Goodyear (1998) suggested that informed consent should occur at three levels: client consent to treatment, client consent to supervision of their case, and supervisee consent to supervision. I would expand their list to consider five levels:

1. client consent to treatment by the supervisee
2. client consent to supervision of his or her case
3. supervisor consent to assume supervisory responsibility for the supervisee
4. supervisee consent to supervision with a given supervisor
5. institutional consent to comply with the clinical, ethical, and legal parameters of supervision for the discipline(s) involved

Let's examine standards and precedents at each level of consent.

Informed Consent by Clients

Codes of ethics for all mental health disciplines mandate the need for clients to be fully informed of treatment methods, alternatives, and potential risks. Legal components of informed consent include (a) that recipients be competent to comprehend the information and make autonomous choices, (b) that consent be voluntary and given without coercion, and (c) that the information given be comprehensive enough to make reasonable decisions (Crawford, 1994; Haas & Malouf, 1995; Malley & Reilly, 1999). Viable limitations to informed consent may occur when treating minors (who cannot legally consent but whose guardians must do so); in cases of substituted consent by third parties for clients with diminished capacity; when disclosure of certain information may be expected to cause harm to the client; and if there is delayed informed consent during clinical emergencies (Haas & Malouf, 1995; Younggren, 1995).

From this legal perspective, all therapeutic relationships rest on a contract between therapist and client. "If there is no valid informed consent from a client, a court will construct a contract favoring the client" (Swenson, 1997, p. 133). Legal interpretation of the informed consent doctrine was summarized succinctly by the New York State Supreme Court in *Sangiuolo v. Leventhal* (1986): "Failure to secure a patient's informed consent is generally now regarded as a species of malpractice."

Informed consent is thus a universally acknowledged standard of clinical practice. But who actually monitors this? Most counseling and clinical settings have informed consent documents. It is recommended that clinicians preserve written evidence of client participation in this process (Bennett, Bryant, VandenBos, & Greenwood, 1990; Bertram & Wheeler, 1995; Crawford, 1994; Dickson, 1995; Horejsi & Garthwait, 1999; Huber, 1994; Watkins, 1997a). Supervisors are expected to ensure that supervisees obtain informed consent and that this is appropriately documented in clinical files. In our vignette, this requires that supervisor Jeremy periodically review Georgia's case files on Maria and her other clients to verify this documentation.

In school settings, informed consent typically includes parental receipt of a school handbook that describes all school services available to their children. When school counseling is limited to curriculum or career issues and requires minimum contact with students, additional consent may not be needed (Fischer & Sorenson, 1996; Malley & Reilly, 1999). However, given that Carrie is discussing personal concerns, written consent should be obtained. Guidance Director Smith also needs to ensure that Maria was informed that her daughter is seeing a counseling intern in the school; this is usually accomplished through a letter sent home to parents. In addition to introducing Paul to teachers and students as an intern, Ms. Smith might also consider having him wear a visible name tag that indicates his training status and academic affiliation while on school grounds (Kapp, 1984).

Informed Consent in Supervision

The second level of consent, discussed in an earlier chapter, involves clients being informed that their therapist receives supervision and having access to contact the supervisor directly. When applicable, this should also include consent for their case being discussed with faculty supervisors at an academic institution, among peers in formal group supervision, or with other staff at the training site. Table 6.1 highlights standards of disciplines that address this expectation. Some differences are evident across disciplines regarding this disclosure. The American Association for Marriage and Family Therapy (AAMFT) stipulates obtaining informed consent for supervision only when live observation takes place. The American Psychiatric Association (ApA) and American Association of Pastoral Counselors (AAPC) are silent about this disclosure.

The American Psychological Association (APA) and the National Association of Social Workers (NASW) additionally stipulate that supervisor names be shared with a supervisee's clients. Supervisors working across disciplines need to be aware of these distinctions, as they may affect disclosure of supervised status by trainees from different disciplines. A prudent course of action is to follow the most restrictive guideline affecting either the supervisor or supervisee, as that will provide protection for both parties (American Association for Marriage and Family Therapy, 1991).

A third area of informed consent involves that of the supervisor in accepting a supervisee. Particularly as we become aware of our extent of responsibility for supervisees' performance, it behooves supervisors to exercise discretion in assuming this training role. Aspiring to be nurturant teachers, we also must take seriously our role as vigilant gatekeepers (Robiner, Fuhrman, & Ristredts, 1993). The best risk management tool of all is a screening process that allows supervisors to identify competent and trustworthy applicants. Training programs and agencies should have selection or hiring policies that include personal interviews by potential supervisors of new students or staff. Given their degree of legal and ethical exposure in this role, supervisors should have the authority to accept or refuse to supervise anyone regardless of whether they are admitted to or hired by the institution. This right is best preserved when it is included in the written job description of the supervisor.

The fourth level of informed consent is chronically overlooked. This is the supervisee's right to be informed of the qualifications and approach of his or her supervisor. Although all disciplines acknowledge the critical importance of supervision in one's professional development, in practice supervisors rarely inform supervisees of their credentials. The frequent lack of supervisory training may make such disclosures embarrassing, but Shulman (1993) also attributes this to a general lack of clarity about supervisory roles and purposes, the "taboo nature" of discussing authority issues, and the fear of making an offer one cannot back up.

TABLE 6.1   Informed Consent in Supervision

American Association for Marriage and Family Therapy
Code of Ethics
Standard 1.8: Marriage and family therapists obtain written informed consent from clients before videotaping, audio recording, or permitting third party observations.

American Counseling Association
Code of Ethics and Standards of Practice
Standard F.3.d: Client permission is obtained in order for the students and supervisees to use any information concerning the counseling relationship in the training process.

American Psychological Association
Ethical Principles of Psychologists and Code of Conduct
Standard 1.07(a): When psychologists provide . . . supervision, teaching, consultation, research, or other psychological services to an individual, a group, or an organization, they provide, using language that is reasonably understandable to the recipient of those services, appropriate information beforehand about the nature of such services . . .

Standard 4.01(b): When the psychologist's work with clients or patients will be supervised, the above discussion includes that fact, and the name of the supervisor when the supervisor has legal responsibility for the case.

Standard 4.01(c): When the therapist is a student intern, the client or patient is informed of that fact.

Association for Counselor Education and Supervision
Ethical Guidelines for Counseling Supervisors
Guideline 1.01: Supervisors should have supervisees inform clients that they are being supervised and that observation and-or recordings of the session may be reviewed by the supervisor.

National Association of Social Workers
Guidelines for Clinical Social Work Supervision
Issues of confidentiality and informed consent require that the client or the client's representative (for example, a child's parent) be advised that supervision is taking place, the nature of information that is shared, and the supervisor's name and contact information.

National Board for Certified Counselors
Standards for the Ethical Practice of Clinical Supervision
Standard 1: Clinical supervisors shall ensure that supervisees inform clients of their professional status (e.g., intern) and of all conditions of supervision.

Standard 3: Clinical supervisors shall inform supervisees about the process of supervision, including supervision goals, case management procedures, and the supervisor's preferred supervision model(s).

Standard 14: Clinical supervisors shall ensure that both supervisees and clients are aware of their rights and of due process procedures.

McCarthy, Kulakowski, and Kenfield (1994) conducted a survey of 232 experienced psychologists and found that 72% were unsure whether their own supervisors had been trained in supervision. These authors recommended that informed consent be documented in supervisory relationships. McCarthy et al.

(1995) subsequently specified topics to be addressed in such a document. These topics parallel the information relevant for supervisory contracts: a professional disclosure statement, practical aspects of the relationship, methods and format of supervision, evaluation and due process procedures, ethical and legal parameters, and a statement of agreement signed by all parties.

Supervisees should also give informed consent when their disclosures in supervision will be shared with faculty, training peers in group supervision, or other staff members (Ladany, Lehrman-Waterman, Molinaro, & Wolgast, 1999). Particularly in settings where "layered supervision" occurs (e.g., doctoral students supervise master's students and in turn are supervised on their supervision by faculty), the potential for violating a supervisee's rights increases dramatically. Safeguards must be taken to protect these rights (Hardcastle, 1991). This would most likely affect Paul in our vignette, as he is enrolled in an academic training program while concurrently completing his internship. He should have an informed understanding, documented in the supervision contract, of what types of information will be shared between site and faculty supervisors, as well as with other program or site professionals. Further, he should have the option to disclose certain information (e.g., personal history) to only those supervisors he wishes to notify.

A final level of informed consent engages the institution in a commitment to support legal and ethical requirements of supervision. Although seldom addressed in the literature, the reality for many practicing supervisors is that their employers fail to consistently provide the time or resources to conduct competent supervision. This includes protecting the supervision from cancellation or intrusion, limiting supervisory caseloads to the number stipulated by professional guidelines, supporting training and supervisory consultation, allotting time for supervisor documentation, and updating agency policies as case law and evolving state statutes impact on supervisory as well as clinical practices.

DANGEROUS LIAISONS: DUAL RELATIONSHIPS IN TREATMENT

Given our discussion of institutional support, it is important to acknowledge the supervisory relationship in its institutional context. Supervision is an educational experience, but not purely intellectual. It is at times an emotional experience, but carefully distinguished from therapy. It is a collegial experience, but imbalanced and thus vulnerable to exploitation. Ultimately, supervision serves as the watchdog guarding entry into professional practice. Rubinstein (1992) points out that "supervisors have tremendous influence not only on the personal and professional development of supervisees, but on their formal advancement as well" (p. 114). Thus, although the relationship may directly involve only several people, supervisors need to remain vigilant of the larger professional context within which their role is sanctioned.

A fundamental tenet of the human services professions is to avoid dual relationships. All professional ethics codes are explicit about these boundary violations in counseling or clinical relationships. Dual relationships must be avoided or, in cases where that is not feasible (e.g., Georgia's community contact with Maria's sister), the burden is squarely on the professional to ensure that they remain harmless to the client. Most states have enacted laws making sexual relationships with clients, as well as their exploitation in other ways, either a civil violation or a criminal offense that can result in fines, imprisonment, and/or loss of license (Association of State and Provincial Psychology Boards, 1998b; Dickson, 1995; Haas & Malouf, 1995; Swenson, 1997). Each discipline has also established guidelines proscribing sexual and nonsexual dual relationships in supervision (Table 6.2). There is no ambiguity in this standard of practice except regarding when, or if, relationships with clients or supervisees may change at some point after their professional contract ends.

Why, then, are dual relationships evidently so common among mental health professionals? Psychotherapist–patient sexual violations represent the major cause of financial losses in malpractice suits, licensing disciplinary actions, and ethics complaints (Pope & Vasquez, 1998). Lawsuits arising out of sexual boundary violations from 1976 to 1991 accounted for one-fifth of all claims against the major psychology insurance carrier (Stromberg & Dellinger, 1993; Swenson, 1997). Similarly, a review of the major social worker insurance carrier over a 20-year period revealed sexual improprieties to be the most common cause of claims (Dickson, 1995). Across eight national self-report surveys that polled psychologists, psychiatrists, and/or social workers, nearly 7% of male and 2% of female therapists reported engaging in sex with at least one client (Pope & Vasquez, 1998). Among complaints filed with state licensing boards, sexual violations account for over 20% of complaints against counselors (Disney & Stephens, 1994) and 35% of complaints against psychologists (Pope & Vasquez, 1998). Finally, annual reports of the APA Ethics Committee show that sexual violations consistently represent over half of the cases reviewed that result in loss of membership. These statistics are clearly troubling.

Sexual intimacies with clients are destructive to both parties. Yet statistics suggest that up to 90% of mental health professionals have been tempted by the possibility at least once (Rutter, 1989). The lack of clinician training in how to appropriately handle sexual feelings toward clients can easily become a supervisor's nightmare.

Several legal cases demonstrate how supervisors assume direct liability for their response to supervisee sexual transgressions with clients. In *Simmons v. United States* (Case 6.1), a social worker encouraged his client of 5 years to act on her professed attraction toward him and subsequently engaged in a sexual and romantic relationship with her for over a year while treatment continued. This was brought to the attention of his supervisor, who took no action. Several years later, after treatment ended, the client attempted suicide and was advised

TABLE 6.2 Dual Relationships in Supervision

American Association for Marriage and Family Therapy
*Responsibilities and Guidelines for AAMFT Approved Supervisors
and Supervisors-in-Training*
A supervisor must not supervise his or her family members, former family members, clients in therapy, or any other person with whom the nature of the relationship prevents or makes difficult the establishment of a professional supervisory relationship.

American Association of Pastoral Counselors
Code of Ethics
Principle V.A: We do not engage in ongoing counseling relationships with current supervisees, students and employees.

Principle V.B: We do not engage in sexual or other harassment of supervisees, students, employees, research subjects or colleagues.

Principle V.C: All forms of sexual behavior . . . with our supervisees, students, research subjects and employees (except in employee situations involving domestic partners) are unethical.

American Psychiatric Association
Principles of Medical Ethics
Principle 4.14: Sexual involvement between a faculty member or supervisor and a trainee or student, in those situations in which an abuse of power can occur, often takes advantage of inequalities in the working relationship and may be unethical because: (a) any treatment of a patient being supervised may be deleteriously affected; (b) it may damage the trust relationship between teacher and student; and (c) teachers are important professional role models for their trainees and affect their trainees' future professional behavior.

Association for Counselor Education and Supervision
Ethical Guidelines for Counseling Supervisors
Guideline 2.09: Supervisors who have multiple roles (e.g., teacher, clinical supervisor, administrative supervisor, etc.) with supervisees should minimize potential conflicts. Where possible, the roles should be divided among several supervisors. Where this is not possible, careful explanation should be conveyed to the supervisee as to the expectations and responsibilities associated with each supervisory role.

Guideline 2.10: Supervisors should not participate in any form of sexual contact with supervisees. Supervisors should not engage in any form of social contact or interaction which would compromise the supervisor–supervisee relationship. Dual relationships with supervisees that might impair the supervisor's objectivity and professional judgment should be avoided and/or the supervisory relationship terminated.

Association of State and Provincial Psychology Boards
Supervision Guidelines
Guideline II.D: Supervisors avoid entering into dual relationships with their supervisees. Psychologists do not exploit or engage in sexual relationships with supervisees. Supervisors attempt to resolve any unforeseen interference that may be potentially harmful to the supervisory relationship with due regard for the best interests of the supervisee and after appropriate consultation.

National Association of Social Workers
Guidelines for Clinical Social Work Supervision
To protect objectivity and guard against conflict of interest, the supervisor should not supervise his or her own parents, spouse, former spouses, siblings, children, anyone sharing the same household, or anyone with whom there is a romantic, domestic, or familial relationship.

National Board for Certified Counselors
Standards for the Ethical Practice of Clinical Supervision
Standard 5: Clinical supervisors shall avoid all dual relationships with supervisees that may interfere with the supervisor's professional judgment or exploit the supervisee.

CASE

6.1

Simmons v. United States

805 F.2d 1363 (9th Cir. 1986)   *United States Court of Appeals, Ninth Circuit*

FACTS

During a 7-year counseling relationship with a social worker at a government health service on a Native American reservation, the plaintiff (Ms. Simmons) was eventually encouraged by the therapist to act on her transference feelings for him. Believing it was part of the treatment, the plaintiff and social worker engaged in sexual relations over several years, which subsequently caused the plaintiff to suffer increased anxiety and depression. After being hospitalized for attempted suicide years later, the plaintiff learned that the relationship encouraged by the social worker was inappropriate and damaging. During the course of this relationship, the tribal chairwoman of the reservation apparently knew of the sexual nature of the relationship and had expressed concern to the social worker's supervisor, who made no attempt to intervene or take any action against the social worker.

HOLDING OF THE COURT

The court ultimately concluded that the social worker was acting within the scope of his employment when he encouraged the sexual relationship with the plaintiff. The court reasoned that transference is a part of the therapeutic process and that, because the social worker encouraged the sexual relationship *as part of the therapy*, he was acting within his job as a therapist (albeit he was acting inappropriately). As a result of this social worker's actions occurring within the scope of his employment, he was found liable for malpractice. Regarding the supervisor, the court found that he should have known about "the negligent acts of a subordinate." *Id.* at 1371. The supervisor had actual knowledge (from the tribal chairwoman) or, at the very least, reason to suspect that something inappropriate was taking place. As a result of his failing to act, he was liable for the negligent supervision that contributed to the injuries suffered by Ms. Simmons.

IMPLICATIONS

Ideally, everyone reading this understands the reasoning for holding the social worker liable for malpractice as a result of his sexual misconduct with the plaintiff. It is hard to think of a more powerful argument to support the need for supervision. It was even worse in this case because the relationship could have been stopped and the injuries minimized to the plaintiff if only the supervisor had fulfilled his duty of care to the plaintiff. What many of us may be asking is why the supervisor didn't act on the information given to him. There may be 100 reasons, but the court didn't care. As a supervisor, you have the responsibility of overseeing the counseling relationship between the supervisee and client, and you *should* know what is taking place. Ignorance will never be an excuse.

Timothy E. Bray (2000). Reprinted with permission.

by a treating psychiatrist that this therapist's mishandling of her transference caused her psychological problems. She brought suit. Because this therapist worked for the Indian Health Service and the violation occurred within the scope of his employment, the government as well as the therapist and supervisor were held liable. Among its findings, the court ruled that the supervisor was negligent in failing to act to prevent further harm to the client once he was informed of the abusive relationship (*Simmons v. United States*, 1986).

What if a supervisor learns of possible sexual improprieties of his or her supervisee and does act? How far does the supervisor's action need to go? This question was raised in *Andrews v. United States* (Case 6.2). Here the supervisor did confront the supervisee about his alleged behavior but, upon the supervisee's denial, took no further action. The court deemed that did not go far enough and again found for negligent supervision.

In our vignette, Georgia has contact with her client's sister based on shared community activities. This becomes a dual relationship as she joins the family therapy meetings. How should it be managed? Does it disqualify Georgia from participating in the family sessions? How can supervisors become aware of these sometimes subtle yet important treatment complications? It is clear that supervisors must act swiftly to minimize additional harm by thoroughly investigating possible violations as soon as they become aware of them. This may include some or all of the following actions (Ellis, 1991; Richard & Rodway, 1992):

- Confront supervisee about the allegation and document his or her response.
- Place "critical incident" report in supervisee's file pending resolution.
- Question the client and any other party who reported the violation.
- Consult with colleagues regarding appropriate responses.
- Monitor supervisee's cases closely (including live supervision).
- Address possible attraction to clients regularly in supervision.
- Report the alleged incident to employer for investigation.
- Report the alleged incident to state licensing board or ethics committee.
- Document all actions and the reasons for them.

BREAKING THE FAITH: DUAL RELATIONSHIPS WITH SUPERVISEES

Not only clients but also supervisees are vulnerable to sexual boundary violations. Although sexual relationships between supervisors and trainees are explicitly prohibited by every ethical code (Table 6.2), evidence that graduate students have sexual relationships with faculty supervisors abounds (Bartell & Rubin, 1990; Neufeldt, 1999). Glaser and Thorpe (1986) surveyed former female psychology students and found that 17% reported having had sexual contact with faculty members or supervisors during their graduate training. A survey of licensed psychologists found that 6% reported sexual boundary

Andrews v. United States

732 F.2d 366 (4th Cir. 1984)   *United States Court of Appeals,*
Fourth Circuit

FACTS

A physician's assistant (P.A.) at a navy clinic was certified to provide counseling and to prescribe psychiatric medication. Mrs. Andrews came to the P.A. for medical problems, after which he informed her that she appeared depressed and would benefit from counseling with him. She agreed and began counseling sessions and taking the antidepressant he prescribed. During the counseling sessions, the P.A. told Mrs. Andrews that she "needed an affair," that it was important for her treatment and psychological health, and that he was available to have the affair with her. Under the guise of treatment, he began to fondle her and ultimately convinced her to have sexual relations with him. A friend of Mrs. Andrews, who had knowledge of this relationship, informed the attending physician (the P.A.'s supervisor). When his supervisor confronted him, the P.A. denied the allegations and the supervisor did not pursue the matter. As a result of the "treatment," Mr. and Mrs. Andrews both suffered severe depression and subsequently alleged that this inappropriate sexual relationship caused their divorce.

**HOLDING OF
THE COURT**

The court found that the P.A. was working under the scope of his employment when he had sex with Mrs. Andrews and that she only did so because he had convinced her that it was part of her treatment. Clients do *not* have to know what is ethical or legal when entering a course of treatment; that burden always falls on the mental health professional. Second, the court found that the supervising physician had acted negligently in his duties when, upon having knowledge of the allegations, he failed to investigate the matter further. Specifically, the appeals court upheld the trial court's finding that "had proper supervision been formulated once the allegations of sexual intimacies and improprieties were made . . . these matters would have been properly and promptly investigated and in all likelihood would have terminated the counseling relationship . . . and would have averted the subsequent sexual intercourse and irreparable emotional harm being caused to both plaintiffs in this action." *Id*. at 368, quoting 548 F.Supp. 603 at 609.

IMPLICATIONS

This case further illuminates the supervisor's ultimate responsibility to protect client welfare. When a supervisor becomes aware of information regarding highly questionable professional conduct, either through direct observation or from a third party, the supervisor has a duty to look into the matter to a substantial extent. This certainly includes personal investigation, and it may also involve reporting the questionable conduct to employers, state regulatory boards, or ethics committees. Their investigation will either shed light upon damaging practices by the supervisee or prove the allegations unfounded. In either case, as supervisor you will have fulfilled your duty and obligation to the client. If negligence by the supervisee is identified and the supervisor had no prior knowledge of it, and no reason to have such knowledge, by fulfilling the foregoing duty the supervisor's exposure to liability is reduced.

Timothy E. Bray (2000). Reprinted with permission.

violations by their supervisors, 8% by educators, and 2% by their therapists (Lamb & Catanzaro, 1998). This study supports other findings that place rates of supervisor–supervisee sexual contact between 3% and 8%.

It's not hard to appreciate that the vast majority of these trainees feel vulnerable, reluctant to refuse a supervisor's advances, unaware of appropriate professional boundaries, and/or afraid to report violations for fear of their degree, recommendation, or license being jeopardized. Most later recall the violations as unethical and harmful (Glaser & Thorpe, 1986). Because both the client in treatment and the supervisee in training are consumers of the supervisor's level of ethical decision making (Kurpius, Gibson, Lewis, & Corbet, 1991), supervisors engaging in such behavior are at very high risk. Bonosky (1995) drives home this point:

> A supervisor's standard of care is very specific. A supervisor can be held responsible for not "properly training" a student. If a supervisor is involved in a sexual relationship with a supervisee, a client could argue a strong case for malpractice, based on negligent and injurious supervision. The trainee, the supervisor, the agency and the educational institution may all be named as defendants. (p. 90)

Although sexual boundary violations are the most egregious of dual relationships, they certainly are not the only ones. We all exist in social worlds and interact with people in many contexts (Haas & Malouf, 1995). Faculty supervisors, senior clinical staff, and business, church, or school acquaintances all represent potential future training relationships that may involve dual roles. At what point do those relationships impair the supervisor's objectivity?

Due to the close, collegial nature of supervisory relationships, one might "lose track of the evaluative component of those relationships and begin to see supervisees as friends or fully qualified colleagues" (Welfel, 1998b, p. 273). This is particularly likely when supervising junior colleagues rather than students. "Affectional and collegial aspects of the supervisor/supervisee relationship are primary benefits for the supervisor and a major motive for people to stay in the profession" (Alonso, 1985, p. 97). This can cloud our judgment, however. Surveying a sample of 321 field-based supervisors, Navin, Beamish, and Johanson (1995) reported that 25% were aware of social interactions between supervisors and supervisees that they viewed as incompatible with the supervisor's duties.

State licensing board applications frequently ask about any preexisting relationships between the applicant and supervisor(s), and some have established regulations prohibiting the admissibility of hours accrued in dual supervisory relationships (Disney & Stephens, 1994; Hall, 1988b). When such complications are unavoidable (e.g., in rural areas where alternative supervisors are not available), it is imperative to consult with one's state board and professional association for guidance prior to assuming a supervisory role. If you fail to do this, a supervisee who subsequently becomes disgruntled with your supervision or evaluation may have grounds for an ethical or civil complaint (American Association for Marriage and Family Therapy, 1991).

Another dual relationship that has been addressed in supervision theory and practice literature occurs when supervisors assume a therapeutic stance with their supervisees (Baltimore, 1998; Bernard & Goodyear, 1998; Bonosky, 1995; Kadushin, 1992; Munson, 1993; Watkins, 1997b). Given that most supervisors are themselves clinicians, and often have received little training as supervisors, this is a fairly common problem. Jacobs, David, and Meyer (1995) outline critical parallels and distinctions between these relationships:

> Both psychotherapy and supervision are dyadic situations that carefully monitor serious life events and different individuals' emotional experience of those events. Both psychotherapy and supervision are revelatory processes: they are self-reflective and self-conscious; both generate and reveal unanticipated affective responses in the context of an unequal power relationship; and each fosters a level of dependency and/or regression. . . . However, the essential differences between psychotherapy and supervision have been less clearly appreciated. . . . The information available to trainee and supervisor in psychotherapy supervision is very different. No shared history, personal or professional, is comprehensively elaborated in the supervisory dialogue, nor is information about the trainee's functioning in any settings other than the therapeutic hours being discussed. . . . The relationship between supervisor and therapist . . . is not customarily available for collaborative examination. (pp. 151–152)

Whether one adheres to an educational model, treatment model, parallel process model, or developmental model, the supervisor's methods and techniques differ from those of the psychotherapist. Although they may occasionally overlap, any explorations of personal history or professional functioning with supervisees should only occur when they are clearly in the service of assisting them to become more effective with their clients (Bernard & Goodyear, 1998). Supervisors need to know how to frame the training environment. This includes knowing when to refer supervisees to psychotherapy to resolve recurring issues that limit their clinical effectiveness, as evidenced in supervisory case reviews.

How can supervisors effectively avoid dual relationships? They can and should take preventive steps that include the following:

- Do not supervise current or former clients.
- Do not supervise current or former sexual partners, business associates, family members, or friends.
- If supervising students, clarify teaching and supervisory roles.
- Do not engage in social activities with supervisees that may impair objectivity.
- Avoid excessive self-disclosure in supervision.
- Avoid comments or actions that might be interpreted as sexual.
- Recognize and respect professional boundaries in supervision.
- If concerned about your objectivity, consult with colleagues.

Although we can substantially control our own behavior, it is more difficult to monitor possible dual relationships between our supervisees and their clients. It is *not* prudent to expect supervisees to initiate discussion of these conflicts, as they may be embarrassed or fearful of the consequences of such a disclosure. Sexual feelings, in particular, tend not to be reported in supervision (Neufeldt, 1999). In research on supervisee disclosures, Ladany, Hill, Corbett, and Nutt (1996) studied 108 graduate-level trainees in practicum and internship settings. They found that almost all (97%) withheld material they rated as "moderately important" to their functioning as a therapist from their supervisors. These nondisclosures included negative reactions to the supervisor (90%); personal issues (60%); clinical mistakes (44%); evaluation concerns (44%); aspects of the client or the clinical relationship (43%); negative reactions to clients (36%); countertransference issues (22%); and client–counselor attraction (9%). This finding is particularly troubling given that supervisors may be liable if supervisees provide incompetent service but withhold relevant information from them (Welfel, 1998b). Obviously, if supervisees are engaged in what they know to be substandard, unethical, or illegal behavior with a client, that is likely to be the very information they withhold in supervision sessions. Finding ways to minimize this possibility is an important risk management task of the supervisor.

Returning once more to our vignette, Jeremy completes a risk management checklist (Figure 6.1) when supervising each of Georgia's clients to target clinical and case management issues that are likely to impact on treatment effectiveness. This prompts him to query Georgia consistently about sensitive topics she may not raise, including dual relationships and sexual misconduct.

SUMMARY AND RECOMMENDATIONS

Therapy was once characterized as "an undefined technique which is applied to unspecified problems with a nonpredictable outcome" (Lehner, 1952, p. 547). This definition no longer suffices. Clients are entitled to know what, why, how, and by whom therapy techniques are administered and monitored. Supervisors are also enjoined to apply a "clean, well-lit room" standard to judge ethical and legal appropriateness of their own and their supervisee's conduct (Haas & Malouf, 1995). Dual relationships with clients or supervisees very seldom meet this standard.

Responsibility for the actions of supervisees is always tempered by (a) the extent of supervisors' power over them, (b) the aspect of treatment in which negligence or misconduct occurs, (c) circumstances of the actions, (d) motivation of the supervisee, and (e) the likelihood that the supervisor could have reasonably predicted the supervisee's actions (Disney & Stephens, 1994). We

FIGURE 6.1   FoRMSS Current Risk Management

Observations and Training Recommendations: _____

_____

_____

CURRENT RISK MANAGEMENT ISSUES

☐ Informed Consent	☐ Child Abuse/Neglect	☐ Supervisee Expertise	☐ Releases Needed
☐ Parental Consent	☐ Risk of Significant Harm	☐ Supervisor Expertise	☐ Vol./Invol. Hospitalization
☐ Confidentiality	☐ Duty to Warn	☐ Institutional Conflict	☑ 3rd Party/UR Review
☐ Recordkeeping	☐ Substance Abuse	☐ Dual Relationship	☐ Discharge/Termination
☐ Records Security	☐ Medical Exam Needed	☐ Sexual Misconduct	☐ _____

Action Taken: *UR in 3 weeks; counselor to discuss with client options for extending reimbursement vs. self-pay.*

are not expected to be omniscient, but we are required to be diligent in our supervision. Ensuring that proper informed consent occurs and that supervisees avoid dual relationships are clearly defined areas of this diligence. In addition to the specific recommendations outlined in this chapter, there are several general policies that help alert supervisors to potential problems in these areas (Falvey, Caldwell, & Cohen, 2002; Kaiser, 1999; Weiner & Wettstein, 1993; Welfel, 1998b):

◆ Meet with each client of your supervisees, either during the screening and assignment process or early in treatment.
◆ Provide a comprehensive legal and ethical orientation that includes clarification of the informed consent and dual relationship mandates.
◆ Distribute relevant codes of ethics to all supervisees and have them sign a statement that they will abide by them.
◆ Require supervisees to record their sessions on a rotating basis to provide direct samples of their clinical work.
◆ Ask about a supervisee's personal reactions to his or her clients and to supervision on a regular basis.
◆ Document and follow up on all clinical and training recommendations given to supervisees.
◆ Do not permit clients to be seen or allow supervision to occur "after hours."
◆ Require that both supervisor and supervisee carry liability insurance for the duration of the supervisory relationship.

CLINICAL OVERSIGHT: CONFIDENTIALITY AND ITS LIMITS

CASE UPDATE

Georgia contacted her supervisor immediately following the next Monday morning appointment with Maria, requesting Jeremy's help regarding a potentially dangerous situation. Jeremy met with her later that same day and Georgia reported the following events.

Following the family meeting last week, Maria phoned the school to implement their plan for the guidance office to contact Ringo about the incident involving Carrie. The guidance director agreed to this plan and contacted Ringo by phone the next day (Friday). Maria reported that, after that call and over the weekend, Ringo called her twice to discuss the incident and also spoke briefly with Carrie (who would not tell him any details). He reportedly became "loud and crazy" at times on the phone, threatening several times (to both Maria and Carrie) to kill the boy. He finally calmed down and agreed to attend the family session this week to discuss the situation before taking any action.

Meanwhile, Maria and Carrie had spoken with a Sexual Assault Support Services (SASS) advocate on Friday. Carrie accepted that the boy's parents had been informed of the incident by the Division of Children, Youth and Families (DCYF) but refused to consider pressing charges against him. She felt that he "just got a bit rough" and had stopped short of forcing her to have sex. She wants to "just write him off as a jerk and get on with my life." Maria is inclined to accept Carrie's decision.

In her session with Georgia, Maria shared her fear of Ringo "taking over" in the next family session and worries that he might try to hurt the boyfriend. Although he reportedly assured both the guidance director and Maria that he wouldn't "do anything rash," Georgia is now concerned. She asks for Jeremy's help in deciding whether to warn this young man of potential danger. Georgia is particularly anxious because she has never met Ringo and feels guilty for not trusting Maria's initial portrayal of him. She wonders if Ringo is a "loose cannon" who could be destructive to the family and to others.

While clearly Ringo is not Georgia's client, this turn of events raises sensitive questions about how to proceed with treatment, whether there is a risk of harm, and whether Georgia has an ethical or legal mandate to act on her concerns. What if Ringo repeats his threat in the family session this week? What if he fails to attend that session? Given that none of the professionals working with this family have heard Ringo make threats, do they have any responsibility to warn a potential victim based solely on report by their clients of his intentions? How do confidentiality rights and duty-to-warn mandates balance in situations such as this? And what are the supervisors' responsibilities once they become aware of the threat?

According to Disney and Stephens (1994), "any confidential communication made to the supervisor, whether directly by the client or by the supervisee at a later time, imposes the duty of confidentiality on the supervisor" (p. 24). Jeremy Marcas, Edith Smith, and Professor Olan all need guidelines for how to proceed as their supervisees bring this clinical dilemma to them. This requires that they understand the complex and sometimes contradictory requirements surrounding confidentiality and its limits. Let's examine how disciplines, circumstances, and legal doctrines inform supervisory practice regarding confidentiality.

PROMISES, PROMISES: CONFIDENTIALITY IN TREATMENT

"Little else in psychotherapy commands as much agreement as the belief that therapists have a responsibility to safeguard information obtained during the treatment process" (Huber, 1994, p. 18). Privacy is a basic right protected under the Constitution. Clients' knowledge of their right to privacy in psychotherapy forms the very foundation for therapeutic trust. Confidentiality is recognized by all professional associations and by the courts as essential to elicit the full disclosure necessary for effective treatment (Fischer & Sorenson, 1996; Malley & Reilly, 1999).

Confidential communications include a client's verbal and written disclosures, case documentation and records, test or evaluation results, and any electronic materials (e.g., audio- or videotapes) recorded during treatment (Disney & Stephens, 1994). As we have noted, supervisors are also bound by the confidential nature of clinical and personal material discussed with them by their supervisees.

Table 7.1 compares professional guidelines for confidentiality in supervisory relationships. There is consensus across disciplines that information about both client and supervisee shared in supervision is considered confidential and must be protected. But from whom? This standard often comes in conflict with institutional policies or personal values and creates a powerful ethical dilemma for supervisors. For example, in working with adolescents such as

TABLE 7.1   Confidentiality in Supervision

American Association for Marriage and Family Therapy
Code of Ethics
Standard 4.3: Marriage and family therapists do not disclose supervisee confidences except:
(a) as mandated by law; (b) to prevent a clear and immediate danger to a person or persons;
(c) where the therapist is a defendant in a civil, criminal, or disciplinary action arising from
the supervision (in which case supervisee confidences may be disclosed only in the course
of that action); (d) in educational or training settings where there are multiple supervisors,
and then only to other professional colleagues who share responsibility for the training of
the supervisee; or (e) if there is a waiver previously obtained in writing, and then such information may be revealed only in accordance with the terms of the waiver.

American Association of Pastoral Counselors
Code of Ethics
Principle IV.C: Except in those situations where the identity of the client is necessary to
the understanding of the case, we use only the first names of our clients when engaged in
supervision or consultation. It is our responsibility to convey the importance of confidentiality to the supervisor/consultant; this is particularly important when the supervision is
shared by other professionals, as in a supervisory group.

American Psychiatric Association
Principles of Medical Ethics
Section 4.4: The ethical responsibility of maintaining confidentiality holds equally for the
consultations in which the patient may not have been present and in which the consultee
was not a physician. In such instances the physician consultant should alert the consultee
to his/her duty of confidentiality.

Association for Counselor Education and Supervision
Ethical Guidelines for Counseling Supervisors
Guideline 1.03: Supervisors should make supervisees aware of clients' rights, including
protecting clients' rights to privacy and confidentiality in the counseling relationship and
the information resulting from it. Clients should also be informed that their right to
privacy and confidentiality will not be violated by the supervisory relationship.

Guideline 1.04: Records of the counseling relationship . . . are considered to be confidential professional information. Supervisors should see that these materials are used . . . with
the full knowledge of the client and that permission to use these materials is granted by
the applied counseling setting offering service to the client. . . . Written consent from the
client (or legal guardian, if a minor) should be secured prior to the use of such information
for instructional, supervisory, and/or research purposes.

Association of State and Provincial Psychology Boards
Supervision Guidelines
Guideline III.D: The supervisory process addresses legal, ethical, social, and cultural
dimensions that impact not only the professional practice of psychology, but also the
supervisory relationship. Issues of confidentiality, professional practice, and protection of
the public are central.

National Association of Social Workers
Guidelines for Clinical Social Work Supervision
The supervisor must handle supervisory material in a confidential manner. The parameters
for the sharing of information about the supervisee's performance should be made clear at
the beginning of supervision and be made part of the supervisory contract.

National Board for Certified Counselors
Standards for the Ethical Practice of Clinical Supervision
Standard 2: Clinical supervisors shall ensure that clients have been informed of their rights
to confidentiality and privileged communication when applicable. Clients also should be
informed of the limits of confidentiality and privileged communication.

Standard 4: Keep and secure supervision records and consider all information gained in
supervision as confidential.

Carrie, how confidential are their disclosures? Do behaviors such as satanic worship, heavy drug use, or underage sexual activity constitute sufficiently extreme situations that must set confidentiality aside? What about school district policies that require school counselors to report certain student confidences to the principal? How would supervisor Jeremy ethically respond to a request for information about Georgia's marital history in recommending her for agency-funded family therapy training? And how should the supervisor handle threats made by the relative of a client, as in our vignette?

Ethical and legal guides cannot provide simple templates for such complex questions. Even across disciplines, there is some discrepancy about the release of confidential information, particularly in group, family, or couples settings. For example, although the American Association for Marriage and the Family (AAMFT) and the American Association of Pastoral Counselors (AAPC) clearly proscribe release without consent of all parties, the National Association of Social Workers' (NASW) ethical guidelines suggest that social workers have some discretion in this decision. This could become important in our vignette because Jeremy is a social worker, whereas Georgia is a counselor. Whose standards guide whether to share information about Maria's immediate family with other relatives, with the school counselor, or with others?

"Ethics, standards or rules can never legitimately serve as a substitute for a thoughtful, creative, and conscientious approach to our work. They can never relieve us of the responsibility to struggle with competing demands, multiple perspectives, evolving situations, and the prospect of uncertain consequences" (Pope & Vasquez, 1998, p. 57). Even among the best-trained professionals, ethical dilemmas have been found to lead to intentional noncompliance with ethical or legal mandates. Pope and Bajt (1988) surveyed 60 senior psychologists, all of whom had been members of state or national ethics committees, authors of texts on legal or ethical aspects of psychology, and/or diplomates of the American Board of Professional Psychology. Over one half (57%) of these professionals acknowledged violating a law or ethical mandate at least once "in light of a client's welfare or other deeper value" (Pope & Bajt, 1988, p. 829). Divulgence of confidential information accounted for 21% of these violations. Another 27% of the violations related to refusal to carry out the duty to report suspected child abuse or the duty to warn victims of dangerousness. Over 75% of this select group endorsed the belief that "psychologists should sometimes violate formal legal and ethical standards, and a majority have actually done so" (Pope & Bajt, 1988, p. 829). Perhaps this finding contributed to the senior author's subsequent warning to supervisors a decade later: "if we [were] completely truthful in describing to our supervisor what we actually thought, felt, and did with our clients, we might be advised to look for another line of work" (Pope & Vasquez, 1998, p. 4).

The need for sound clinical judgment in protecting confidentiality was emphasized in a national survey of 226 school psychologists (Jacob-Timm, 1999). In this study, 36% of the respondents identified ethically troubling incidents related to administrative pressure to act unethically or concerns about the confidentiality of information (Jacob-Timm, 1999). Supervisors in school, university, and business settings are often working in cultures that are unaccustomed to the high level of confidentiality necessary in therapy relationships (Hobbs & Collison, 1995; Welfel, 1998b). In these settings, therapists may have a variety of interactions with clients or students that take place in public areas such as hallways or the cafeteria (Fischer & Sorenson, 1996). They may use technologies to fax, phone, or copy materials that potentially compromise the confidentiality of those materials. What is confidential or not may become confused.

Because school counselors, social workers, and psychologists work with minors *in loco parentis*, these professionals may respond from a guidance rather than a clinical model of case management. In such settings, there is often a temptation to trade client confidentiality for the perception of being a team player among educators, parents, and colleagues (Isaacs & Stone, 1999; Welfel, 1998b). Thus, when teachers query Paul about Carrie's progress in counseling, his supervisors need to assist this intern in learning how to field their requests cordially but without compromising confidential information.

Some argue that holding ourselves to ethical standards is not an option determined by surrounding circumstances (Steinman, Richardson, & McEnroe, 1998), but most practitioners find themselves faced with dilemmas for which existing standards do not provide absolute direction. Good clinical judgment must prevail in these circumstances. This is where supervision and consultation often prove invaluable. A few guiding considerations can also help frame decisions in a consistent and clinically defensible manner. Haas and Malouf (1995) developed a series of questions to assist clinicians and supervisors in determining whether there are viable alternatives to breaching client confidentiality in a given situation:

◆ Does a relevant professional, legal, or social standard for confidentiality exist?
◆ Is there a compelling reason to deviate from that standard?
◆ Can a feasible solution that doesn't require deviation from the existing standard be generated?
◆ Can a primary ethical dimension guiding this decision be identified?
◆ Does the alternative course of action appear to satisfy the needs and preferences of the affected parties?
◆ Does the alternative course of action present any new ethical dilemmas?
◆ Can this course of action be implemented?

CONFIDENTIALITY IN THE COURTROOM

Although confidentiality is a client right in therapy relationships, it may become a legal privilege during litigation. Confidentiality regarding the testimony of therapists or their supervisors in court is referred to as privileged communication. This privilege allows clients to prevent their therapy communications from being revealed in legal proceedings without their consent. The privileged communication doctrine is generally agreed to rest on four requirements (Wigmore, 1961):

1. The communications must originate in confidence that they will not be disclosed.
2. The confidentiality must be essential to full and satisfactory maintenance of the relationship between the parties.
3. The relationship must be one which, in the opinion of the community, should be sedulously fostered.
4. The injury to that relation, caused by disclosure, would be greater than the benefit gained by the process of litigation.

Privileged communication is not extended to all therapists or therapies. Which mental health professionals warrant this privilege has been hotly debated in a number of legal cases. The recent Supreme Court appeal of *Jaffee v. Redmond* (Case 7.1) resulted in a landmark ruling that now establishes a standard for patient–therapist privilege in all federal cases. The court held that "confidential communications between a licensed psychotherapist and the psychotherapist's patient in the course of diagnosis or treatment are protected from compelled disclosure" (*Jaffee v. Redmond,* 1996). While extending this privilege specifically to licensed psychiatrists, psychologists, and social workers, the court noted that drawing distinctions among different mental health professionals who provide essentially the same service to patients served no discernible purpose (DeBell & Jones, 1997; Knapp & VandeCreek, 1997b). The court also cautioned that this privilege would not apply in certain cases, such as in mandated duty-to-warn situations.

Jaffee v. Redmond (1996) sets a new standard for privileged communications and appears to open the door to this privilege for a variety of mental health professionals. However, this ruling is binding only in federal court. Individual states vary widely in their determination of which mental health disciplines qualify for privileged communication and the circumstances under which that privilege will be respected (Fischer & Sorenson, 1996). In the case of unlicensed supervisees, they may or may not be covered under the privilege of a licensed supervisor. In judicial hearings, judges are the ultimate interpreters of when and how privileged communication applies; they may compel disclosure in certain cases regardless of statute (Weiner & Wettstein, 1993). To complicate matters even further, statutes change frequently as evolving case law sets new

Jaffee v. Redmond

518 U.S. 1 (1996)   *Supreme Court of the United States*

(opinion by Justice Stevens)

FACTS

After a police officer shot and killed a man, she sought counseling from a licensed social worker. A federal civil suit was brought by the deceased's family for wrongful death. As part of the litigation, the family sought to obtain information from the police officer's therapist about statements she had allegedly made about the incident. The question arose whether, under the federal rules of evidence (FRE), there existed a "psychotherapist privilege" that would prevent the disclosure of the information sought.

HOLDING OF THE COURT

Couched in the language of the federal rules of evidence, the court concluded that a "psychotherapist privilege" does exist for *licensed* therapists beyond licensed psychiatrists and psychologists. "We have no hesitation in concluding in this case that the federal privilege should also extend to confidential communications made to licensed social workers in the course of psychotherapy." *Id.* at 15. The court recognized that all 50 states and the District of Columbia have enacted legislation that creates a privilege for licensed psychotherapists (most state statutes define who is considered a "psychotherapist") and that this privilege is vital to the practice of effective psychotherapy. The court further reasoned that, for the sake of consistency, it was appropriate to expand the definition of the FRE in this case to avoid a schism between the federal and state courts' protection of confidential information. Interestingly, the court also seems to rely on an economic component, first expressed by the Court of Appeals, 51 F.3d 1346, 1358: "[D]rawing a distinction between the counseling provided by costly psychotherapists and the counseling provided by more readily accessible social workers serves no discernible public purpose." 518 U.S. at 17.

IMPLICATIONS

This Supreme Court decision is very important. Prior to this decision and on the federal level, "psychotherapist" only included licensed psychiatrists and psychologists, defined as such to be eligible for privileged communications (lawyers and physicians also enjoy this privilege). As master's level clinicians have begun to have more of an impact in the delivery of mental health services, and as licensure has expanded to include them in many states, the need for equal protection of confidential communications with clients has become increasingly important. As a result of this, states have begun passing statutes extending the privilege to *licensed* social workers and other master's level disciplines. This decision extends the privilege to licensed psychotherapists only at the federal level. Supervisors should be aware that because this privilege covers licensed therapists, unlicensed supervisees *may* be covered by your license (that is determined by individual states). However, if the degree of involvement and control by the supervisor is not sufficient to establish a supervisory relationship (as discussed in previous chapters), the unlicensed supervisee will not enjoy privileged communications with clients.

Timothy E. Bray (2000). Reprinted with permission.

legal precedents in the various jurisdictions. Glosoff, Herlihy, Herlihy, and Spence (1997) provide a comparative analysis of various state laws and exceptions to privileged communication that visually depict these discrepancies.

Supervisors need to keep informed of current statutes regarding privileged communication in their state, for their discipline, and as it extends to their supervisees. Some national and state professional organizations provide this watchdog service. Periodic consultation or in-service training with an attorney familiar with mental health laws in your state is also recommended.

Ethical codes often serve as the recognized standard of care in legal challenges to client–therapist confidentiality. Although litigation against mental health professionals is still relatively rare, it doubled in the 1990s. Breach of confidentiality ranks among the top five charges in successful lawsuits brought against psychologists and social workers (Dickson, 1995; Weiner & Wettstein, 1993; Zuckerman, 1997). Clinical supervisors are vulnerable to direct and vicarious liability for their own or supervisees' breaches of confidentiality. For example, in *Rost v. State Board of Psychology* (1995), the Pennsylvania court upheld that state licensing board's reprimand of a psychologist supervisor for releasing medical records of her supervisee's client without the client's consent. The court rejected the supervisor's claim of lack of adequate training in this area and asserted that, as a licensed psychologist, she was obligated to be aware of her ethical duties regarding confidentiality. Again, we see how the courts readily apply ethical codes in their interpretation of the standard of practice.

LIMITS TO CONFIDENTIALITY: THE CLINICAL MIRANDA WARNING

When therapists (or supervisors) betray their client's (or supervisee's) trust, it can result in pervasive and lasting damage (Pope & Vasquez, 1998). The exploitation of trust is exquisitely captured by Adrienne Rich: "When we discover that someone we trusted can be trusted no longer, it forces us to reexamine the whole instinct and concept of trust. For a while, we are thrust back into some bleak, jutting ledge . . . in a world before kinship, or naming, or tenderness exist . . . " (quoted in Pope & Vasquez, 1998). Perhaps no other aspect of therapy evokes as much anguish for professionals as our struggles over when, if, and how a client's right to confidentiality may be limited in a given situation.

Confidentiality as a clinical responsibility is clearly articulated in the ethical codes of every mental health discipline. Confidentiality must be maintained unless (somewhat) clearly defined circumstances demand disclosure to protect the welfare of a client or the public at large. These extenuating circumstances include the following situations (Association of State and Provincial Psychology

Boards, 1998b; Corey, Corey, & Callanan, 1998; Huber, 1994; Stromberg, Lindberg, Mishkin, & Baker, 1993):

◆ when a client gives informed consent to disclosure
◆ when a therapist is acting in a court-appointed capacity
◆ when there is suicidal risk or some other life-threatening emergency
◆ when a client initiates litigation against the therapist
◆ when a client's mental health is introduced as part of a civil action
◆ when a child under the age of 16 is the victim of a crime
◆ when a client requires psychiatric hospitalization
◆ when a client expresses intent to commit a crime that will endanger society or another person (duty to warn)
◆ when a client is deemed to be dangerous to him- or herself
◆ when required for third-party billing authorized by the client
◆ when required for properly utilized fee collection services

These situations are reasonably clear, but there are a variety of other contexts in which limits to confidentiality are quite murky. Professionals and agencies often create their own internal policies to handle (a) requests for information from family members having a legitimate "need to know"; (b) information revealed in group, couples, or family settings; (c) subpoenas from attorneys; (d) sharing of information among interdisciplinary professionals and staff internal to the agency; (e) sharing of information in peer training seminars; (f) confidentiality of adolescent client disclosures; and (g) confidentiality of supervisee disclosures that may impair the supervisee's clinical effectiveness (Haas & Malouf, 1995).

Whatever criteria are used to determine the extent and limits of confidentiality, they must be communicated to the client (or supervisee) at the start of a relationship. This encompasses a "psychological Miranda warning" (Swenson, 1997, p. 72) that enables recipients to make informed choices about what they will subsequently share in therapy. Supervisors must ensure that their supervisees cover this information thoroughly (preferably in writing as well as orally) in informed consent procedures with clients. Supervisors must similarly inform their supervisees of the limits to confidentiality in the supervisory relationship. This includes what kinds of information—disclosed during supervision or identified in evaluations—will be shared with training programs, licensing boards, current employers, or potential future employers through letters of reference.

Three responsibilities affecting both therapists and supervisors, which are increasingly guided by legal as well as ethical mandates, include the duty to warn potential victims of dangerous clients, the duty to protect clients at risk of serious harm to themselves, and the duty to report certain information revealed in confidence. The following sections focus on supervisory implications of these mandates.

Supervisory Oversight of the Duty to Warn

Virtually every therapist is familiar with the landmark ruling in *Tarasoff v. Regents of the University of California* (1976) that established the duty to warn the intended victims of dangerous clients. But how many of us are aware of the supervisors involved and their liability in this case? As described in Case 7.2, the supervising psychiatrist was found liable, along with the treating psychologist, for their failure to take adequate measures to warn and protect the intended victim. The California Supreme Court ultimately defined the duty-to-warn doctrine very broadly:

> When a therapist determines, or pursuant to the standards of his profession should determine, that his [client] presents a serious danger of violence to another, he incurs an obligation to use reasonable care to protect the intended victim against such danger. The discharge of this duty may require the therapist to take one or more of various steps, depending upon the nature of the case. Thus it may call for

CASE

7.2

Tarasoff v. Regents of the University of California
551 P.2d 334 (Cal. 1976)   *Supreme Court of California*

FACTS
This was a suit by Tatiana Tarasoff's parents alleging her wrongful death. Prosenjit Poddar had been seeing a psychologist, Dr. Moore, as a voluntary outpatient at a hospital affiliated with University of California, Berkeley. During a session on August 20, 1969, Poddar informed Dr. Moore of his homicidal ideation toward Tatiana, stating that he wanted to kill her when she returned from her trip to Brazil. Dr. Moore felt that hospitalization was needed but had to consult his superiors before that decision could be made. Two additional psychiatrists examined Poddar and came to the same conclusion. Dr. Moore then sent a letter to the police asking for their assistance in detaining Poddar. The police held and interviewed Poddar but ultimately released him as the police felt he was not a threat to himself or others because he was then denying his threats. The clinical supervisor and director of the hospital, Dr. Powelson (a psychiatrist), then directed that Poddar not be admitted involuntarily for a 72-hour observation (despite the recommendation of Dr. Moore and two staff psychiatrists) and told Dr. Moore to have the letter to the police returned and destroyed along with other written material. Two months later, on October 27, 1969, Poddar killed Tatiana Tarasoff.

HOLDING OF THE COURT
The California Supreme Court concluded that the clinicians owed a duty of care to Tatiana (i.e., a third party) beginning with their actual knowledge of potential danger to her and when the victim was readily identifiable. This duty warranted action by the clinicians to protect her from danger. Simply report-

him to warn the intended victim or others likely to apprise the victim of the danger, to notify the police, or to take whatever other steps are reasonably necessary under the circumstances. (*Tarasoff v. Regents of the University of California*)

Particularly relevant was the court's finding that at least one of this psychologist's supervisors shared in this responsibility.

Despite the fact that two decades later only 14 jurisdictions outside of California have explicitly adopted and applied the *Tarasoff* ruling, its symbolic value has been so compelling as to reflect a national standard of practice (Perlin, 1997). The *Tarasoff* ruling is referred to in many court opinions regarding confidentiality of therapeutic disclosures. It has been significantly extended in more recent cases to include a therapist duty to warn in the case of serious property damage (Case 4.2), as well as when a potentially dangerous client acquires weapons while making unspecified threats (*Lipardi v. Sears, Roebuck & Co.,* 1980) or threatens foreseeable victims (Case 7.3). *Tarasoff* has, however, been limited in court cases where there was no identified victim,

---

ing to the police was not enough, and breaking confidentiality would be allowed to notify Tatiana of the danger. Most important here, the court concluded that Dr. Powelson (the supervisor) could be held liable because he had direct knowledge and control over Poddar's treatment. As a result of this direct knowledge and treatment control, he assumed a duty of care to Tatiana, as if he were acting as the primary therapist. The case was sent back to a lower court for a jury to determine if Dr. Powelson, given this court's guidelines, was negligent. There is no official report of subsequent proceedings, suggesting an out-of-court settlement.

IMPLICATIONS   After this decision, for those clinicians practicing in California, the question of "who is the client?" in a crisis situation became more difficult. The duty of care owed now went beyond the immediate client to other identifiable persons in the community. The important piece for supervisors to know is that, in guiding the treatment of the client (having direct knowledge and participating in the treatment decision-making process), you may be held liable for negligence for failing to warn a third party, even if that instruction was delegated to the supervisee to carry out. A supervisor has the same duty to protect a third party (when there is reasonable belief of impending danger) as does the supervisee. In this case, Dr. Moore was claiming that he was subordinate to Dr. Powelson and that he shouldn't be held liable because he lacked ultimate control. The court seemed to suggest that this might work but left it for a lower court to decide. If upheld, this would have left the supervisor solely liable.

Timothy E. Bray (2000). Reprinted with permission.

where the therapist lacked control over the client, and where the therapist could have reasonably believed that a client's fantasies did not pose a genuine threat to an identified person (Perlin, 1997).

A particularly disturbing application of the duty-to-warn mandate was the ruling in *Jablonski v. United States* (Case 7.3). In this case, both the therapist and supervisor were found negligent for failing to accurately predict a homicide based on the "psychological profile" of a patient, even though they had each warned the victim of his potential dangerousness! A key to this decision appears to have been their failure to obtain the patient's prior medical record, which documented past violent intentions. It has elsewhere been noted that "clinicians appear to question patients more often about a history of violence to self or current suicidal ideation, than about a history of violence to others or current violent fantasies" (Monahan, 1993, p. 245). As supervisors, we are prudent to ensure that supervisees ask these questions, obtain past clinical records

---

CASE

7.3

Jablonski v. United States

712 F.2d 391 (9th Cir. 1983)   *United States Court of Appeals, Ninth Circuit*

FACTS   Meghan Jablonski brought this lawsuit against the V.A. hospital for the wrongful death of her mother, Melinda Kimball. Phillip Jablonski ("Jablonski"), Meghan's father, attacked Kimball's mother. Although no charges were brought, Jablonski agreed to undergo a psychiatric evaluation. The police contacted the V.A. hospital where the evaluation would take place, and when the physician assigned to his case (Dr. Kopiloff) was unavailable, the police conveyed the information to Dr. Berman. However, this information was not passed along to Dr. Kopiloff. Jablonski was evaluated by Dr. Kopiloff with Kimball present and was deemed to be ineligible for involuntary admission. At this evaluation, some aspects of Jablonski's violent past were exposed. Even though Jablonski refused to divulge information on past treatment, no attempt was made to locate his medical records through the V.A. At this and a subsequent evaluation, Kimball expressed concern for her safety and was advised to leave Jablonski while he was being evaluated. At the second evaluation, Dr. Kopiloff and his supervisor evaluated Jablonski, and the same conclusions were reached. Another psychiatrist noted Kimball's distress at this meeting and also advised her to stay away from Jablonski. The day before his third scheduled evaluation, Jablonski murdered Kimball.

HOLDING OF THE COURT   The court upheld the finding that the psychiatrists involved committed malpractice when they: (a) failed to record and transmit the information from the police; (b) failed to obtain past medical records; and (c) failed to ad-

whenever possible, and interview significant others when in doubt regarding the violence potential of a client.

Generally accepted legal criteria for predicting dangerousness include the following (Stromberg, Schneider, & Joondeph, 1993): past violent behaviors, specific or detailed threats, threats repeated on numerous occasions, violent ideation and poor impulse control, expressed fear of the client by others, possession of the means to carry out a threat, a history of irrational or unpredictable behavior, and the existence of a likely precipitant. Although supervisors and clinicians are not expected to be clairvoyant, including these inquiries in an assessment of dangerousness will establish that appropriate criteria were considered.

There are, unfortunately, no uniform standards guiding the duty to warn. *Tarasoff* suggests that notifying the police, the intended victim, and others in a position to protect the victim are minimum precautions. When voluntary hospitalization or involuntary commitment is warranted by the client's condition,

---

equately warn Kimball of Jablonski's dangerousness. Had the psychiatrists reviewed Jablonski's medical records, given the information he conveyed to them at the initial evaluation, they could have diagnosed his "dangerousness" and taken appropriate safety measures. Although the court offers little guidance on what an "adequate" warning would be, the mere warnings by the psychiatrists to Kimball to stay away from Jablonski were insufficient.

IMPLICATIONS   Even though the psychiatrists heard no specific threats from Jablonski, they had (or should have had) sufficient information from Kimball, the police, and his past medical records to determine that he was potentially dangerous and in need of hospitalization. This decision suggests that even when there are no words to indicate dangerousness, mental health practice has developed such that there are reliable sources of information beyond the client that we should use to influence our determination of "dangerousness." Also, having Dr. Kopiloff's supervisor evaluate Jablonski did not ease the duty imposed upon them to obtain his medical records or to "adequately" warn Kimball of Jablonski's dangerousness. The four pieces of the analysis used by the court that must be satisfied to constitute malpractice are: (a) a psychotherapist–client relationship existed; (b) the psychotherapist knew, or should have known, that Jablonski was dangerous; (c) Kimball was a foreseeable target of Jablonski's dangerousness; and (d) the psychotherapist did not take necessary steps to discharge his duty. Whether a supervisor or not, the potential targets of a client's dangerousness are owed a duty of protection by clinicians, whose diligence and accuracy will serve to reduce their exposure to liability.

Timothy E. Bray (2000). Reprinted with permission.

it should be instituted directly following the meeting in which threats are made. In a more recent case (*Davis v. Lihm,* 1988), the Michigan Supreme Court established eight factors to consider in determining whether a client might act on threats to a third party:

1. clinical diagnosis
2. the manner and context in which the threat was made
3. the client's opportunity to act on the threat
4. the client's history of violence
5. factors provoking the threat
6. whether threats are likely to continue
7. the client's relationship with the potential victim
8. the client's response to treatment

Of course, supervisors as well as therapists need to document all consultations, decisions, and the reasons for decisions that justify their protective actions in such cases.

There are also no clear guidelines regarding the duty to warn among counselors and psychotherapists who work with minors. Isaacs and Stone (1999) provide the following recommendations, geared particularly toward professionals working in school settings:

◆ Conduct a periodic update on current laws and district policies regarding situations that require confidentiality to be breached.
◆ Monitor one's own values and experiences to identify biases regarding dangerous behaviors among minors of various ages.
◆ Establish in advance which behaviors and issues may warrant breach of confidentiality and communicate these to clients/parents.
◆ Establish a peer network of professionals to consult with in confidence when potentially dangerous situations arise.
◆ Identify alternative actions to breaching confidentiality to protect students and clients when danger is not imminent.
◆ Engage in professional development and advocate for revision of existing prevention and risk management policies as needed.
◆ Purchase liability insurance and consult with carriers to determine appropriate actions to take with dangerous clients.
◆ Educate all stakeholders regarding the rationale for confidentiality and its limits.
◆ Develop and use a written, consistent informed consent protocol with all clients.

Supervisors are responsible for ensuring that their supervisees understand and implement duty-to-warn mandates (Munson, 1993). Many states stipulate steps the professional must take to meet this requirement; the supervisor is expected to monitor their implementation. In the absence of a law, supervisors should communicate and oversee that institutionally approved procedures are carried out by supervisees.

Supervisory Oversight of the Duty to Protect

Another area in which confidentiality must be breached is when clients exhibit serious self-destructive tendencies, especially suicidal intent. Supervisors need to manage the problem of suicide competently, as its ramifications are profound for all those affected. The scope of suicide in the United States is significant. Over 30,000 reported suicides occur annually, and clinicians work with a disproportionately high percentage of persons at high risk for suicide. Mental health professionals repeatedly rank working with suicidal patients as the most stressful of all clinical endeavors (Bongar, 1991; Pope & Vasquez, 1998). Suicide also represents one of the most common causes of malpractice cases against these professionals. One of six graduate psychology students reportedly experiences client suicide at some point during training (Kleespies, Smith, & Becker, 1990), and the odds of losing a patient to suicide during one's career have been estimated at about 20% for psychologists to over 50% for psychiatrists (Chemtob, Bauer, Hamada, Pelowski, & Muraoka, 1989).

Most states have imposed a duty on psychiatrists as well as other licensed psychotherapists to foresee and prevent suicide among their patients (Swenson, 1997). This duty is tempered by the degree to which the patient is judged to have been competent and thus responsible for his or her own actions. Careful diagnosis and formal assessment of suicide risk factors are imperative in working with any self-destructive client. Whether to attempt to manage the potentially suicidal client on an outpatient basis or to seek involuntary commitment is a difficult decision, currently made even more difficult by managed-care restrictions on inpatient reimbursement. From an ethical perspective, professionals must balance factors favoring commitment, such as more clinical resources for treatment and better control over a client's impulses, against loss of liberty and the impact this is likely to have on a distraught client (Amchin, Wettstein, & Roth, 1990).

There is debate in the field, and in the courts, about who bears responsibility for a suicide. One side of the argument holds that clients are accountable for their actions, make a moral choice in taking their own life, and are solely responsible for their suicide if they do not seek professional help to prevent it (Szasz, 1986). The opposing argument is that suicide is a permanent solution to an often temporary crisis and that, if professionals can reasonably predict suicidal intent, they have an ethical and legal responsibility to act affirmatively to prevent it (Corey et al., 1998).

Which actions are taken appear paramount in this crisis. All ethical codes stipulate that breaching confidentiality is necessary when clients pose a "clear," "immediate," "serious," and/or "imminent" danger to themselves. In the eyes of the law, supervisors and institutions bear "a duty to avoid conduct that could cause an abnormal mental state that would shift responsibility for the suicide away from the victim" (Swenson, 1997). Weiner and Wettstein (1993) go even further, cautioning us that "mental health professionals should assume that the duty to protect the public from violent deaths is now a reality, even if there is no specific case law or statute on the subject in every state . . . " (p. 249).

Suicide rates peak during the adolescent years. Because suicide is the second leading cause of death among adolescents, suicide prevention has become a critical case management issue for schools. Duty to protect in these situations has become a clear legal standard. In *Eisel v. The Board of Education of Maryland* (1991), a school counselor was informed of a 13-year-old student's suicidal ideation. After a meeting with the girl (Eisel) in which she denied the threats, no further action was taken to notify the administration or Eisel's parents. Shortly thereafter, the girl and a peer completed a suicide pact in a public park. The appeals court found Eisel's counselor negligent for failure to warn her parents of the danger; the school administration was also found to share in liability for this counselor's inaction (*Eisel v. The Board of Education of Maryland,* 1991). The court of appeals ruled that "school counselors have a duty to use reasonable means to attempt to prevent a suicide when they are on notice of a child or adolescent student's suicidal intent. . . . "

There are three additional ways in which professionals can be legally implicated when working with potentially suicidal clients (Moline, Williams, & Austin, 1998). These include assisting in the suicide, negligent diagnosis, and abandonment. Assistance may be inferred, for example, if a therapist directs a client to suicide as a paradoxical intervention or if they encourage the abuse of medications. Negligent diagnosis results from the failure to assess symptoms or predisposing factors accurately. Client abandonment occurs if the therapist abruptly terminates treatment, fails to respond to emergencies, or fails to obtain competent coverage during an absence (Moline et al., 1998). The supervisor as well as the therapist will likely be held legally accountable for such misconduct in these high-risk situations.

Supervisors cannot assume that their supervisees have been adequately trained in suicide assessment and prevention. They should ensure that both they and their supervisees complete current readings, training, and workshops in this area on a regular basis. If supervisees are not themselves licensed, the supervisor should consider intervening directly with clients at risk for suicide to assess lethality personally. In inpatient settings, there need to be careful procedures and staff training around suicide watches, patient passes, and discharge criteria. School or agency policies and procedures regarding potentially suicidal clients should be reviewed and updated at least annually. Current statutes and case law surrounding the duty to warn in your jurisdiction should be regularly monitored. Supervisors should always consult with colleagues, employers, attorneys, state ethics boards, and/or liability insurance carriers regarding suicide prevention steps to take in specific situations. Finally, careful documentation of the rationale for steps taken in these crises will demonstrate sound professional judgment of the supervisor.

Supervisory Oversight of the Duty to Report

A third limit to confidentiality, in which all disciplines as well as state statutes mandate reporting by mental health professionals, occurs when clients are suspected victims of child abuse or neglect. This is defined under the Child Abuse Prevention and Treatment Act of 1974 (PL 93-247):

> Physical or mental injury, sexual abuse or exploitation, negligent treatment, or maltreatment of a child under the age of eighteen or the age specified by the child protection law of the state in question, by a person who is responsible for the child's welfare, under circumstances which indicate that the child's health or welfare is harmed or threatened thereby.

The federal government makes funds available to states that implement its child abuse reporting guidelines and standards. All states have done so; thus, they require reporting and grant immunity from civil or criminal prosecution to mandated reporters acting in good faith (Huber, 1994). Many states also impose liability on mandated reporters who fail to report suspected abuse (Association of State and Provincial Psychology Boards, 1998b; Corey et al., 1998).

Although this seems straightforward, it seldom is in practice. States vary in how certain one must be, whom the information comes from, and whether the abuse was recent or remote in considering whether to report it. In some states, mandatory reporting of suspected elderly abuse has also been enacted. Mental health professionals sometimes do not adhere to these reporting laws. The case of *Pesce v. J. Sterling Morton High School, District 201* (Case 7.4) illustrates how even a thoughtful weighing of circumstances and confidentiality rights against duty-to-warn mandates can leave the professional vulnerable to loss of employment, ethical complaints, or legal action.

Despite these sanctions, many professionals acknowledge failing to report suspected abuse. Concern for child safety, cultural differences in child rearing, fear of alienating clients, confidentiality rights, age of the child, type of abuse, and lack of familiarity with or confidence in the child protective services to whom reports are made are among the myriad of reasons cited for noncompliance. In Pope and Bajt's (1988) survey, 21% of their sample of psychologists, fully knowledgeable of these legal and ethical mandates, nevertheless indicated failing to report suspected child abuse in certain situations. Corey et al. (1998) acknowledge the dilemma of many therapists in reconciling ethical or

Pesce v. J. Sterling Morton High School, District 201

830 F.2d 789 (7th Cir. 1987)   *United States Court of Appeals, Seventh Circuit*

FACTS

A tenured teacher and school psychologist (Dr. Pesce) sued the school district, claiming it violated his constitutional rights by disciplining him for failing to disclose suspected child abuse. Dr. Pesce learned from another student that J.D. (a student) had been hinting about suicide, was struggling with his sexual identity, and had visited the home of another teacher where "something sexual" happened. Dr. Pesce spoke with J.D. that same day. J.D. denied any suicidal ideation or sexual acts with the other teacher but stated that the teacher had once shown him some "pictures." J.D. requested help and was referred to an outside therapist. Upon consultation and careful consideration of the ethical and legal implications, Dr. Pesce chose not to notify school officials of the rumored sexual activity or suicidal ideation. The following week, upon learning that J.D. had canceled an appointment with the other therapist, Dr. Pesce again spoke with him at school. At this meeting, J.D. acknowledged that something sexual had taken place between him and the teacher. It was agreed upon by Dr. Pesce and J.D. that this should now be reported to school officials. The superintendent subsequently suspended Dr. Pesce for failure to report this student's situation promptly.

HOLDING OF THE COURT

The court agreed with Dr. Pesce that the confidentiality of the initial meeting with J.D. was very important but concluded that the duty imposed by law to

moral values with legal obligations: "Therapists may feel that they have been placed in the predicament of either behaving unethically (by reporting and thus damaging the therapy relationship) or illegally (by ignoring the mandate to report all cases of suspected child abuse)" (p. 180).

Supervisors may be caught in the middle of such dilemmas. Regardless of whether their supervisee informs them, they are liable for failure to report abuse. As in the duty to protect, supervisors must ensure that supervisees know and implement duty-to-report responsibilities. It is advisable to have procedures in place that alert supervisors immediately to any situation in which abuse may be suspected so that they direct the supervisee appropriately. Developing a personal relationship with case workers from the child protective services also enables supervisors to consult with them in ambiguous situations. Finally, cultivating avenues to consult with colleagues and medical personnel increases the expertise brought to bear on complex clinical decisions.

report suspected child abuse superseded that confidentiality (note that this was not a privilege). Indeed, this was expressly written into the statute regarding the reporting of suspected child abuse in that state: "The privileged quality of communication between any professional person required to report and his patient or client shall not apply to situations involving abused or neglected children. . . . " *Id.* at 791. Between the competing interests of keeping information confidential and the mandatory reporting law, the court conceded that the law is not settled on what standard of review should be used. However, the court in this instance found that the public policy implicated in the mandatory reporting statute is strong evidence that a constitutional confidentiality cannot prohibit disclosure.

IMPLICATIONS   Even though the psychologist ultimately reported the suspected abuse of J.D., the law said it needed to be done immediately rather than at the discretion of the psychologist. It is a difficult situation to be in, trying to find the best remedy for the client but the law dictates what *must* be done regardless of the situation. The court seemed to suggest that Dr. Pesce's efforts were valiant but that the need for mandatory immediate reporting is too important to be ignored, if even for a while. Mandatory reporting is a complex and hotly debated issue because it is an area where law and psychology both intersect and diverge. It is crucial for supervisors in youth services and school settings to understand this area of the law, as it will inevitably become an issue with a trainee, intern, or other staff.

Timothy E. Bray (2000). Reprinted with permission.

Summary and Recommendations

As we have seen in earlier chapters, it is imperative to keep in mind that, with the possible exception of fully licensed providers, the supervisee cannot be expected to assume final responsibility for clients. That responsibility rests with supervisors and the agency or institution (Harrar, VandeCreek, & Knapp, 1990). "Often the person at fault is not the primary provider, but the staff or clinic auxiliary. Laws of agency and respondeat superior require a principle to accept responsibility for the actions of her agents so long as the agent is acting within the scope of her employment" (Association of State and Provincial Psychology Boards, 1998b, p. 14). Particularly in high-risk situations such as those reviewed in this chapter, supervisors need to be cautious and thorough in their overview of supervisee actions. As in other areas of difficult clinical practice, supervisor familiarity with legal requirements, conducting thorough risk evaluations, independent consultation, and careful documentation of their decision-making processes are the best defense against ethical or legal charges (Mitchell, 1991; Soisson, VandeCreek, & Knapp, 1987; Weiner & Wettstein, 1993).

It is particularly important for supervisors to develop well-defined procedures for case review that routinely cover potentially high-risk topics. It is also critically important to document supervisee adherence to these procedures. Vesper and Brock (1991) developed a model to implement sound clinical procedures that is readily adapted to address client confidentiality and its limits within the supervisory structure:

◆ Provide a clearly defined outline of the frequency of supervision, including frequency of supervisory review of high-risk cases.
◆ Use a consistent format for supervisees to describe and conceptualize client problems that addresses potential legal and ethical dilemmas.
◆ Carefully review initial treatment plans with supervisees, including informed consent and crisis management contingencies.
◆ Discuss impediments to successful treatment and their management.
◆ Document supervisor feedback and directives for intervention for every clinical case reviewed in supervision.
◆ Provide supervisees with a written summary of recommendations, referrals, and risk management actions discussed in supervision.
◆ Obtain direct work samples (e.g., observation, audiotapes, cotherapy) of the supervisee–client relationship and treatment in high-risk cases.

EVALUATION AND DOCUMENTATION IN SUPERVISION

Let's shift our view from the details of Maria's family and focus on the two counselors involved. What have Georgia and Paul learned from this case, have they responded appropriately, and how can their supervisors provide helpful feedback and evaluation regarding their clinical skills and professional development? If we were to interview them, we would probably hear some version of the following summaries.

SUPERVISEE UPDATE

Georgia found the work with Maria to be challenging. What initially appeared to be treatment of this woman for clinical depression evolved into the need for family intervention, cultural sensitivity, and a systemic perspective. Trained as an adult outpatient clinician, she did not feel well prepared for this shift, yet recognized her responsibility not to abandon her client. Georgia struggled with a personal response to Carrie's assault and with some feelings of competition and inadequacy when her supervisor joined in the treatment. She also grew concerned about the potential for danger in Ringo's reaction to the alleged assault and questioned whether it met the threshold to invoke a duty-to-warn mandate. She was able to bring these concerns to her supervisor.

School counseling intern Paul relied on immediate and concrete supervisory guidance to respond appropriately to Carrie's report of the assault. As a trainee, he recognized his inexperience in moving beyond school adjustment and career counseling issues with this student. While continuing to meet with Carrie, Paul welcomed his supervisor's handling the Division of Children, Youth and Families (DCYF) reporting, the consultation with Georgia, and notification of the family about this incident. He also turned to his campus supervisor for direction regarding the limits to confidentiality of Carrie's disclosures to him.

Both of these counselors used supervision appropriately. They brought up relevant concerns in a timely manner and accepted their supervisors' recommendations and interventions. In both cases, the supervisors were available and responsive to their supervisees' as well as the clients' needs. Supervision of this case thus appears to have served its dual functions of providing a productive learning environment for the supervisee as well as ensuring client welfare (Barretta-Herman, 1993; Carlozzi, Romans, Boswell, Ferguson, & Whisenhunt, 1997; Dye & Borders, 1990; Ronnestad & Skovholt, 1993).

But let's play devil's advocate as the hypothetical situation unfolds further. What if Ringo subsequently harms Carrie's boyfriend, and his family brings suit against these therapists and their supervisors? Or suppose Georgia acknowledges Maria's depression to Ringo, he uses that as a basis to seek custody of the children, and Maria subsequently files an ethical complaint against Georgia for breach of confidentiality? What if Paul had failed to share Carrie's report with his supervisor out of fear or ignorance of the significance of this allegation? Or imagine if Georgia and Jeremy become romantically involved, and he thus loses objectivity in his supervision of her clinical work. These may seem like far-fetched scenarios, but they clearly can occur. Accountability systems and risk management strategies become valuable tools in preventing or at least anticipating such possibilities.

Supervisors need to have mechanisms in place to demonstrate accountability in their professional roles (Beis, 1984; Calfee, 1997; Glenn & Serovich, 1994; Kutcher & Jones, 1996). Accountability systems for supervisors should include informal and formal evaluation procedures; an organized documentation format; written criteria for supervisee recommendations, retention, and dismissal; and due process rights of supervisees. Although they ideally will never be needed in a courtroom or before an ethics board, these systems support important supervisor functions that include:

◆ providing ongoing informal feedback to supervisees
◆ documenting the content and outcomes of supervisory sessions
◆ formally evaluating supervisee progress at given intervals
◆ serving as professional gatekeepers in recommending supervisees for academic credit, licensure, employment, or conversely, remediation or termination from training
◆ providing risk management for the supervisor

This chapter examines how accountability systems enhance our competence in supervisory roles.

SUPERVISORY FEEDBACK AND EVALUATION

Many of us vividly recall our earliest experiences as a supervisee. As new professionals, we were likely to be doubtful of our clinical abilities, fearful of making mistakes, frustrated by differences in values or theoretical orientation between ourselves and our supervisor(s), and concerned about being less than completely truthful in supervision due to the anticipation of being evaluated (Greben & Ruskin, 1994; Pope & Vasquez, 1998). We were torn between the need to reveal our vulnerabilities in order to grow and the impulse to shield our shaky competence and confidence from the supervisor's view. As many contemporary models of supervision point out, the balance between support and challenge in supervision shifts markedly depending on where the supervisee is along this dynamic developmental continuum. We were, as supervisees, experiencing a personal and professional "growth spurt" through which our supervisors (ideally) mentored us (Berger & Buchholz, 1993; Inskipp, 1999).

Supervisors thus wield a great deal of power, no matter how egalitarian they attempt to be. The most visible manifestation of this power is evident in their responsibility to evaluate supervisees. As Table 8.1 depicts, each mental health discipline except psychiatry explicitly stipulates the need for ongoing supervisory feedback as well as periodic formal evaluation. What is not addressed in these guidelines is the high level of discomfort both parties often have with the evaluative component of supervision. Judging others runs counter to the principle of unconditional acceptance that underlies much clinical theory and training in this field. How, then, do we model a nonjudgmental stance with clients and yet make judgments about the adequacy of our supervisees' efforts to do this? Discomfort leads to resistance, clarifying why the lack of timely feedback has become the most common basis of formal ethics complaints regarding supervision (Koocher & Keith-Spiegel, 1998).

Supervisory evaluation is required for preservice trainees, but among professionals, this is not always the case. Many supervisors avoid this responsibility completely or give uniformly positive evaluations to sidestep possible criticism, career implications, and the potential for grievance associated with negative assessments (Shulman, 1993). For example, Garrett and Barretta-Herman (1995) studied licensed school social workers and found that 40% of them had not been formally evaluated by their supervisors in 3 or more years. In fact, many practicing school-based mental health professionals have been found to receive no clinical supervision at all (Crespi & Lopez, 1998; Davis & Mickelson, 1994; Hayes, 1998; Henderson & Lampe, 1992; Roberts & Borders, 1994). How can their work be valued if it is never evaluated?

Evaluation may be distinguished as *formative feedback,* which is ongoing and informal, versus *summative assessment,* which is periodic and formal (Robiner, Fuhrman, & Bobbitt, 1990). Most supervisors are comfortable with the former, recognizing that such feedback "represents the bulk of the supervisor's work with the trainee . . . and stresses process and progress" (Bernard & Goodyear, 1998, p. 153). Freeman (1985) and Kadushin (1992) outline the major characteristics of effective formative feedback:

TABLE 8.1   Guidelines for Supervisory Evaluations

American Association for Marriage and Family Therapy
Responsibilities and Guidelines for AAMFT Approved Supervisors
and Supervisors-in-Training
The progress of trainees should be periodically reviewed according to pre-determined
supervisory goals, and evaluations should be shared and discussed with trainees. . . .
Supervisors and trainees must have a clear understanding about responsibility for
evaluations as well as specific details about how the evaluation will be shared.

American Counseling Association
Code of Ethics
Principle F.2.c: Counselors clearly state to students and supervisees, in advance of
training, the levels of competency expected, appraisal methods, and timing of evaluations
for both didactic and experiential components. Counselors provide students and supervisees with periodic performance appraisal and evaluation feedback throughout the
training program.

American Psychological Association
Ethical Principles of Psychologists
Principle 6.05(a): In academic and supervisory relationships, psychologists establish an
appropriate process for providing feedback to students and supervisees.

Principle 6.05(b): Psychologists evaluate students and supervisees on the basis of their
actual performance on relevant and established program requirements.

Association for Counselor Education and Supervision
Ethical Guidelines for Counseling Supervisors
Guideline 2.08: Supervisors should provide supervisees with ongoing feedback on their
performance. This feedback should take a variety of forms, both formal and informal, and
should include verbal and written evaluations. It should be formative during the supervisory experience and summative at the conclusion of the experience.

Association of State and Provincial Psychology Boards
Supervision Guidelines
Guideline IV.A: Based on the job description, written and oral evaluation is necessary to
ensure that supervisors achieve identified employment objectives. Evaluations provide
objective assessment and direct feedback about the supervisee's competence in meeting
the needs of the employment setting.

Guideline IV.B: Direct feedback should be ongoing with written evaluations provided at
least semi-annually. At the outset of the supervisory period each supervisor together with
the supervisee shall establish a written contract that specifies: (1) the competencies to be
evaluated as well as the goals to be attained; (2) the standards for measuring performance;
and (3) the job description.

National Association of Social Workers
Guidelines for Clinical Social Work Supervision
Supervision creates a hierarchical relationship. The supervisor must abide by the authority
vested in the supervisory context (licensing body, employer, third-party payer, and so
forth). These responsibilities may include specific tasks such as preparing personnel
evaluations, providing recommendations for licensure. . . .

National Board for Certified Counselors, Inc.
Standards for the Ethical Practice of Clinical Supervision
Standard 7: Clinical supervisors shall provide supervisees with adequate and timely
feedback as part of an established evaluation plan.

- ◆ It is systematic: consistent, reliable, and minimally influenced by subjective variables.
- ◆ It is timely: provided in close proximity to performance to maximize supervisee motivation, reinforcement, and interest in learning.
- ◆ It is clear: based on explicit and objective criteria that are directly related to aspects of the supervisee's performance.
- ◆ It is descriptive: focused on supervisee behaviors and actions rather than assessments or judgments of his or her personality.
- ◆ It is tentative: offered for consideration rather than presented for acceptance.
- ◆ It is constructive: accompanied by specific suggestions for future application or potentially useful alternative behaviors.
- ◆ It is selective: provided in consideration of when and how much feedback the supervisee can use at a given time.

Formative feedback lets supervisees know how the supervisor sees their professional work evolving over time. Because it is generally attached to the discussion of cases, formative feedback is grounded in reported, observed, or recorded clinical material. This feedback provides a mutually understood basis for subsequent formal assessments. Surprises don't occur in formal evaluations when formative feedback has been honest and accurate.

Supervisors appear to have considerably more difficulty providing appropriate oversight in summative evaluations. Nowhere else in supervision does the power differential become more evident and, for many supervisors, distasteful. A national survey of supervision ideals and practices among 329 counselor educators (Freeman & McHenry, 1996) revealed that, while respondents viewed evaluation as an important function of supervision, less than 3% mentioned screening and evaluation as a focus of their supervisory approach. Welfel (1998b) and Erera and Lazar (1994) note that the collegial nature of supervisory relationships may cause supervisors to lose sight of their evaluation responsibilities. Research by Navin, Beamish, and Johanson (1995) supports this contention, finding that over 25% of a multidisciplinary sample of field supervisors were aware of social interactions between supervisors and trainees that they viewed as incompatible with the supervisor's evaluative duties.

This is an important risk management consideration in assuming supervisory roles. Formal evaluation moves beyond the supportive and corrective nature of formative feedback to a summary of the supervisee's competencies at that time. These evaluations are often used in administrative decisions related to one's academic, employment, or credentialing status. Without previously established evaluation criteria and ongoing feedback linked to those criteria, supervisees are left "unprotected from a potentially capricious and irresponsible evaluation on the part of the supervisor" (Sherry, 1991, p. 572). Formal evaluations thus can incur ethical and legal liability for supervisors.

Unfortunately, our responsibility in this area may not be matched by available resources. Ladany, Lehrman-Waterman, Molinaro, and Wolgast (1999) suggest that supervisors have little to guide them in this effort: "there are no known supervisee evaluation instruments with adequate psychometric properties" (p. 458). Similarly, Bernard and Goodyear (1998) point to the criterion problem in supervision: "evaluation becomes a problematic area when there is virtually no research to determine what is essential for supervisees to learn under supervision" (p. 154).

Although evaluation guidelines often identify general areas for assessment—such as skills and knowledge, clinician's use of self, use of supervision, and future goals to enhance skills and remedy deficiencies (Crespi & Lopez, 1998; Kadushin, 1992; Taibbi, 1995)—specific criteria within these categories are largely left to the individual supervisor and institution to establish. It is important that those criteria be closely linked to job descriptions, the supervision contract, and specific needs of the organization. Further, performance criteria must distinguish between competent and incompetent levels of behavior (Blodgett, 1995; Hanna & Smith, 1998). Supervisors who are expected to develop institutional evaluation procedures and forms would benefit from formal training in performance appraisal techniques.

Ethical complaints by supervisees against clinical supervisors remain infrequent. Presumably, this is due in large measure to the competence of their supervisors. However, given that their professional future may rest on a supervisor's evaluation, it is understandable that supervisees avoid actions that could result in negative repercussions. For example, Ladany et al. (1999) studied 151 former graduate trainees in psychology and found that 33% identified ethical violations of their supervisors in failing to monitor their activities and/or conduct performance evaluations adequately. However, only 35% of that sample reported discussing this directly with their supervisor, choosing instead to talk with a peer (84%), significant other (33%), or another supervisor (21%) (Ladany et al., 1999).

Trainees are not the only ones who can be affected by such violations. Ramifications for the supervisor if supervisees do choose to report can be significant. The Report of the Ethics Committee (American Psychological Association, 1998) highlights a case that illustrates this vividly:

> An intern filed a complaint alleging that her supervisor did not meet with her for supervision, and allowed her and other trainees to provide services for which they were not qualified. The supervisor stated in his response that the supervision was provided through weekly staff meetings, and that he considered the supervision appropriate. His responses to follow-up questions indicated that the staff meetings did not include review of the intern's treatment sessions with clients. The Ethics Committee found violations of Standard 1.22.b (delegation to and supervision of subordinates) and Standard 6.05.a (assessing student and supervisee performance) as charged, and recommended censure with a directive of a 10-session tutorial in

the ethics of supervision. An appeal and subsequent adjudication upheld the Committee's recommendation. The member's employer, licensure board and state psychological association, ASPPB and the National Register were all informed of this ruling by the APA Ethics Committee. (p. 978)

Guest and Dooley (1999) see the potential for supervisee ethics complaints or litigation against their supervisors to create an important new area of risk management. How can supervisors avoid this outcome while providing fair and accurate evaluations of their supervisees?

Bernard and Goodyear (1998) suggest some conditions that favor more positive evaluation experiences. These include:

♦ acknowledging and discussing the power differential and oversight responsibilities inherent in supervision
♦ addressing defensiveness and individual/cultural differences openly in supervision
♦ providing a clear, mutual, and continuous feedback process
♦ modeling flexibility in accommodating short-term disruptions in a supervisee's performance
♦ ensuring a strong administrative structure that will support both supervisor evaluations and due process rights of supervisees
♦ encouraging feedback from supervisees throughout the process

Shulman (1993) proposed a seven-step collaborative evaluation process for supervisors that minimizes the potential for unexpected conflicts regarding the supervisee's performance:

1. Discuss evaluation criteria. Review what specific information, instruments, and sources of evidence will be used in evaluations. Supervisees should be given written copies of the final evaluation criteria and their due process rights at the onset of a supervisory relationship.
2. Refer to criteria frequently. Include an informal review of these criteria in ongoing case presentations and performance discussions.
3. Provide formative feedback. Structure time for feedback in the supervision sessions so that all parties acknowledge the supervisee's progress as well as areas that need concentration. Supervisor attention to a diversity of viewpoints, cultures, and theoretical allegiances is an important component of these discussions.
4. Develop a joint evaluation process. Have both supervisor and supervisee prepare a draft evaluation based on the criteria, sources of evidence, and formative feedback provided up to this point in supervision.
5. Anchor evaluations in documentation. Both supervisor and supervisee should cite examples or critical incidents from the supervisee's work to support strengths and weaknesses identified in their draft evaluations.
6. Conduct a supervisory conference. Identify agreed-on areas of strength

and weakness as well as areas of disagreement early in the meeting to allow for adequate discussion. Negotiate modifications where appropriate.

7. Write the final evaluation. Supervisors are responsible for final decisions regarding content of the evaluation report. If disagreements are not resolved in the supervisory conference, it is important to note them in the evaluation. Supervisees should know in advance with whom the evaluation report will be shared.

SUPERVISORS AS PROFESSIONAL GATEKEEPERS

Evaluations are designed to monitor the supervisee's knowledge and skills as well as to protect clients and the professional community from incompetent practitioners (Goodyear & Bernard, 1999; Haber, 1996; McConnell, 1993). What if an evaluation suggests that a given supervisee is not providing acceptably competent service? This becomes a complex and troubling issue for supervisors as well as for employers, credentialing bodies, and training programs. Table 8.2 provides ethical and professional guidelines that some disciplines have developed to aid supervisors in carrying out decisions and actions that accompany this finding. It is curious that neither the American Psychiatric Association nor the American Psychological Association has developed guidelines regarding this duty, given that a significant proportion of their members report clinical supervision among their professional activities.

Feedback, remediation efforts, dismissal from training programs, and refraining from endorsement are difficult tasks for the supervisor. Field site supervisors as well as academic training programs should have formal written policies regarding impaired or incompetent trainees. These policies should be given to all supervisees at the start of their training. They should be discussed in initial supervision sessions as well as between campus and site supervisors on a regular basis. In addition, supervisees must be given notice of their due process rights to appeal such actions. What does that mean and when does it apply?

Due process is a constitutional right, granted under the 14th Amendment, that protects individuals from state actions depriving them of life, liberty, or property without first allowing that person the opportunity to challenge the action. Procedural due process ensures that notice and a hearing must be given before an important right, such as the right to education or to practice one's profession, can be removed even temporarily (Disney & Stephens, 1994). Due process rights accrue to all persons working in public or government-funded institutions. Due process applies to private organizations only if the policies of those organizations stipulate it (Welfel, 1998b). Supervisees in settings mandated to provide due process have the legal right to be periodically evaluated and to file grievances regarding evaluations or decisions they believe are unfair (Robke, 1993; Tyler & Tyler, 1997; Welfel, 1998b).

TABLE 8.2   Supervisory Guidelines for Professional Gatekeeping

American Association for Marriage and Family Therapy
*Responsibilities and Guidelines for AAMFT Approved Supervisors
and Supervisors-in-Training*
Should a supervisor develop significant concerns about the abilities, philosophical beliefs, or practices of a trainee, the concerns must be shared with the trainee and documented in writing as early as possible.

American Counseling Association
Code of Ethics
Principle F.1.h: Counselors do not endorse students or supervisees for certification, licensure, employment, or completion of an academic or training program if they believe students or supervisees are not qualified for the endorsement. Counselors take reasonable steps to assist students or supervisees who are not qualified for endorsement to become qualified.

Principle F.3.a: Counselors, through ongoing evaluation and appraisal, are aware of the academic and personal limitations of students and supervisees that might impede performance. Counselors assist students and supervisees in securing remedial assistance when needed, and dismiss from the training program supervisees who are unable to provide competent service due to academic or personal limitations. Counselors seek professional consultation and document their decision to dismiss or refer students or supervisees for assistance. Counselors assure that students and supervisees have recourse to address decisions made, to require them to seek assistance, or to dismiss them.

Association for Counselor Education and Supervision
Ethical Guidelines for Counseling Supervisors
Guideline 2.12: Supervisors, through ongoing supervisee assessment and evaluation, should be aware of any personal or professional limitations of supervisees which are likely to impede future professional performance. Supervisors have the responsibility of recommending remedial assistance to the supervisee and of screening from the training program, applied counseling setting, or state licensure those supervisees who are unable to provide competent professional services. These recommendations should be clearly and professionally explained in writing to the supervisees who are so evaluated.

Guideline 2.13: Supervisors should not endorse a supervisee for certification, licensure, completion of an academic training program, or continued employment if the supervisor believes the supervisee is impaired in any way that would interfere with the performance of counseling duties. The presence of any such impairment should begin a process of feedback and remediation wherever possible so that the supervisee understands the nature of the impairment and has the opportunity to remedy the problem and continue with his/her professional development.

Guideline 2.14: Mechanisms for due process appeal of individual supervisory actions should be established and made available to all supervisees.

National Association of Social Workers
Guidelines for Clinical Social Work Supervision
The supervisor has the authority to enforce recommendations and can use sanctions such as a personnel evaluation, a reporting to the regulatory body, refusal to recommend for credentials, and others. . . . The supervisor may need to take the actions necessary within his or her scope of authority to lead a social worker out of the profession.

National Board for Certified Counselors, Inc.
Standards for the Ethical Practice of Clinical Supervision
Standard 10: Clinical supervisors shall refrain from endorsing an impaired supervisee when such impairment deems it unlikely that the supervisee can provide adequate counseling services.

Supervisors struggle with their seemingly incompatible functions of educator, trainer, and administrator when substandard supervisee evaluations require that remedial or disciplinary actions be taken (Erera & Lazar, 1994). It is no wonder that many training as well as employment settings have yet to establish formal guidelines for responding to impaired or incompetent trainees and supervisees (Bernard & Goodyear, 1998; Haas & Hall, 1991; Pope & Vetter, 1992; Rubin, 1997).

Several models for handling this situation do exist, however. Frame and Stevens-Smith (1995) outlined a three-step process for monitoring and dismissal procedures in graduate training programs. Their model includes the following steps to be taken with students receiving substandard ratings on an evaluation form used in all classes:

1. Students are presented with results of the evaluation, along with the supervising professor's written comments. A copy of this evaluation is given to program faculty and discussed at the next student review meeting. After this meeting, the supervising professor and the student meet to discuss the evaluation and recommended steps toward remediation.
2. If the student receives more than one substandard evaluation during a semester, or receives a substandard rating from more than one professor over two semesters, the student is required to meet with his or her faculty adviser to discuss remediation or possible reconsideration of continuation in the program. Copies of all evaluations are given to the student and are placed in his or her academic file.
3. If the student receives three or more substandard evaluations in one semester, the student is required to meet with his or her adviser and two other faculty members to discuss continuation in the program. If this committee determines that the student's personal or professional behavior is inappropriate to the discipline and would be detrimental to working with others, the student is denied continuance in the program (Frame & Stevens-Smith, 1995).

A four-step model for responding to impaired supervisees has been proposed for trainees in internship settings. Lamb, Cochran, and Jackson (1991) identified the following due process steps:

Step 1   Early in the evaluation process, supervisors who identify areas of concern about intern performance consult with one another to assess impairment based on the presence of several of the following traits:

- the intern does not acknowledge, understand, or address the problematic behavior when it is identified
- the problematic behavior is not merely a reflection of a skill deficit that can be rectified by academic or didactic training
- the quality of service delivered by the intern is consistently negatively affected

◆ the problematic behavior is not restricted to one area of professional functioning

◆ the problematic behavior of the intern has potential for ethical or legal ramifications if not addressed

◆ a disproportionate amount of attention by training personnel is required

◆ the intern's behavior does not change as a function of feedback, remediation efforts, or time

◆ the intern's behavior negatively affects the public image of the agency

These consultations are documented, followed by internal adjustments to supervision and intern opportunities to respond to the supervisory feedback in writing.

Step 2   If the foregoing initial review does not result in improvement of the intern's performance, additional discussion and documentation of the problematic behaviors, their manifestation and impact, and the intern's response to evaluative feedback take place. Training staff explore the full range of possible interventions and their potential impact on the intern. Modifications to supervision such as changing its focus, providing additional supervision time, assigning readings, or recommending personal therapy may be sufficient to address the identified concerns.

Step 3   If further intervention is required, probation or dismissal from training is considered. If probation is necessary, the intern is notified in writing of the conditions and duration of the probation. He or she has the option to challenge this decision in a meeting with relevant training personnel. The sponsoring academic program is apprised in writing of the intern's change in status, and ongoing feedback is provided to the intern throughout the probationary period. If a decision for dismissal is made, agency and institutional implications of the decision are reviewed, letters are simultaneously sent to the intern and academic program, the timing of departure is considered, and the intern is given the opportunity to appeal the decision within a given time frame.

Step 4   All probation or dismissal decisions are considered systemic interventions. Thus, their impact on clients, other interns and staff, the sponsoring program, and on the intern him- or herself must be noted and sensitively addressed (Lamb et al., 1991).

Among credentialed professionals, a determination of impairment or incompetence leaves colleagues and supervisors with a number of unpleasant options (Haas & Hall, 1991):

◆ to ignore the questionable behavior

◆ to support the filing of a complaint by a consumer

◆ to report the behavior to a formal regulatory body

◆ to consult with other colleagues about how to respond

◆ to discuss the concerns directly with the professional

Informal resolution of these problems generally involves providing the professional with training, information, and/or supervision to improve performance. When such problems come to the attention of state boards or professional associations, they may mandate an evaluation in which the professional has the opportunity to respond to the concerns in person or in writing. If concerns are upheld through this process, they will sanction the professional in light of the discipline's responsibility to protect the public from potential harm by its members.

OLD STORY WITH A NEW TWIST: DOCUMENTING SUPERVISION

Along with consultation and liability insurance, documentation is unquestionably a crucial risk management tool for clinical supervisors. "The supervisory record should be a tool for promoting ongoing growth and development of the practitioner. Under the best conditions, it aids the supervisor in fostering professional growth. . . . In difficult adversary conditions, the record is a documented defense against unrecognized and unacceptable practitioner failure at performance" (Munson, 1993, p. 221).

It is astounding to recognize that supervision remains infrequently documented in the mental health disciplines. As is evident in Table 8.3, there is little attention to this standard in the professional codes. This is in sharp contrast to

TABLE 8.3   Supervision Documentation Guidelines

Association of State and Provincial Psychology Boards
Code of Conduct
Rule 6.d: For each person professionally supervised, the psychologist shall maintain for a period of not less than five years after the last date of supervision a record of the supervisory session that shall include, among other information, the type, place, and general content of the session.

National Association of Social Workers
Guidelines for Clinical Social Work Supervision
The supervisor should document: date of contact; progress toward learning goals outlined in the contract; specific recommendations including additional consultation for supervisee or supervisee's client, suggested readings, and educational activities.

The supervisee should document: date of contact; questions and issues brought to the supervisor; supervisor's recommendations; follow-up action plan with rationale.

The client records should document: the client's knowledge that supervision is taking place; the nature of information that is shared; verification that the client has the name, address, and phone number of the supervisor or other person with administrative authority.

National Board for Certified Counselors, Inc.
Standards for the Ethical Practice of Clinical Supervision
Standard 4: Clinical supervisors shall keep and secure supervision records. . . .

the clearly defined standards across disciplines for maintaining and storing clinical records. Furthermore, it ignores the legal doctrine that an absent or inadequate record will itself be viewed as evidence of substandard care, no matter what care was actually provided (Moline, Williams, & Austin, 1998; Weiner & Wettstein, 1993; Welch, 1998).

Suslovich v. New York State Education Department (Case 8.1), while involving a direct service provider rather than a clinical supervisor, illustrates the court's general stance regarding recordkeeping in the mental health professions. In this appeal, the New York Supreme Court upheld that state's licensing board sanctions against a practitioner for failing to maintain adequate clinical records. Sanctions included suspending that psychologist's license, requiring 1 year of supervision to monitor his practice, and mandating enrollment in a course on professional ethics. How would a supervisor fare under similar scrutiny following an ethics complaint by a supervisee?

Documentation is no longer an option in supervision. Supervisors are crucial links in any effective mental health service delivery system. Legal precedents suggest that we are both ethically and legally responsible for quality control of our supervisees' work (Falvey, Caldwell, & Cohen, 2002). The supervision record is a useful and necessary part of that professional accountability. It "builds the record" of our professionalism and is an essential exposure-limiting strategy (Monahan, 1993). However, in stark contrast to the numerous clinical documentation forms available, a scarcity of documentation formats has forced supervisors to rely on personal style in recording their supervisory activities.

What should be included in the supervisory record? Weiner and Wettstein (1993) suggest that there are pitfalls in both overdocumenting and underdocumenting. Examples of overdocumentation in supervisory records include disparaging staff or clients, including extraneous or sensitive supervisee data, altering the record at a later time, illegible handwriting, and improper abbreviations. Underdocumentation includes the failure to document decision processes regarding significant supervisory events, failure to document informed consent, destroying supervision records prematurely, and the failure to obtain and review past supervision records (Weiner & Wettstein, 1993).

Taibbi (1995) reports that accreditation and licensing reviews increasingly require that some record be kept of supervision sessions. He suggests that "a file on each clinician, including a list of his or her caseload, notes about a particular case, the supervisor's clinical recommendations, and impressions of the session, helps the supervisor keep track of what's going on and . . . provide ready information for formal evaluations" (p. 124).

Munson (1993) observes that, at a minimum, the supervision record should include a supervisory contract; a brief summary of the supervisee's experience, training, and learning needs; a summary of all performance evaluations; notation of all supervision sessions, including the cases discussed and

Suslovich v. New York State Education Department
174 A.D.2d 802 (N.Y. App. Div. 1991)   *New York Supreme Court, Appellate Division*

FACTS

This case is an appeal following the Commissioner of Education's suspension of a psychologist's license for 3 months for unprofessional conduct related to failure to maintain proper medical records. The psychologist had agreed to see a client for ten sessions. After attending only five, the client terminated treatment. However, the psychologist submitted an insurance reimbursement claim for all ten sessions. This prompted concern about other questionable practices, so the insurance company filed a complaint with the Department of Education (licensing body in New York) for unprofessional conduct. In connection with the fraudulent billing concerns, the Department of Education's subsequent investigation revealed a lack of recordkeeping for this case by Dr. Suslovich. New York law requires licensed psychologists to maintain adequate records to "ensure that meaningful information is recorded in case the patient should transfer to another professional or the treating professional should become unavailable." *Id.* at 803. Dr. Suslovich admitted that he maintained the records in this case "in his head," claiming that the insurance claim form would serve as the medical record. However, the insurance form was sparse in information as well.

HOLDING OF THE COURT

The court upheld the license suspension on the ground that there was more than enough evidence to show that the psychologist failed to maintain proper records for the five sessions he had with the client. Simply keeping the records in his head was not sufficient to provide an adequate medical record, and Dr. Suslovich did not substantiate any intent at the time to have the insurance claim serve as the client record.

IMPLICATIONS

While the New York licensing laws are very vague, only requiring "adequate" medical records to be kept, this case makes clear that storing client records in your head is *not* adequate. All therapists at some point have experienced a time crunch; it is hard to get all of the necessary paperwork done when clients are scheduled all day long. However, medical record information is equally as important as insurance documentation. While the court in this case illuminated several reasons for maintaining records, there are other rationales that bear directly on your exposure to liability. Although medical records are subject to confidentiality or privilege, they can serve as strong extrinsic evidence for or against you if ordered admitted into evidence by a court. If you have not adequately documented session and client information, but have to "recall" the information from memory and are required by a court to disclose it, a jury may not put as much credibility on your information.

Timothy E. Bray (2000). Reprinted with permission.

significant decisions made; notation of canceled or missed supervision sessions; and significant problems encountered in supervision and how they were resolved. This information helps the supervisor track the supervisee's clinical work and provides evidence of supervision should a grievance or client lawsuit subsequently arise.

Several authors have developed standardized formats for the documentation of supervision. Bridge and Bascue (1990) developed the Supervisory Record Form (SRF), a one-page outline for recording supervision sessions that is organized into three sections: identifying information, supervisory activity, and supervisor recommendations. Glenn and Serovich (1994) designed a Case Review Form (CRF), a one-page outline for use by supervisors having diverse orientations working with individuals, couples, or families. This form includes a checklist of "milestone events" in therapy (e.g., initial client contact, first session, treatment planning, termination) for supervisors to date as they occur. Williams (1994) developed a similarly brief format for marital and family counseling supervisors to document their recommendations.

By far the most comprehensive documentation system for clinical supervisors was developed by Falvey et al. (2002). The Focused Risk Management Supervision System (FoRMSS) includes forms to document the following supervisory information and activities:

- *emergency contact information* to facilitate rapid communication between the supervisee and supervisor or a designated backup
- a *supervisee profile* to summarize the supervisee's training and experience as well as to identify supervisory goals
- a *log sheet* that enables supervisors to track the supervisee's changing caseload as well as cases reviewed in supervision sessions, thus alerting supervisors to anticipate and schedule future case reviews in a timely manner
- an *initial case overview* that provides a brief overview of new cases, documents treatment goals and plans, tracks referrals and record requests, and highlights priority issues and risks to be addressed
- a *supervision record* that documents each case as it is reviewed in supervision, updating the client's progress, noting supervisory discussions and recommendations, and alerting supervisors to training or risk management issues in oversight of that case
- a *termination summary* that records the circumstances of client terminations, client status at termination, and any follow-up or referrals needed

A unique feature of FoRMSS is the various highlighted risk management boxes that alert supervisors to monitor potential clinical, ethical, or legal risks associated with a supervised case. This assists supervisors in providing adequate clinical oversight, tracking their supervisee's professional development, and minimizing negative outcomes. The FoRMSS system has been adopted in a variety of academic and agency settings and "represents a new standard for supervision record keeping. . . . [It] benefits the entire therapy system by keeping supervision focused on its multiple levels from a variety of angles" (Bernard & Goodyear, 1998, p. 219).

It is important that the reader be convinced of the need to keep supervision records. But how long should they be kept? The American Psychological Association's *Record Keeping Guidelines* (1993a) recommend retaining full clinical records for at least 3 years and a summary for an additional 12 years. State statutes have established standards ranging from 5 to 30 years for clinical record retention (Moline et al., 1998). Given that client lawsuits may arise years after treatment, and considering that there is no statute of limitations regarding complaints of professional ethics violations (Weiner & Wettstein, 1993), it would seem prudent to retain supervision records for at least as long as your state requires clinical records to be kept.

Final Reflections on Supervisory Risk Management

As a therapist, educator, and supervisor for the past two decades, I have had the opportunity to experience a variety of challenging and rewarding aspects of the mental health field. In the early years of my career, supervision, although widely practiced, was relegated to a peripheral position in many inpatient, community agency, and school settings. Training was virtually nonexistent, methods were borrowed from clinical theories, and supervision time was often unprotected from intrusion or cancellation. Much of what passed for supervision was in fact administrative oversight that did little to help the clinician with difficult treatment issues.

That has changed, at least in theory. We now have numerous models and a growing empirical base that establish supervision as a clinical specialty. Training in supervision, while not yet plentiful, is more available than in the past. Certainly, our awareness of ethical and legal issues has been sharpened by both professional associations and the social climate of our times. As I complete this book, I am headed to a national conference on supervision, which is one of several that now occur regularly in the mental health disciplines.

While the scaffolding of our specialty is thus much more elaborate than even a decade ago, the need for supervisors to pay careful attention to the responsibilities and risks of their mentoring roles is stronger than ever. As preceding chapters illustrate, there is considerable exposure on the part of the professional who supervises a trainee whom they cannot fully control and oversees the treatment of clients with whom they seldom have contact.

Although that knowledge may deter some from supervising others, for many the opportunity to train and support junior colleagues in the field is among the most rewarding of professional activities. Benefiting our own clinical practice as well, supervision and peer consultation challenge us to remain current and accountable in our interventions. As colleagues and I struggled with the supervision issues that ultimately led to this book, the need to balance risk with prudent action in supervisory practice came into bold relief.

Many recommendations have been offered in each chapter to assist supervisors in conducting themselves competently and in accordance with evolving legal and ethical standards of care. This text will conclude with the "top 10" risk management strategies most frequently cited in the current supervision and legal literature. Following these guidelines, the supervisor's invaluable service as a professional mentor within his or her discipline is augmented by management practices that benefit clients, supervisees, and society at large.

1. *Maintain written policies.* Have policies and procedures addressing clinical emergencies, client–supervisee rights, and your state's legal and ethical mandates. Train staff and supervisees to follow them.
2. *Monitor supervisee competence.* Select supervisees carefully. Obtain direct work samples periodically, monitor all supervisee cases, and provide ongoing feedback as well as formal evaluations.
3. *Have a supervision contract.* Develop a written agreement that clearly delineates goals, objectives, duties, and responsibilities of all parties to the supervisory relationship.
4. *Be accessible to supervisees.* Conduct supervision regularly. Ensure competent supervisory coverage when you are unavailable and have an emergency contact plan in place for supervisees to reach you or appropriate backup personnel at any time.
5. *Get informed consent for supervision.* Be sure that clients and supervisees are apprised of procedures, their rights, and any limitations to confidentiality associated with supervision.
6. *Document supervisory activities.* Record content of supervision sessions, supervisory recommendations and their implementation, and decision processes used in high-risk clinical or supervisory situations.
7. *Consult regularly.* Confer with colleagues, administrators, state boards, ethics committees, and/or attorneys when in doubt or at risk of liability exposure.
8. *Read and discuss ethical codes.* Talk about ethics regularly in supervision. Monitor supervisee compliance with ethical codes.
9. *Know current laws and statutes.* Keep informed of state statutes and regulations. Follow emerging case law that affects clinical as well as supervisory practice in your jurisdiction.
10. *Purchase professional liability insurance.* Be sure that both your employers' and your own professional liability policies cover supervisory activities. Require supervisees to maintain current liability insurance.

Supervision Guidelines *A*

ASSOCIATION OF STATE AND PROVINCIAL PSYCHOLOGY BOARDS

Preamble

The Association of State and Provincial Psychology Boards' charge to its 1996 Task Force on Supervision Guidelines was to: 1) review and develop guidelines for the supervision of credentialed non-doctoral personnel; 2) review and develop guidelines for the supervision of doctoral level candidates for licensure; and 3) review the current Guidelines for Supervision of Uncredentialed Personnel and suggest revisions, if necessary. This publication offers recommendations made by the task force and approved by the ASPPB Board of Directors in December 1997. Given the complexity of the licensure process and the practice of psychology, the task force recognizes that these recommendations can only serve as a model that must be adapted to suit the context, realities and needs of the jurisdictions in which they will be implemented.

Supervision has long been an essential component of pre- and postdoctoral training in psychology. Guidelines for accreditation identify supervision as a central ingredient in psychology training programs. Most jurisdictions regulating the practice of psychology specifically address both pre- and postdoctoral supervision in their laws and regulations. Supervised experience is recognized by statute in most jurisdictions as one of the prerequisites for licensure for independent practice as a psychologist.

Supervision is regulated for a variety of personnel in a variety of settings. An increasing number of psychologists are involved in some form of supervision as a component of their professional practice. Changes in the delivery of health services, the advent of managed care, and increased litigiousness provide compelling reasons for attending to the quality and extent of supervision for licensure and regulation of psychologists. In addition, consensus among jurisdictions regarding statutory requirements for supervised experience and practice would enhance efforts to secure reciprocity.

Given the critical role of supervision in the protection of the public and in the training and practice of psychologists, it is surprising that organized psychology has failed to establish graduate level training in supervision or training standards for supervisors (e.g., qualifications, content of supervision, evaluation). Few supervisors report having had formal courses on supervision, and most rely on their own experience as a supervisee. In addition, the complexity of the supervisory process as well as the reality that supervision itself serves multiple purposes prevents simplistic guidelines. The intent is to identify the most salient ethical and legal components of the supervisory process. Concerns for protection of the public and accountability are paramount.

Supervision is defined as the relationship focused on the development, enhancement and evaluation of the supervisee's skills, knowledge and behavior in the practice of psychology. A psychologist may supervise a psychology research student, a practicum or extern student, a pre- or postdoctoral trainee, individuals trained at the masters or doctoral level in psychology who are not yet licensed, another licensed psychologist, uncredentialed personnel such as a psychological associate, psychometrician, or a student or mental health professional in another specialty area such as psychiatry or social work.

Certain concepts should be kept in mind while reviewing and applying these guidelines on supervision. Supervision is neither psychotherapy nor consultation. The ultimate effectiveness and success of supervision depends to a large extent upon the nature and quality of the relationship between the supervisor and supervisee and the characteristics of each. Supervision has a central role in the development of professional identity and commitment to ethical behavior. The intent of these guidelines is to identify measurable components known to be critical in meeting goals of supervision.

The development of the following guidelines is founded on an intensive review of existing statutes and regulations dealing with supervision from 18 U.S. and Canadian jurisdictions and a summary review from other states and provinces as well as a review of professional literature on supervision and relevant ASPPB, American Psychological Association (APA) and other organizational documents.

These guidelines are meant to assist jurisdictions and supervisors by providing recommendations for: the supervision setting; supervisor qualifications; the duration and frequency of supervisory contact; the conduct of supervision; and evaluation, regulation and enforcement issues for the three categories of supervisee.

Guidelines for Supervision of Doctoral Level Candidates for Licensure

The following supervision guidelines are applicable to doctoral level candidates for licensure. This category includes both the pre- and postdoctoral supervised experience. These supervisees, who are in or have completed a doctoral program in psychology, or in some cases a related field, may be referred to as: interns, residents, fellows, trainees or some other descriptive title. These guidelines apply to predoctoral candidates who have completed the minimum graduate credits required by a regionally accredited program prior to internship experience and who are in good standing in their program and to postdoctoral candidates who have completed their regionally accredited doctoral training program. APA approved pre- or postdoctoral training programs are recognized as meeting the following recommendations regarding the components of supervised experience.

I. Setting of Supervised Experience

A. An acceptable training setting provides ongoing psychological services in a well-defined and established program. Physical components must be available such as office, support staff, and equipment necessary for the supervisee to be successful. The program meets the broad and specialized needs of the supervisee that are congruent with the supervisee's interests and level of training. Predoctoral settings should offer full spectrum training and provide a foundation for a career in psychology. Postdoctoral experience is intended to focus the training in areas of intended, advanced or specialized practice. The major focus of the setting is on training rather than on generating funds. There is sufficient administrative and financial support to maintain integrity as a training program.

B. Both the pre- and postdoctoral programs are organized education and training programs with a planned sequence of supervised experience. Postdoctoral programs offer a range of education and training building on the doctoral program and the predoctoral internship. The setting must provide the prospective supervisee with a written document specifying the rules and regulations of the program, as well as the roles, goals and objectives expected from both supervisee and supervisor. At the onset of training, the supervisor will be responsible for developing, along with the supervisee, a written individualized training plan that meets the needs of the supervisee and is consistent with the purpose of the setting. The supervisor is responsible for determining the adequacy of the trainee's preparation for the tasks to be performed. These documents serve as the foundation for quarterly, written evaluations.

C. The program must have a full-time licensed psychologist on site who is clearly responsible for the integrity and quality of the program and as many additional psychologists as are necessary to meet the training needs of the supervisee. The program should offer a variety of professional role models and diverse client populations. The predoctoral program has an identifiable group of supervisees who are of sufficient number to ensure meaningful peer interaction and support. The postdoctoral program makes every effort to provide meaningful peer interaction and support. The training status of the supervisee must be identified by an appropriate title such as intern, resident, fellow, etc., such that their training status is clearly identifiable to clients, third party payers and other entities.

II. Qualifications of Supervisors

A. Supervising psychologists shall be licensed or certified for the practice of psychology and must be aware of and abide by the ethical principles and state or provincial statutes pertaining to the practice of psychology in general and to supervision in particular. Supervisors have adequate training, knowledge and skill to render competently any psychological service that their supervisee undertakes. They shall not permit their supervisee to engage in any psychological practice that they cannot perform competently themselves. The supervisor has the responsibility to interrupt or terminate the supervisee's activities whenever necessary to ensure adequate training and protection of the public. The supervisor has at least three (3) years of postlicensure experience and has had training and/or experience in supervision.

B. The supervisor is ethically and legally responsible for all of the professional activities of the supervisee. For those jurisdictions that allow "interim" licensure of a doctoral level psychologist during the postdoctoral supervised experience, both the supervisor and the doctoral level psychologist share legal and ethical responsibilities. The supervisor's overall responsibility for the supervisee's professional practice of psychology is limited by the extent the credentialed supervisee is functioning independently and has been provided with competent and adequate supervision. The level of supervision should be commensurate with the level of competence of the supervisee.

C. The supervisor, or a qualified designee who meets the requirements as a supervisor, provides 24-hour availability to both the supervisee and the supervisee's clients. The psychologist shall have sufficient knowledge of all clients, including face-to-face contact when necessary, in order to plan effective service delivery procedures. The supervisor makes reasonable effort to provide for another qualified supervisor in case of any interruption of supervision due to such factors as the supervisor's illness, unavailability, or relocation.

D. Supervisors avoid entering into dual relationships with their supervisees. Psychologists do not exploit or engage in sexual relationships with supervisees. Supervisors attempt to resolve any unforeseen interference that may be potentially harmful to the supervisory relationship with due regard for the best interests of the supervisee and after appropriate consultation.

E. Predoctoral—The individual supervisor shall supervise no more than three (3) supervisees. Postdoctoral—The individual supervisor shall supervise no more than four (4) supervisees.

III. Nature and Duration of Supervisory Contact

A. Predoctoral—The predoctoral supervised internship consists of a minimum of 1500 hours of actual work experience (exclusive of holidays, sick leave, vacations, or other such absences) completed in not less than 48 weeks nor more than 104 weeks. The predoctoral experience averages at least 16 hours but not more than 40 hours a week. During the predoctoral supervision the supervisor shall provide a minimum of two (2) hours per week of face to face supervision and two (2) hours of additional learning activities such as group supervision, seminars, and case conferences regardless of whether the predoctoral internship is completed in one year or two. At least 50 percent of the predoctoral supervised experience must be in clinical service-related activities such as assessment, interviews, report writing, case presentations, treatment and consultation with at least 25 percent of that time devoted to face to face direct patient/client contact. No more than 25 percent of time shall be allocated for research.

B. Postdoctoral—The postdoctoral supervised experience consists of a minimum of 1500 hours of actual work experience (exclusive of holidays, sick leave, vacations, or other such absences) completed in not less than 48 weeks nor more than 104 weeks. The postdoctoral experience averages at least 16 hours but not more than 40 hours a week. The postdoctoral experience shall include one (1) hour of individual supervision and one (1) additional hour of learning activities per week. There may be special circumstances, e.g., geographical or confirmed physical hardship, when a jurisdiction may consider a variance in the frequency of the supervision sessions so that a minimum of four (4) hours per month of one-to-one supervision shall be maintained. The postdoctoral supervised experience shall consist of at least 25 percent and not more than 60 percent of the time devoted to direct service per week with the majority of work being in the intended area of practice.

C. Payment for supervisory services by the predoctoral supervisee is not acceptable. If payment is required for supervision for postdoctoral experience, supervisors should pay particular attention to the impact of the financial arrangements on the supervisory relationship.

D. The supervisory process addresses legal, ethical, social, and cultural dimensions that impact not only the professional practice of psychology but also the supervisory relationship. Issues of confidentiality, professional practice, and protection of the public are central.

IV. Written and Oral Evaluation

A. Evaluations provide objective assessment and direct feedback about the supervisee's competence in order to facilitate skill acquisition and professional growth. They are necessary to ensure that supervisees achieve identified objectives. At the outset of the supervisory period each supervisor together with the supervisee shall establish a written contract that specifies: a) the competencies to be evaluated and the goals to be attained, b) the standards for measuring performance, and c) the time frame for goal attainment. Direct feedback should be ongoing with written evaluations provided at least quarterly. Written evaluation of the supervisor by the supervisee should be provided at the end of the training program.

V. Regulation and Enforcement Issues

A. In order to assure quality supervision, supervisors must register with the jurisdiction. Registrants shall submit: academic credentials, applied training and experience as well as formal and informal training in supervision. Based on those materials, the jurisdiction will evaluate the supervisor's qualifications for providing supervision.

B. Boards should make available detailed information specifying supervisory responsibilities, supervision guidelines, and sample supervisee evaluation forms. All evaluations, both of the supervisor and supervisee, shall be maintained for a minimum of five (5) years and should be made available to the Board if requested.

C. Reports of successful completion of pre- and postdoctoral supervised experience will be forwarded to the licensing board as required by the individual jurisdictions. The jurisdiction's complaint and grievance procedures shall be followed where applicable.

GUIDELINES FOR SUPERVISION OF CREDENTIALED NON-DOCTORAL PERSONNEL

These guidelines apply to personnel providing psychological supervision to those who have a statutory license, registration, or certificate in psychology or in another mental health discipline and who must by statute or terms of employment provide psychological services under the direct supervision of a licensed psychologist.

I. Setting of Supervised Experience

A. An acceptable employment setting provides ongoing psychological services in a well defined and established program. Physical components must be available such as office space, support staff, and equipment necessary for the supervisee to be successful. The setting meets the broad and specialized needs of the supervisee that are congruent with the supervisee's job description.

B. The work setting must provide the employee with a written document specifying the administrative policies as well as the roles, goals and objectives of the position. At the onset of employment, the supervisor will be responsible for developing, along with the supervisee, a written individualized job description that is consistent with the qualifications of the supervisee and needs of the setting. The supervisor is responsible for determining the adequacy of the employee's preparation for the tasks to be performed. The level of supervision should be commensurate with the level of competence of the supervisee. These documents serve as the foundation for written evaluations.

C. The setting must have a licensed psychologist who is legally and ethically responsible for oversight of the integrity and quality of the services as well as other resources necessary to meet the employment needs of the supervisee.

D. The status of the supervisee must be identified by an appropriate title such as psychological assistant such that their status is clearly identifiable to clients, third party payers as well as other entities.

E. Titles of employees must clearly indicate their supervised status. Work assignments shall be commensurate with the skills of the uncredentialed person. All procedures shall be planned in consultation with the supervisor.

II. Qualifications of Supervisors

A. Supervising psychologists shall be licensed or certified for the practice of psychology and must be aware of and abide by the ethical principles and state or provincial statutes pertaining to the practice of psychology in general and to supervision in particular. The supervisor has at least three (3) years of postlicensure experience and has had training and/or experience in supervision. Both the supervisor and the credentialed non-doctoral supervisee share legal and ethical responsibilities. The supervisor's overall responsibility for the supervisee's professional practice is limited by the extent the credentialed supervisee is functioning independently and has been provided with competent and adequate supervision.

B. Supervisors have adequate training, knowledge and skill to render competently or have available consultation for any psychological service that their supervisee undertakes. They shall not permit their supervisee to engage in any psychological practice that they cannot perform competently. The supervisor has the responsibility to interrupt or terminate the supervisee's activities whenever necessary to ensure adequate development of skills and the protection of the public.

C. The supervisor, or a qualified designee who meets the requirements as a supervisor, provides 24-hour availability to both supervisee and the supervisee's clients for emergency consultation and intervention. The supervisor makes reasonable effort to provide supervision by another qualified supervisor in case of any interruption of supervision due to such factors as the supervisor's illness, unavailability, or relocation.

D. Supervisors avoid entering into dual relationships with their supervisees. They do not exploit or engage in sexual relationships with supervisees. Supervisors attempt to resolve any unforeseen interference that may be potentially harmful to the supervisory relationship with due regard for the best interests of the supervisee and after appropriate consultation.

E. No supervisor shall supervise more than four (4) supervisees.

III. Nature and Duration of Supervisory Contact

A. The supervisor should not be the employee of the supervisee. Supervisors should pay particular attention to the impact of the financial arrangements on the supervisory relationship.

B. The supervisory process addresses legal, ethical, social, and cultural dimensions that impact not only the professional practice of psychology but also the supervisory relationship. Issues of confidentiality, professional practice, and protection of the public are central.

IV. Written and Oral Evaluation

A. Based on the job description, written and oral evaluation is necessary to ensure that supervisors achieve identified employment objectives. Evaluations provide objective assessment and direct feedback about the supervisee's competence in meeting the needs of the employment setting.

B. Direct feedback should be ongoing with written evaluations provided at least semi-annually. At the outset of the supervisory period each supervisor together with the supervisee shall establish a written contract that specifies: 1) the competencies to be evaluated as well as the goals to be attained, 2) the standards for measuring performance, and 3) the job description.

V. Regulation and Enforcement Issues

A. In order to assure quality supervision, supervisors must register with the jurisdiction and shall submit: academic credentials, applied training and experience, as well as formal and informal training in supervision. Based on those materials, the jurisdiction will evaluate the supervisor's qualifications for providing supervision.

B. Boards should make available detailed information specifying supervisory responsibilities, supervision guidelines, and sample supervisee evaluation forms. The jurisdiction's complaint and grievance procedures shall be followed where applicable.

Standards for Counseling Supervisors **B**

ASSOCIATION FOR COUNSELOR EDUCATION AND SUPERVISION

The Standards include a description of eleven core areas of personal traits, knowledge and competencies that are characteristic of effective supervisors. The level of preparation and experience of the counselor, the particular work setting of the supervisor, and counselor and client variables will influence the relative emphasis of each competency in practice.

These core areas and their related competencies have been consistently identified in supervision research and, in addition, have been judged to have face validity as determined by supervisor practitioners, based on both select and widespread peer review.

1. **Professional counseling supervisors are *effective counselors* whose knowledge and competencies have been acquired through training, education, and supervised employment experience.**
   The counseling supervisor:
   1.1 demonstrates knowledge of various counseling theories, systems, and their related methods;
   1.2 demonstrates knowledge of his/her personal philosophical, theoretical and methodological approach to counseling;
   1.3 demonstrates knowledge of his/her assumptions about human behavior; and
   1.4 demonstrates skill in the application of counseling theory and methods (individual, group, or marital and family and specialized areas such as substance abuse, career-life rehabilitation) that are appropriate for the supervisory setting.

2. **Professional counseling supervisors demonstrate personal *traits and characteristics* that are consistent with the role.**
   The counseling supervisor:
   2.1 is committed to updating his/her own counseling and supervisory skills;
   2.2 is sensitive to individual differences;
   2.3 recognizes his/her own limits through self-evaluation and feedback from others;
   2.4 is encouraging, optimistic and motivational;
   2.5 possesses a sense of humor;

2.6 is comfortable with the authority inherent in the role of supervisor;

2.7 demonstrates a commitment to the role of supervisor;

2.8 can identify his/her own strengths and weaknesses as a supervisor; and

2.9 can describe his/her own pattern in interpersonal relationships.

3. **Professional counseling supervisors are knowledgeable regarding *ethical, legal and regulatory aspects* of the profession, and are skilled in applying this knowledge.**

The counseling supervisor:

3.1 communicates to the counselor a knowledge of professional codes of ethics (e.g., ACA, APA);

3.2 demonstrates and enforces ethical and professional standards;

3.3 communicates to the counselor an understanding of legal and regulatory documents and their impact on the profession (e.g., certification, licensure, duty to warn, parents' rights to children's records, third party payments, etc.);

3.4 provides current information regarding professional standards (NCC, CCMHC, CRC, CCC, licensure, certification, etc.);

3.5 can communicate a knowledge of counselor rights and appeal procedures specific to the work setting; and

3.6 communicates to the counselor a knowledge of ethical considerations that pertain to the supervisory process, including dual relationships, due process, evaluation, informed consent, confidentiality, and vicarious liability.

4. **Professional counseling supervisors demonstrate conceptual knowledge of the *personal and professional nature of the supervisory relationship*, and are skilled in applying this knowledge.**

The counseling supervisor:

4.1 demonstrates knowledge of individual differences with respect to gender, race, ethnicity, culture and age and understands the importance of these characteristics in supervisory relationships;

4.2 is sensitive to the counselor's personal and professional needs;

4.3 expects counselors to own the consequences of their actions;

4.4 is sensitive to the evaluative nature of supervision and effectively responds to the counselor's anxiety relative to performance evaluation;

4.5 conducts self-evaluations, as appropriate, as a means of modeling professional growth;

4.6 provides facilitative conditions (empathy, concreteness, respect, congruence, genuineness, and immediacy);

4.7 establishes a mutually trusting relationship with the counselor;

4.8 provides an appropriate balance of challenge and support; and

4.9 elicits counselor thoughts and feelings during counseling or consultation sessions, and responds in a manner that enhances the supervision process.

5. **Professional counseling supervisors demonstrate conceptual knowledge of *supervision methods and techniques*, and are skilled in using this knowledge to promote counselor development.**

The counseling supervisor:

5.1 states the purposes of supervision and explains the procedures to be used;

5.2 negotiates mutual decisions regarding the needed direction of learning experiences for the counselor;

5.3 engages in appropriate supervisory interventions, including role-play, role-reversal, live supervision, modeling, interpersonal process recall, micro-training, suggestions and advice, reviewing audio and video tapes, etc.;

5.4 can perform the supervisor's functions in the role of teacher, counselor, or consultant as appropriate;

5.5 elicits new alternatives from counselors for identifying solutions, techniques, responses to clients;

5.6 integrates knowledge of supervision with his/her style of interpersonal relations;

5.7 clarifies his/her role in supervision;

5.8 uses media aids (print material, electronic recording) to enhance learning; and

5.9 interacts with the counselor in a manner that facilitates the counselor's self-exploration and problem solving.

6. Professional counseling supervisors demonstrate conceptual knowledge of the *counselor developmental process*, and are skilled in applying this knowledge.

The counseling supervisor:

6.1 understands the developmental nature of supervision;

6.2 demonstrates knowledge of various theoretical models of supervision;

6.3 understands the counselor's roles and functions in particular work settings;

6.4 understands the supervisor's roles and functions in particular work settings;

6.5 can identify the learning needs of the counselor;

6.6 adjusts conference content based on the counselor's personal traits, conceptual development, training, and experience; and

6.7 uses supervisory methods appropriate to the counselor's level of conceptual development, training and experience.

7. Professional counseling supervisors demonstrate knowledge and competency in *case conceptualization and management*.

The counseling supervisor:

7.1 recognizes that a primary goal of supervision is helping the client of the counselor;

7.2 understands the roles of other professionals (e.g., psychologists, physicians, social workers) and assists with the referral process, when appropriate;

7.3 elicits counselor perceptions of counseling dynamics;

7.4 assists the counselor in selecting and executing data collection procedures;

7.5 assists the counselor in analyzing and interpreting data objectively;

7.6 assists the counselor in planning effective client goals and objectives;

7.7 assists the counselor in using observation and assessment in preparation of client goals and objectives;

7.8 assists the counselor in synthesizing client psychological and behavioral characteristics into an integrated conceptualization;

7.9 assists the counselor in assigning priorities to counseling goals and objectives;

7.10 assists the counselor in providing rationale for counseling procedures; and

7.11 assists the counselor in adjusting steps in the progression toward a goal based on ongoing assessment and evaluation.

8. Professional counseling supervisors demonstrate knowledge and competency in client *assessment and evaluation*.

The counseling supervisor:

8.1 monitors the use of tests and test interpretations;

8.2 assists the counselor in providing rationale for assessment procedures;

8.3 assists the counselor in communicating assessment procedures and rationales;

8.4 assists the counselor in the description, measurement, and documentation of client and counselor change; and

8.5 assists the counselor in integrating findings and observations to make appropriate recommendations.

9. Professional counseling supervisors demonstrate knowledge and competency in *oral and written reporting and recording*.

The counseling supervisor:

9.1 understands the meaning of accountability and the supervisor's responsibility in promoting it;

9.2 assists the counselor in effectively documenting supervisory and counseling-related interactions;

9.3 assists the counselor in establishing and following policies and procedures to protect the confidentiality of client and supervisory records;

9.4 assists the counselor in identifying appropriate information to be included in a verbal or written report;

9.5 assists the counselor in presenting information in a logical, concise, and sequential manner; and

9.6 assists the counselor in adapting verbal and written reports to the work environment and communication situation.

10. Professional counseling supervisors demonstrate knowledge and competency in the *evaluation of counseling performance*.

The counseling supervisor:

10.1 can interact with the counselor from the perspective of evaluator;

10.2 can identify the counselor's professional and personal strengths, as well as weaknesses;

10.3 provides specific feedback about such performance as conceptualization, use of methods and techniques, relationship skills, and assessment;

10.4 determines the extent to which the counselor has developed and applied his/her own personal theory of counseling;

10.5 develops evaluation procedures and instruments to determine program and counselor goal attainment;

10.6 assists the counselor in the description and measurement of his/her progress and achievement; and

10.7 can evaluate counseling skills for purposes of grade assignment, completion of internship requirements, professional advancement, and so on.

11. **Professional counseling supervisors are knowledgeable regarding *research in counseling and counselor supervision*, and consistently incorporate this knowledge into the supervision process.**

The counseling supervisor:

11.1 facilitates and monitors research to determine the effectiveness of programs, services and techniques;

11.2 reads, interprets, and applies counseling and supervisory research;

11.3 can formulate counseling or supervisory research questions;

11.4 reports results of counseling or supervisory research and disseminates as appropriate (e.g., inservice, conferences, publications); and

11.5 facilitates an integration of research findings in individual case management.

The Education and Training of Supervisors

Counseling supervision is a distinct field of preparation and practice. Knowledge and competencies necessary for effective performance are acquired through a sequence of training and experience which ordinarily includes the following:

1. Graduate training in counseling;
2. Successful supervised employment as a professional counselor;
3. Credentialing in one or more of the following areas: certification by a state department of education, licensure by a state as a professional counselor, and certification as a National Certified Counselor, Certified Clinical Mental Health Counselor, Certified Rehabilitation Counselor, or Certified Career Counselor;
4. Graduate training in counseling supervision including didactic courses, seminars, laboratory courses, and supervision practica;
5. Continuing educational experiences specific to supervision theory and practice (e.g., conferences, workshops, self-study); and
6. Research activities related to supervision theory and practice.

The supervisor's primary functions are to teach the inexperienced and to foster their professional development, to serve as consultants to experienced counselors, and to assist at all levels in the provision of effective counseling services. These responsibilities require personal and professional maturity accompanied by a broad perspective on counseling that is gained by extensive, supervised counseling experience. Therefore, training for supervision generally occurs during advanced graduate study or continuing professional development. This is not to say, however, that supervisor training in the pre-service stage is without merit. The presentation of basic methods and procedures may enhance students' performance as counselors, enrich their participation in the supervision process, and provide a framework for later study.

The Standards include a description of eleven core areas of personal traits, knowledge and competencies that are characteristic of effective supervisors. The level of preparation and experience of the counselor, the particular work setting of the supervisor, and counselor and client variables will influence the relative emphasis of each competency in practice.

Ethical Guidelines for Counseling Supervisors

ASSOCIATION FOR COUNSELOR EDUCATION AND SUPERVISION

Preamble

The Association for Counselor Education and Supervision (ACES) is composed of people engaged in the professional preparation of counselors and people responsible for the ongoing supervision of counselors. ACES is a founding division of the American Counseling Association (ACA) and as such adheres to ACA's current ethical standards and to general codes of competence adopted throughout the mental health community.

ACES believes that counselor educators and counseling supervisors in universities and in applied counseling settings, including the range of education and mental health delivery systems, carry responsibilities unique to their job roles. Such responsibilities may include administrative supervision, clinical supervision, or both. Administrative supervision refers to those supervisory activities which increase the efficiency of the delivery of counseling services; whereas, clinical supervision includes the supportive and educative activities of the supervisor designed to improve the application of counseling theory and technique directly to clients.

Counselor educators and counseling supervisors encounter situations which challenge the help given by general ethical standards of the profession at large. These situations require more specific guidelines that provide appropriate guidance in everyday practice. The Ethical Guidelines for Counseling Supervisors are intended to assist professionals by helping them:

1. observe ethical and legal protection of clients' and supervisees' rights;
2. meet the training and professional development needs of supervisees in ways consistent with clients' welfare and programmatic requirements;
3. establish policies, procedures, and standards for implementing programs.

The specification of ethical guidelines enables ACES members to focus on and to clarify the ethical nature of responsibilities held in common. Such guidelines should be reviewed formally every five years, or more often if needed, to meet the needs of ACES members for guidance.

The Ethical Guidelines for Counseling Supervisors are meant to help ACES members in conducting supervision. ACES is not currently in a position to hear complaints about alleged non-compliance with these guidelines. Any complaints about the ethical behavior of any ACA member should be measured against the ACA Ethical Standards and a complaint lodged with ACA in accordance with their procedures for doing so.

One overriding assumption underlying this document is that supervision should be ongoing throughout a counselor's career and not stop when a particular level of education, certification, or membership in a professional organization is attained.

Definitions of Terms

Applied Counseling Settings—Public or private organizations of counselors such as community mental health centers, hospitals, schools, and group or individual private practice settings.

Supervisees—Counselors-in-training in university programs at any level who are working with clients in applied settings as part of their university training program, and counselors who have completed their formal education and are employed in an applied counseling setting.

Supervisors—Counselors who have been designated within their university or agency to directly oversee the professional clinical work of counselors. Supervisors also may be persons who offer supervision to counselors seeking state licensure and so provide supervision outside of the administrative aegis of an applied counseling setting.

1. CLIENT WELFARE AND RIGHTS

1.01 The primary obligation of supervisors is to train counselors so that they respect the integrity and promote the welfare of their clients. Supervisors should have supervisees inform clients that they are being supervised and that observation and/or recordings of the session may be reviewed by the supervisor.

1.02 Supervisors who are licensed counselors and are conducting supervision to aid a supervisee to become licensed should instruct the supervisee not to communicate or in any way convey to the supervisee's clients or to other parties that the supervisee is himself/herself licensed.

1.03 Supervisors should make supervisees aware of clients' rights, including protecting clients' right to privacy and confidentiality in the counseling relationship and the information resulting from it. Clients also should be informed that their right to privacy and confidentiality will not be violated by the supervisory relationship.

1.04 Records of the counseling relationship, including interview notes, test data, correspondence, the electronic storage of these documents, and audio and videotape recordings are considered to be confidential professional information. Supervisors should see that these materials are used in counseling, research, and training and supervision of counselors with the full knowledge of the client and that permission to use these materials is granted by the applied counseling setting offering service to the client. This professional information is to be used for the full protection of the client. Written consent from the client (or legal guardian, if a minor) should be secured prior to the use of such information for instructional, supervisory, and/or research purposes. Policies of the applied counseling setting regarding client records also should be followed.

1.05 Supervisors shall adhere to current professional and legal guidelines when conducting research with human participants such as Section D-1 of the ACA Ethical Standards.

1.06 Counseling supervisors are responsible for making every effort to monitor both the professional actions, and failures to take action, of their supervisees.

2. SUPERVISORY ROLE

Inherent and integral to the role of supervisor are responsibilities for:

a. monitoring client welfare;
b. encouraging compliance with relevant legal, ethical, and professional standards for clinical practice;
c. monitoring clinical performance and professional development of supervisees; and
d. evaluating and certifying current performance and potential of supervisees for academic, screening, selection, placement, employment, and credentialing purposes.

2.01 Supervisors should have had training in supervision prior to initiating their role as supervisors.

2.02 Supervisors should pursue professional and personal continuing education activities such as advanced courses, seminars, and professional conferences on a regular and ongoing basis. These activities should include both counseling and supervision topics and skills.

2.03 Supervisors should make their supervisees aware of professional and ethical standards and legal responsibilities of the counseling profession.

2.04 Supervisors of post-degree counselors who are seeking state licensure should encourage these counselors to adhere to the standards for practice established by the state licensure board of the state in which they practice.

2.05 Procedures for contacting the supervisor, or an alternative supervisor, to assist in handling crisis situations should be established and communicated to supervisees.

2.06 Actual work samples via audio and/or videotape or live observation in addition to case notes should be reviewed by the supervisor as a regular part of the ongoing supervisory process.

2.07 Supervisors of counselors should meet regularly in face-to-face sessions with their supervisees.

2.08 Supervisors should provide supervisees with ongoing feedback on their performance. This feedback should take a variety of forms, both formal and informal, and should include verbal and written evaluations. It should be formative during the supervisory experience and summative at the conclusion of the experience.

2.09 Supervisors who have multiple roles (e.g., teacher, clinical supervisor, administrative supervisor, etc.) with supervisees should minimize potential conflicts. Where possible, the roles should be divided among several supervisors. Where this is not possible, careful explanation should be conveyed to the supervisee as to the expectations and responsibilities associated with each supervisory role.

2.10 Supervisors should not participate in any form of sexual contact with supervisees. Supervisors should not engage in any form of social contact or interaction which would compromise the supervisor–supervisee relationship. Dual relationships with supervisees that might impair the supervisor's objectivity and professional judgment should be avoided and/or the supervisory relationship terminated.

2.11 Supervisors should not establish a psychotherapeutic relationship as a substitute for supervision. Personal issues should be addressed in supervision only in terms of the impact of these issues on clients and on professional functioning.

2.12 Supervisors, through ongoing supervisee assessment and evaluation, should be aware of any personal or professional limitations of supervisees which are likely to impede future professional performance. Supervisors have the responsibility of recommending remedial assistance to the supervisee and of screening from the training program, applied counseling setting, or state licensure those supervisees who are unable to provide competent professional services. These recommendations should be clearly and professionally explained in writing to the supervisees who are so evaluated.

2.13 Supervisors should not endorse a supervisee for certification, licensure, completion of an academic training program, or continued employment if the supervisor believes the supervisee is impaired in any way that would interfere with the performance of counseling duties. The presence of any such impairment should begin a process of feedback and remediation wherever possible so that the supervisee understands the nature of the impairment and has the opportunity to remedy the problem and continue with his/her professional development.

2.14 Supervisors should incorporate the principles of informed consent and participation; clarity of requirements, expectations, roles and rules; and due process and appeal into the establishment of policies and procedures of their institution, program, courses and individual supervisory relationships. Mechanisms for due process appeal of individual supervisory actions should be established and made available to all supervisees.

3. Program Administration Role

3.01 Supervisors should ensure that the programs conducted and experiences provided are in keeping with current guidelines and standards of ACA and its divisions.

3.02 Supervisors should teach courses and/or supervise clinical work only in areas where they are fully competent and experienced.

3.03 To achieve the highest quality of training and supervision, supervisors should be active participants in peer review and peer supervision procedures.

3.04 Supervisors should provide experiences that integrate theoretical knowledge and practical application. Supervisors also should provide opportunities in which supervisees are able to apply the knowledge they have learned and understand the rationale for the skills they have acquired. The knowledge and skills conveyed should reflect current practice, research findings, and available resources.

3.05 Professional competencies, specific courses, and/or required experiences expected of supervisees should be communicated to them in writing prior to admission to the training program or placement/employment by the applied counseling setting, and, in the case of continued employment, in a timely manner.

3.06 Supervisors should accept only those persons as supervisees who meet identified entry level requirements for admission to a program of counselor training or for placement in an applied counseling setting. In the case of private supervision in search of state licensure, supervisees should have completed all necessary prerequisites as determined by the state licensure board.

3.07 Supervisors should inform supervisees of the goals, policies, theoretical orientations toward counseling, training, and supervision model or approach on which the supervision is based.

3.08 Supervisees should be encouraged and assisted to define their own theoretical orientation toward counseling, to establish supervision goals for themselves, and to monitor and evaluate their progress toward meeting these goals.

3.09 Supervisors should assess supervisees' skills and experience in order to establish standards for competent professional behavior. Supervisors should restrict supervisees' activities to those that are commensurate with their current level of skills and experiences.

3.10 Supervisors should obtain practicum and fieldwork sites that meet minimum standards for preparing students to become effective counselors. No practicum or fieldwork setting should be approved unless it truly replicates a counseling work setting.

3.11 Practicum and fieldwork classes should be limited in size according to established professional standards to ensure that each student has ample opportunity for individual supervision and feedback. Supervisors in applied counseling settings should have a limited number of supervisees.

3.12 Supervisors in university settings should establish and communicate specific policies and procedures regarding field placement of students. The respective roles of the student counselor, the university supervisor, and the field supervisor should be clearly differentiated in areas such as evaluation, requirements, and confidentiality.

3.13 Supervisors in training programs should communicate regularly with supervisors in agencies used as practicum and/or fieldwork sites regarding current professional practices, expectations of students, and preferred models and modalities of supervision.

3.14 Supervisors at the university should establish clear lines of communication among themselves, field supervisors, and the students/supervisees.

3.15 Supervisors should establish and communicate to supervisees and to field supervisors specific procedures regarding consultation, performance review, and evaluation of supervisees.

3.16 Evaluations of supervisee performance in universities and in applied counseling settings should be available to supervisees in ways consistent with the Family Rights and Privacy Act and the Buckley Amendment.

3.17 Forms of training that focus primarily on self understanding and problem resolution (e.g., personal growth groups or individual counseling) should be voluntary. Those who conduct these forms of training should not serve simultaneously as supervisors of the supervisees involved in the training.

3.18 A supervisor may recommend participation in activities such as personal growth groups or personal counseling when it has been determined that a supervisee has deficits in the areas of self understanding and problem resolution which impede his/her professional functioning. The supervisor should not be the direct provider of these activities for the supervisee.

3.19 When a training program conducts a personal growth or counseling experience involving relatively intimate self disclosure, care should be taken to eliminate or minimize potential role conflicts for faculty and/or agency supervisors who may conduct these experiences and who also serve as teachers, group leaders, and clinical directors.

3.20 Supervisors should use the following prioritized sequence in resolving conflicts among the needs of the client, the needs of the supervisee, and the needs of the program or agency. Insofar as the client must be protected, it should be understood that client welfare is usually subsumed in federal and state laws such that these statutes should be the first point of reference. Where laws and ethical standards are not present or are unclear, the good judgment of the supervisor should be guided by the following list:

a. relevant legal and ethical standards (e.g., duty to warn, state child abuse laws, etc.);
b. client welfare;
c. supervisee welfare; and
d. program and/or agency service and administrative needs.

Standards for the Ethical Practice of Clinical Supervision

NATIONAL BOARD FOR CERTIFIED COUNSELORS, INC.

In addition to following the NBCC Code of Ethics pertaining to the practice of professional counseling, clinical supervisors shall:

1. Ensure that supervisees inform clients of their professional status (e.g., intern) and of all conditions of supervision.

    Supervisors need to ensure that supervisees inform their clients of any status other than being fully qualified for independent practice or licensed. For example, supervisees need to inform their clients if they are a student, intern, trainee or, if licensed with restrictions, the nature of those restrictions (e.g., associate or conditional). In addition, clients must be informed of the requirements of supervision (e.g., the audiotaping of all counseling sessions for purposes of supervision).

2. Ensure that clients have been informed of their rights to confidentiality and privileged communication when applicable. Clients also should be informed of the limits of confidentiality and privileged communication.

    The general limits of confidentiality are when harm to self or others is threatened; when the abuse of children, elders or disabled persons is suspected; and in cases when the court compels the counselor to testify and break confidentiality. These are generally accepted limits to confidentiality and privileged communication, but they may be modified by state or federal statute.

3. Inform supervisees about the process of supervision, including supervision goals, case management procedures, and the supervisor's preferred supervision model(s).

4. Keep and secure supervision records and consider all information gained in supervision as confidential.

5. Avoid all dual relationships with supervisees that may interfere with the supervisor's professional judgment or exploit the supervisee.

    Although all dual relationships are not in themselves inappropriate, any sexual relationship is considered to be a violation. Sexual relationship means sexual contact, sexual harassment, or sexual bias toward a supervisee by a supervisor.

6. Establish procedures with their supervisees for handling crisis situations.

7. Provide supervisees with adequate and timely feedback as part of an established evaluation plan.
8. Render assistance to any supervisee who is unable to provide competent counseling services to clients.
9. Intervene in any situation where the supervisee is impaired and the client is at risk.
10. Refrain from endorsing an impaired supervisee when such impairment deems it unlikely that the supervisee can provide adequate counseling services.
11. Refrain from offering supervision outside of their area(s) of competence.
12. Ensure that supervisees are aware of the current ethical standards related to their professional practice, as well as legal standards that regulate the practice of counseling.

    Current ethical standards would mean standards published by the National Board for Certified Counselors (NBCC) and other appropriate entities such as the American Counseling Association (ACA). In addition, it is the supervisor's responsibility to ensure that the supervisee is aware that state and federal laws might regulate the practice of counseling and to inform the supervisee of key laws that affect counseling in the supervisee's jurisdiction.

13. Engage supervisees in an examination of cultural issues that might affect supervision and/or counseling.
14. Ensure that both supervisees and clients are aware of their rights and due process procedures.

Guidelines for Clinical Social Work Supervision

National Association of Social Workers

The National Council on the Practice of Clinical Social Work (Clinical Council) of the National Association of Social Workers (NASW) views supervision as one of the essential tools for ensuring quality social work services. Supervision early in a social worker's professional development, especially during the first two years after graduation, and the use of consultation throughout his or her professional career increases the social worker's proficiency in service delivery and ultimately improves clients' clinical status and functional outcomes.

The following guidelines provide a framework for the broad range of supervisory circumstances in which clinical social workers participate. The focus of this document is on the clinical supervision of clinical social workers by clinical social workers. These guidelines do not address supervision of students, volunteers, or paraprofessionals, or the supervision of other forms of social work practice, although many of the elements discussed may apply in those circumstances. Further, it is the opinion of the Clinical Council that only social workers can appropriately supervise social work functions. However, it is recognized that some settings may label as "supervision" the appropriate function of other professionals to provide instruction and consultation and, similarly, social workers may provide these same services to non social workers. It is also recognized that administrative supervision may cross professional lines.

Supervision serves a critical role in the ongoing development of clinical social work expertise. The mutual responsibilities and obligations of the supervisor and supervisee must be taken seriously and implemented with great care. Supervision provides the opportunity for interactive guidance and support that is not available through any other source of professional development. Supervision has the potential of enhancing the quality of work for both the supervisee and the supervisor. Ultimately, it is the client who experiences the ultimate benefit of good supervision.

Definitions

Clinical Social Work

This document uses the definition of clinical social work found in the *NASW Standards for the Practice of Clinical Social Work:* Clinical social work shares with all social work practice the goal of enhancement and maintenance of psychosocial functioning of individuals, families, and small groups. Clinical social work practice is the professional application of social work theory and methods to the treatment and prevention of psychosocial dysfunction, disability, or impairment, including emotional and mental disorders. It is based on knowledge of one or more theories of human development within a psychosocial context.

Supervision is differentiated from *education* in two ways:

1. Education starts with the goal of imparting knowledge and teaching models of practice and human behavior, constructs, and theories; cases are used to illustrate general principles and elements. Supervision is organized around performance, using specific cases and theory targeted to the supervisee's learning and practice needs.
2. The supervisory process creates a relationship in which educational techniques and processes can be applied to enhance social worker functioning. Through supervision, the supervisee learns to apply educational knowledge to specific practice situations.

PURPOSE AND INTENT OF SUPERVISION

The primary purpose of supervision is to maintain and enhance the knowledge and skill of the clinical social worker to provide improved services to and clinical outcomes for the client population. Supervision includes the development of professionalism and the evaluation of function.

Supervision may occur for the purpose of aiding professional growth and development; fulfilling the requirements for licensing, credentialing, third-party reimbursement; and meeting internal administrative requirements, external regulatory or accreditation requirements and corrective or disciplinary functions.

Professional Growth and Development

Together with continuing education and consultation, supervision enables a professional to enhance competent practice and lifelong professional growth and satisfaction. As social workers increase their experience and skills, the support they receive in their professional practice will shift away from supervision to emphasize input from consultation and continuing education.

Licensing

Supervision to meet licensure requirements continues the process of imparting integrated didactic knowledge into practice situations so the practitioner can attain a level of expertise sufficient to practice within specified levels of autonomy. Content of supervision includes the ethical, legal and risk-management issues related to clinical social work practice.

Credentialing

In addition to continuing the integration of didactic knowledge into practice situations, supervision for credentialing concentrates on developing formally recognized expertise in general clinical practice or in the specific practice area that is the focus of the credential.

Third-Party Reimbursement

Supervision may be a necessary requirement to receive third-party reimbursement for social work services. Supervisory requirements for third-party payment are determined by state law and individual health care plans.

Administrative Requirements

Administrative requirements for supervision by employers or contractors may have several purposes including quality assurance, performance evaluation, and risk management.

Regulatory/Accreditation

An organization may be required to meet certain stipulated supervisory standards to satisfy government regulations or accreditation requirements.

Corrective and Disciplinary Functions

A state regulatory board, professional association, or employer may require corrective action as a consequence of a finding of misconduct. Supervision with a specified focus may be required as part of a corrective plan.

SETTINGS

Supervision is recommended in all settings where clinical social work is practiced. In an agency or institutional setting, the social work clinical supervisor should be an employee within the setting. Such settings may include hospitals, schools, mental health centers, child welfare agencies, family service agencies, nursing homes, home health agencies, residential treatment centers, and public and private service delivery systems.

When clinical social work supervision is not available from staff, outside supervision should be secured. In seeking outside clinical social work supervision, the following three factors must be considered:

1. The supervisor needs to function as an integral part of the organization by having a solid grasp of the agency's mission, policy, and procedures.

2. The extent of the supervisor's responsibility for the supervisee needs to be clearly defined and delineated in terms of cases to be supervised, role in personnel evaluations, and other aspects.
3. Responsibility for payment needs to be stipulated. Agencies are strongly encouraged to pay for outside supervision, but, even if the supervisee pays directly for the supervision, the supervisor must be responsible to the agency.

In the situation of a private multidisciplinary group practice, supervision should come from a social worker who is more clinically advanced than the supervisee. If such a social worker is not available within the practice, outside social work supervision should be secured. Although NASW recommends profession-specific supervision, it assumes that professionals from all disciplines enter group practice with the perspective that professionals from each discipline will make meaningful and unique contributions to each other.

Social workers who feel the need for additional guidance and education beyond that available from the institutional setting or group practice should feel free to contract for independent consultation on a per-case or ongoing basis with or without payment as another educational resource. It should be made clear that accountability for care rests with the social worker, designated supervisor, and setting of practice.

The clinical social worker in independent private practice should maintain a consultation arrangement throughout the time he or she is in practice. Because the practitioner is solely accountable for his or her own practice, what many have called "supervision" is more precisely a consultation relationship. The following examples represent situations in which a clinical social worker in independent practice is actually receiving supervision:

1. Supervision is provided for the acquisition of credentials. In this case, the supervisor has the authority to sanction the social worker by recommending that the social worker not receive the credential.
2. The clinical social worker is also a student and supervision is being provided for the acquisition of new skills. The supervisor has the authority of an evaluation or grade.
3. Supervision is provided at the recommendation of a regulatory board or professional disciplinary board to ensure that corrective measures are implemented for quality practice.

QUALIFICATIONS

To be a qualified clinical social work supervisor, a social worker should:

- ◆ Possess a master's or doctoral degree in social work from an educational institution with a graduate social work program accredited by the Council on Social Work Education.
- ◆ Be licensed/certified by the state at the clinical level or the most advanced level available if there is no clinical license.

◆ Have at least three years postmaster's direct clinical social work practice experience in an organized setting (that is, one year in excess of the requirements for autonomous practice).

◆ Be grounded in the field of social work as evidenced by an affiliation with social work professional organizations or other methods.

◆ Not be actively under sanction from a disciplinary proceeding.

◆ Have undertaken formalized training and participated in ongoing professional development in the practice of supervision (that is, course content, workshops, and continuing education programs that clearly address effective methods of providing clinical supervision including the study of current professional literature on supervision).

◆ Be participating in ongoing professional development related to emerging trends in the field of social work practice, as well as clinical issues, in accordance with the NASW Continuing Education Standards. Forms of professional development may include:

—reading current professional literature routinely

—attending and/or presenting professional clinical social work workshops or seminars at least once a year

—participating in advanced practice training seminars

—participating in peer education/consultation groups

—providing case material for clinical education training programs

—developing written contributions to the field

◆ Have experience and expertise with the supervisee's client population (e.g., children, adolescents, elderly, substance abusers, and so on).

◆ Have experience and expertise with various methods of practice that the supervisee is employing (for example, family therapy, couples therapy, group work, crisis intervention, brief treatment, and so on).

◆ Have an understanding of organizational issues such as administrative policies and procedures related to agency practice.

◆ Possess appropriate supervisory skills such as:

—ability to address both strengths and weaknesses

—ability to teach and train for clinical practice

—recognition of the need to play an active and direct role in preparation and delivery of supervision

—ability to listen to and be supportive

◆ Possess an understanding of issues related to diversity such as racial, language, cross-cultural, gender, gay/lesbian, age, and physically challenged concerns.

◆ Be knowledgeable about the services available in the community and be able to suggest appropriate referrals for clients.

CONSULTATION FOR SUPERVISION

An effective supervisor recognizes that there will be times when it is necessary to secure consultation for his or her work with the supervisee. For example, the supervisee's or client's case needs may be beyond the supervisor's capacity or the relationship between the supervisor and supervisee may be impeding the supervisory process.

CONDUCT OF SUPERVISION

Supervision may be conducted through a variety of methods. Regardless of the specific method, the framework and mutual expectations must be clearly delineated to promote a positive and productive experience.

A written understanding should be signed by both the supervisor and supervisee (and the agency supervisor or administrator when appropriate) at the beginning of supervision and amended or renegotiated to reflect changes. The agreement should clarify the following items:

- ◆ Supervisory context
- ◆ Learning plan
- ◆ Format and schedule
- ◆ Supervisor responsibilities
- ◆ Supervisee responsibilities
- ◆ Accountability
- ◆ Evaluation measures
- ◆ Documentation and reporting
- ◆ Conflict resolution
- ◆ Compensation
- ◆ Client notification
- ◆ Duration and termination

Supervisory Context

When establishing the supervisory contract, the intent and the accountability framework need to be clearly articulated. Although the general intent is to improve professional performance, some of the variables in the supervisory contract are influenced by more detailed objectives between the supervisor and supervisee. The following examples describe some of the possible variations.

- ◆ For state licensure or certification, the state regulatory board may delineate specific issues such as the frequency, methods, and duration of supervision.
- ◆ In agency and institutional settings, administrative supervisory functions must be differentiated from clinical supervisory functions. If two different people provide the different functions, their relationship relevant to personnel evaluation needs to be articulated. The clinical supervision in an agency setting may have the primary intent of quality assurance, quality improvement, and risk management. Ideally, the specifics of frequency, method, and focus of clinical supervision should be negotiated according to the supervisee's needs and the supervisor's resources.

◆ In multidisciplinary practice, the legal structure of the practice has liability implications for the practice and practitioners. In a partnership, all partners share liability; therefore, supervision requirements may highlight the concern for risk management.

Learning Plan

Both the supervisor and the supervisee need to develop a learning plan that describes the goals and objectives of supervision. These goals should include the ongoing assessment of strengths and limitations and the assurance of practice in accordance with sound theory, the *NASW Code of Ethics,* and legal and administrative regulations.

The supervisor is expected to help the supervisee develop clinical assessment and treatment skills; review therapeutic techniques; explore treatment options, including the use of the client's personal network and community resources; and address dilemmas created by conflicting demands (for example, conflict between ethical conduct and agency regulations).

Format and Schedule

Methods of supervision vary on the basis of factors such as practice setting, client population, available technology, supervisor's management style, and supervisee's level of competence and learning style. Face-to-face supervision is recommended, individually and/or in a group. Some states prohibit or limit group supervision for purposes of fulfilling licensing requirements. The value of the face-to-face format is that it provides the opportunity to use verbal and nonverbal communication, to model practice style, to analyze the supervisory relationship and its impact on treatment, and to offer mutual feedback. The content of face-to-face sessions includes presentation of material, feedback, mutual analysis, and demonstration of skill. Group supervision requires special attention to issues such as confidentiality, the feedback process, and group members' role in performance evaluation.

Telephone or other forms of electronic communication such as the Internet are used in special circumstances. For example, the supervisee may work in an isolated rural geographic area, an emergency may arise, or the supervision may be provided by a distant expert. Written and audio or video material will need to be exchanged when telephone or electronic communication is the primary modality.

The supervisor can obtain information on the supervisee's performance by way of a verbal report (case presentation), observation (being physically present or via one way window), audio or video recording, role playing, or review of written case records.

The length of a supervisory session, frequency of supervisory contacts, and duration of supervision are determined according to the context (for example, state regulations, administrative policy, etc.).

The NASW Standards for the Practice of Clinical Social Work recommend, during the first two years of professional experience, at least one hour of supervision for every 15 hours of face-to-face contact with clients. After the first two years, the ratio may be reduced to a minimum of one hour of supervision (or consultation for the social worker in independent practice) for every 30 hours of face-to-face contact with clients. Clinical social workers with five or more years of experience should use supervision when they feel it is needed, based on the supervisory and practice context. Clinical social workers with five or more years of experience who practice in settings where supervision is not required should establish a consultation relationship.

Accountability Parameters

Supervision creates a hierarchical relationship. The supervisor must abide by the authority vested in the supervisory context (licensing body, employer, third-party payer, and so forth). These responsibilities may include specific tasks such as preparing personnel evaluations, providing recommendations for licensure, signing case records or claim forms, and so forth. All requirements need to be clearly articulated in the contract.

In this hierarchical role, the supervisor has the authority to enforce recommendations and can use sanctions such as a personnel evaluation, a reporting to the regulatory body, refusal to recommend for credentials, and others.

The supervisor may need to take the actions necessary within his or her scope of authority to lead a social worker out of the profession.

Documentation and Recording

A written supervision contract should be signed by both parties in all settings. If supervision is contracted by an employing agency or practice group, a written contract should detail the relationship and mutual responsibilities between the agency, supervisor, and supervisee.

The supervisor should document:

♦ date of contact,
♦ progress toward learning goals outlined in the contract, and
♦ specific recommendations, including additional consultation for supervisee or supervisee's client, suggested readings, and educational activities.

The supervisee should document:

♦ date of contact,
♦ questions and issues brought to the supervisor,
♦ supervisor's recommendations, and
♦ follow-up action plan with rationale.

The client records should document:

♦ the client's knowledge that supervision is taking place,
♦ the nature of information that is shared, and
♦ verification that the client has the name, address, and phone number of the supervisor or other person with administrative authority.

Conflict Resolution

A plan should be in place to address circumstances in which there is conflict between supervisor and supervisee. The supervisor should have a resource for consultation and the supervisee should have access to an appeals or mediation process. In addition, the supervisee should have a resource for consultation in the event he or she believes the supervisor is professionally impaired or has violated ethical guidelines.

Compensation Agreement

NASW strongly recommends that the agency, institution, or group practice assume financial responsibility for supervision. (Note: some states prohibit paid supervision for fulfillment of licensing requirements.) There are some circumstances in which the supervisee is responsible for the supervisor's compensation. If there is compensation for supervisory services, the contract should specify who is responsible for payment, the terms of payment, and the mutual obligations and rights of each party.

There is no standard fee schedule for paid supervision, although when fees are charged they are usually based on an hourly rate. The contract should specify whether the charge is for each session or is a flat rate payable at specific intervals such as monthly, quarterly, or annually.

Client Notification

Issues of confidentiality and informed consent require that the client or the client's representative (for example, a child's parent) be advised that supervision is taking place, the nature of information that is shared, and the supervisor's name and contact information. In situations where it is not clinically appropriate for the supervisor's name and contact information to be disclosed, the name and contact information for someone with administrative authority for the case must be disclosed instead.

Duration and Termination

The contract should indicate the time frame in which the agreement is made and the process for termination of supervision.

LEGAL ISSUES

The clinical practice supervisor shares responsibility for the services provided to the client. Liability of supervisors has been determined by the courts and includes direct liability related to negligent or inadequate supervision and vicarious liability related to negligent conduct by the supervisee.

Clinical social work supervisors in agency or institutional settings should be familiar with the scope of their own responsibility and authority. This scope should be specified in writing either as part of the agency's policies, supervisor's position description, or in a written contract. Many factors related to the degree to which the supervisor has responsibility and authority for both the clinical and administrative practices of the supervisee affect the supervisor's liability. For example, does the supervisor determine the size and nature of the assigned caseloads? Does the supervisor have direct access to outside consultation or is another level of clearance or authority required? Who has authority to respond to requests for access to client records?

The requirements and expectations of the supervisor's position also may affect liability. For example, supervisors who have too many supervisees, too many cases, or other competing demands on their time may not be able to provide adequate supervisory responsibilities. This situation would likely have clinical and ethical implications and could have legal consequences as well.

Direct Liability

Direct liability may be charged whenever harm is caused by erroneous action or omissions by the supervisor, such as inappropriate advice or direction that is carried out to the client's detriment. Direct liability can also be charged when a supervisor assigns duties for which the supervisee is inadequately prepared.

Sexual violations represent the largest number of claims against social workers, and supervisory negligence may be charged in these situations. It is imperative that the supervisor address boundary issues and provide special assistance in dealing with all feelings, including sexual feelings toward a client, and all of the feelings, including sexual feelings, the client may have toward the supervisee.

Vicarious Liability

Vicarious liability may be charged against the supervisor for erroneous acts or omissions. Supervisees can be held to the same standard of care and skill as their supervisors, and they are also expected to abide by the duty to warn or protect as first enunciated in *Tarasoff v. Regents of the University of California* (551 P.2d 334, 131 Cal. Rpter. 141976) and now embodied in statutes and court decisions in most states.

For purposes of risk management, the supervisor should:

- ensure that the services provided to clients by the supervisee are above minimal standards,
- maintain documentation of supervision,
- ensure that the client is informed of who the supervisor or administrative authority is and how to contact him or her,
- monitor the supervisees' professional functioning,
- identify practices that might pose a danger to the health and welfare of the supervisee's clients or to the public and take appropriate remedial measures, and

◆ identify the supervisee's inability to practice social work with reasonable skill and safety due to illness; excessive use of drugs, narcotics, chemicals, or any other substance; or any mental illness, serious personal problem, physical condition, or environmental stress.

To protect objectivity and guard against conflict of interest, the supervisor should not supervise his or her own parents, spouse, former spouses, siblings, children, anyone sharing the same household, or anyone with whom there is a romantic, domestic, or familial relationship.

ETHICAL ISSUES

The supervisor should actively refer to the *NASW Code of Ethics* during the supervisory process as a way to encourage the supervisee to engage in ethical conduct.

The supervisor should abide by ethical standards in his or her own conduct with the supervisee. The following sections from the *NASW Code of Ethics* provide specific guidance.

◆ Section III: The Social Worker's Ethical Responsibility to Colleagues
◆ Section IV: The Social Worker's Ethical Responsibility to Employers and Employing Organizations
◆ Section V: The Social Worker's Ethical Responsibility to the Social Work Profession

The supervisor must treat the supervisee with utmost respect and take care not to abuse the position of authority and power. At the same time, the supervisor must act to protect the client and profession.

Supervisor's Obligations for Professional Respect

The supervisor is obliged to extend to supervisees the utmost respect and regard. The relationship should be entered into in an orderly manner. The supervisor's position of authority should not be used to exploit the supervisee in any way, including sexual harassment or exploitation. Evaluations should be conducted on the basis of fair, objective criteria and shared with the supervisee.

The supervisor must handle supervisory material in a confidential manner. The parameters for the sharing of information about the supervisee's performance should be made clear at the beginning of supervision and be made part of the supervisory contract. In addition, the supervisor must complete evaluation forms and provide verification of the supervision arrangements after the relationship is terminated, without regard to the nature of that relationship or reason for its termination.

Supervisor's Obligation to Protect the Client and Profession

The supervisor has the responsibility to take action through appropriate channels against unethical conduct of a supervisee and to prevent the unauthorized and unqualified practice of social work. If the supervisor has direct knowledge of a supervisee's impairment caused by personal problems, psychosocial distress, substance abuse or mental health difficulties, he or she should consult with the supervisee and help with remedial action.

CONCLUSION

Supervisor Obligations

The supervisor has the responsibility to fulfill obligations to the auspices of supervision and to the supervisee. The supervisor should:

- ensure that the scope of his or her own responsibility and authority in agency settings has been clearly and expressly delineated,
- provide documentation of supervisory qualifications to supervisee or auspices governing the supervisory context,
- provide oversight and guidance in diagnosing, treating, and dealing with the supervisee's clients,
- evaluate the supervisee's role and conceptual understanding in the treatment process, and his or her use of a theoretical base and social work principles,
- conduct supervision as a process distinct from personal therapy or didactic instruction,
- provide supervision in the agreed-upon format,
- maintain documentation of supervision,
- provide periodic evaluation of supervisee,
- provide documentation for supervisee to meet the requirements of the supervisory context (including evaluation forms, recommendation forms, counter-signature of case materials, claim forms, and so on),
- identify practices posing a danger to the health and welfare of the supervisee's clients or to the public, and
- identify supervisee's inability to practice with skill and safety due to illness; excessive use of alcohol, drugs, narcotics, chemicals or any other substance; or as a result of any mental or physical condition.

Supervisee Obligations

The supervisee has the obligation to fully participate in the supervisory process in a responsible manner. The supervisee should:

- obtain and document client's knowledge of supervision and how the supervisor can be contacted,
- in concert with supervisor, develop goals, learning needs, and learning plan, identifying personal strengths and limitations,
- attend and participate in supervision on the agreed-upon basis,
- prepare for sessions, and include case material from sources such as case records, written narratives and audio-visual records that represent the supervisee's practice or an issue where more guidance is needed,

- ◆ seek feedback and evaluation from the supervisor,
- ◆ seek additional resources and references from supervisor, and
- ◆ maintain documentation of supervision.

Supervision requires a delicate balance between the use of power and authority for the purpose of accountability and the establishment of a safe environment, as with a mentor or guide, for sharing to permit professional growth and development. These guidelines provide a framework to negotiate that balance with confidence.

Responsibilities and Guidelines for AAMFT Approved Supervisors and Supervisors-in-Training

AMERICAN ASSOCIATION FOR MARRIAGE AND FAMILY THERAPY

Approved Supervisors and supervisors-in-training are bound by the AAMFT Code of Ethics and Professional Conduct, *and the following Responsibilities and Guidelines.*

CHARACTERISTICS OF MARRIAGE AND FAMILY THERAPY SUPERVISION

Supervision of marital and family therapy is expected to have the following characteristics:

◆ Face to face conversation with the supervisor, usually in periods of approximately one hour each.
◆ The learning process should be sustained and intense.
◆ Appointments are customarily scheduled once a week; three times weekly is ordinarily the maximum and once every other week the minimum.
◆ Supervision focuses on raw data from a supervisee's continuing clinical practice, which is available to the supervisor through a combination of direct live observation, co-therapy, written clinical notes, audio and video recordings, and live supervision.
◆ It is a process clearly distinguishable from personal psychotherapy and is contracted in order to serve professional goals.
◆ It is normally completed over a period of one to three years.
◆ It is recommended that the experience include at least two supervisees with diverse family therapy theoretical orientations.

The following characteristics are not acceptable as marriage and family therapy supervision:

◆ Peer supervision, i.e., supervision by a person of equivalent, rather than superior, qualifications, status and experience
◆ Supervision by current or former family members or any other person where the nature of the personal relationship prevents or makes difficult the establishment of a professional relationship

- Administrative supervision by an institutional director or executive, for example, conducted to evaluate job performance or for case management, not the quality of therapy given to a client
- A primarily didactic process wherein techniques or procedures are taught in a group setting, classroom, workshop or seminar
- Consultation, staff development or orientation to a field program, or role-playing of family interrelationships as a substitute for current clinical practice in an appropriate clinical situation

SUPERVISING FOR THE AAMFT CLINICAL MEMBERSHIP

AAMFT Approved Supervisors and supervisors-in-training (referred to simply as supervisors in this section) may supervise trainees for AAMFT Clinical Membership. When a supervisor-in-training provides the supervision he/she must obtain ongoing supervision-of-supervision from an AAMFT Approved Supervisor who has provided at least 300 hours of supervision since the Approved Supervisor Designation.

A supervisor must not supervise his or her family members, former family members, clients in therapy, or any other person with whom the nature of the relationship prevents or makes difficult the establishment of a professional supervisory relationship. Refer to the *AAMFT Code of Ethics* for more information and guidance about dual relationships.

Supervisors are responsible for an initial screening to evaluate the trainee's knowledge of systems theory, family development, special family issues, gender and cultural issues, systemic approaches and interventions, human development, human sexuality, and ethical responsibilities.

A contract should be developed for the supervision which delineates fees, hours, time and place of meetings, case responsibility, caseload review, handling of suicide threats, other dangerous clinical situations, and so forth. Supervisors should recognize their legal responsibilities for cases seen by supervisees. For more information about these responsibilities, please contact the AAMFT Legal and Risk Management Plan at (202) 452-0109.

The supervision fee is a function of the contract between supervisors and trainees, including amounts and collection procedures. Fees should be in keeping with the community standard. Approved Supervisors are encouraged to commit a portion of their supervision practice to providing pro-bono or reduced fee supervision to deserving supervisees.

The major emphasis on supervision should be on the trainee's work with marriage/couple and family process, whether the trainee is working with individuals, couples or families. During the supervision session, the trainee's cases, not the supervisor's, are to be discussed.

To count toward AAMFT Membership, ***individual supervision*** must be limited to one or two trainees in face-to-face sessions with the supervisor. ***Group supervision*** must be limited to six supervisees. Trainees in group supervision sessions may not count the time as individual supervision when they are presenting a case. They may count time as individual supervision when providing therapy while the supervisor and a group are observing the therapy. Note: A Supervisor-in-Training providing group supervision *may not* count it towards the 180 hour requirement for the Approved Supervisor Designation.

The progress of trainees should be periodically reviewed according to predetermined supervisory goals, and evaluations should be shared and discussed with trainees. Should a supervisor develop significant concerns about the abilities, philosophical beliefs, or practices of a trainee, the concerns must be shared with the trainee and documented in writing as early as possible. Supervisors do not disclose trainee confidences except in limited circumstances described in the *AAMFT Code of Ethics*. Supervisors and trainees must have a clear understanding about responsibility for evaluations as well as specific details about how the evaluation will be shared.

Supervisors must provide supervision reports as needed by trainees, such as those required for AAMFT Membership. The supervisor's signature on the forms verifies the accuracy of the information reported, so the supervisor is responsible for ensuring that the trainee has actually completed the clinical and supervision hours reported.

Supervision Standards

AMERICAN ASSOCIATION OF PASTORAL COUNSELORS

I. SUPERVISION

Supervision is normally expected to be a regular face-to-face meeting to examine the clinical materials of therapeutic interaction, such as audio or video tapes, process notes, or live observation.

A. The minimum expected frequency is twice a month.

B. Individual supervision may include two trainees. When more than two trainees are present, this is considered group supervision.

C. A Member (PCT) is normally expected to have an hour of supervision for each four to six hours of counseling provided.

D. A Member (Certified) or Member Associate is normally expected to have an hour of supervision for each eight to twelve hours of counseling provided.

II. APPROVAL OF NON-AAPC SUPERVISORS

Any supervisor who is not an AAPC Diplomat, a Fellow working under the supervision of supervision, or an approved supervisor on the staff of an AAPC approved Training Program in Pastoral Counseling must be an accredited/licensed and experienced supervisor in a related mental health discipline such as psychiatry, psychology, social work, or family therapy. The supervisor should have at least five years of clinical experience and two years of supervisory experience.

To secure approval for such a supervisor, contact the Association office for the form "Request for Approval of Non-AAPC Supervisor." The completed form and supporting information is to be sent to the Chair, Regional Certification Committee, for a decision.

Reprinted from AAPC "Supervision Standards" in *Certification Committee Operational Manual*, 1999. Copyright © 1999 by American Association of Pastoral Counselors. Reprinted by permission.

Bibliography

Adelson, M. J. (1995). Clinical supervision of therapists with difficult-to-treat patients. *Bulletin of the Menninger Clinic, 59,* 32–53.

Almonte v. New York Medical College, 851 F.Supp. 34 (D. Conn. 1994).

Alonso, A. (1985). *The quiet profession: Supervisors of psychotherapy.* New York: Macmillan.

Amchin, J., Wettstein, R. M., & Roth, L. H. (1990). Suicide, ethics and the law. In S. J. Blumenthal & D. J. Kupfer (Eds.), *Suicide over the life cycle: Risk factors, assessment, and treatment of suicidal patients* (pp. 637–663). Washington, DC: American Psychiatric Association.

American Association for Marriage and Family Therapy. (1991). *Where to draw the line? Ethical and legal issues in supervision* [Videotape]. Dallas, TX: Author.

American Association for Marriage and Family Therapy. (1998). *AAMFT code of ethics.* Washington, DC: Author.

American Association for Marriage and Family Therapy. (1999a). *AAMFT approved supervisors: Mentors and teachers for the next generation of MFTs.* Washington, DC: Author.

American Association for Marriage and Family Therapy. (1999b). Responsibilities and guidelines for AAMFT approved supervisors and supervisors-in-training. In American Association for Marriage and Family Therapy, *AAMFT approved supervisors: Mentors and teachers for the next generation of MFTs* (pp. 23–28). Washington, DC: Author.

American Association of Pastoral Counselors. (1999). Supervision standards. In American Association of Pastoral Counselors, *Certification committee operational manual* (p. 18). Fairfax, VA: Author.

American Counseling Association. (1995). *Code of ethics and standards of practice.* Alexandria, VA: Author.

American Psychiatric Association. (1998). *The principles of medical ethics with annotations especially applicable to psychiatry.* Washington, DC: Author.

American Psychological Association. (1992). Ethical principles of psychologists and code of conduct. *American Psychologist, 47,* 1597–1611.

American Psychological Association. (1993a). Record keeping guidelines. *American Psychologist, 48,* 984–986.

American Psychological Association. (1993b). Report of the Ethics Committee (1991 and 1992). *American Psychologist, 48,* 811–820.

American Psychological Association. (1994). Report of the Ethics Committee (1993). *American Psychologist, 49,* 659–666.

American Psychological Association. (1995). Report of the Ethics Committee (1994). *American Psychologist, 50,* 1–8.

American Psychological Association. (1996). Report of the Ethics Committee (1995). *American Psychologist, 51,* 1279–1286.

American Psychological Association. (1997). Report of the Ethics Committee (1996). *American Psychologist, 52,* 897–905.

American Psychological Association. (1998). Report of the Ethics Committee (1997). *American Psychologist, 53,* 969–980.

American Psychological Association, Ethics Committee. (1999). Report of the Ethics Committee. *American Psychologist, 54,* 701–710.

Andrews v. United States, 732 F.2d 366 (4th Cir. 1984).

Association for Counselor Education and Supervision. (1990). Standards for counseling supervisors. *Journal of Counseling and Development, 69,* 30–32.

Association for Counselor Education and Supervision. (1993). ACES ethical guidelines for counseling supervisors. *ACES Spectrum, 53,* 5–8.

Association of State and Provincial Psychology Boards. (1991). *ASPPB code of conduct.* Montgomery, AL: Author.

Association of State and Provincial Psychology Boards. (1998a). *Supervision guidelines.* Montgomery, AL: Author.

Association of State and Provincial Psychology Boards. (1998b). *Avoiding liability in mental health practice.* Montgomery, AL: Author.

Baltimore, M. J. (1998). Supervision ethics: Counseling the supervisee. *Family Journal, 6,* 312–314.

Barretta-Herman, A. (1993). On the development of a model of supervision for licensed social work practitioners. *The Clinical Supervisor, 11,* 55–64.

Bartell, P. A., & Rubin, L. J. (1990). Dangerous liaisons: Sexual intimacies in supervision. *Professional Psychology: Research and Practice, 21,* 442–450.

Beis, E. B. (1984). *Mental health and the law.* Rockville, MD: Aspen.

Bennett, B. E., Bryant, B. K., VandenBos, G. R., & Greenwood, A. (1990). *Professional liability and risk management.* Washington, DC: American Psychological Association.

Berger, S. S., & Buchholz, E. S. (1993). On becoming a supervisee: Preparation for learning in a supervisory relationship. *Psychotherapy, 30,* 86–92.

Bernard, J. M., & Goodyear, R. K. (1998). *Fundamentals of clinical supervision* (2nd ed.). Boston: Allyn & Bacon.

Bertram, B., & Wheeler, A. M. (1995). *Legal aspects of counseling: Avoiding lawsuits and legal problems.* Workshop sponsored by the American Counseling Association, Portland, ME.

Blodgett, B. P. (1995). Q.A. monitoring: A supervisor's guide to evaluate practice. *The Clinical Supervisor, 13,* 163–174.

Bongar, B. (1991). *The suicidal patient: Clinical and legal standards of care.* Washington, DC: American Psychological Association.

Bonney, W. (1994). Teaching supervision: Some practical issues for beginning supervisors. *Psychotherapy Bulletin, 29,* 31–36.

Bonosky, N. (1995). Boundary violations in social work supervision: Clinical, educational and legal implications. *The Clinical Supervisor, 13,* 79–95.

Borders, L. D., Bernard, J. M., Dye, H. A., Fong, M. L., Henderson, P., & Nance, D. W. (1991). Curriculum guide for training counseling supervisors: Rationale, development, and implementation. *Counselor Education and Supervision, 31,* 58–82.

Borders, L. D., & Cashwell, C. S. (1992). Supervision regulations in counselor licensure legislation. *Counselor Education and Supervision, 31,* 209–218.

Borders, L. D., Cashwell, C. S., & Rotter, J. C. (1995). Supervision of counselor licensure applicants: A comparative study. *Counselor Education and Supervision, 35,* 54–69.

Borders, L. D., & Leddick, G. R. (1987). *Handbook of counseling supervision.* Alexandria, VA: American Association for Counseling and Development.

Bradley, L. J., & Ladany, N. (Eds.). (2001). *Counselor supervision: Principles, process, and practice.* Philadelphia: Brunner-Routledge.

Bramley, W. (1996). *The supervisory couple in broad-spectrum psychotherapy.* London: Free Association Books.

Brashears, F. (1995). Supervision as social work practice: A reconceptualization. *Social Work, 40,* 692–699.

Bridge, P. J., & Bascue, L. O. (1990). Documentation of psychotherapy supervision. *Psychotherapy in Private Practice, 8,* 79–86.

Calfee, B. E. (1997). Lawsuit prevention techniques. In *The Hatherleigh guide to ethics in therapy* (pp. 109–125). New York: Hatherleigh Press.

Canter, M., Bennett, B., Jones, S., & Nagy, T. (1994). *Ethics for psychologists: A commentary on the APA ethics code.* Washington, DC: American Psychological Association.

Carlozzi, A. F., Romans, J. S. C., Boswell, D. L., Ferguson, D. B., & Whisenhunt, B. J. (1997). Training and supervision practices in counseling and marriage and family therapy programs. *The Clinical Supervisor, 15,* 51–60.

Carroll, M. (1999). Training in the tasks of supervision. In E. Holloway & M. Carroll (Eds.), *Training counselling supervisors* (pp. 44–66). Thousand Oaks, CA: Sage.

Cashwell, C. S., Looby, E. J., & Housley, W. F. (1997). Appreciating cultural diversity through clinical supervision. *The Clinical Supervisor, 15,* 75–85.

Chemtob, C. M., Bauer, G. B., Hamada, R. S., Pelowski, S. R., & Muraoka, M. Y. (1989). Patient suicide: Occupational hazard for psychologists and psychiatrists. *Professional Psychology: Research and Practice, 20,* 294–300.

Chiaferi, R., & Griffin, M. (1997). *Developing fieldwork skills.* Pacific Grove, CA: Brooks/Cole.

Cohen, E. D., & Cohen, G. S. (1999). *The virtuous therapist: Ethical practice of counseling and psychotherapy.* Pacific Grove, CA: Brooks/Cole.

Corey, G., Corey, M. S., & Callanan, P. (1998). *Issues and ethics in the helping professions* (5th ed.). Pacific Grove, CA: Brooks/Cole.

Crawford, R. L. (1994). *Avoiding counselor malpractice.* Alexandria, VA: American Counseling Association.

Crespi, T. D., & Lopez, P. G. (1998). Practicum and internship supervision in the schools: Standards and consideration for school psychology supervisors. *The Clinical Supervisor, 17,* 113–126.

Davis v. Lihm, 430 Mich. 326 (1988).

Davis, J. L., & Mickelson, D. J. (1994). School counselors: Are you aware of ethical and legal aspects of counseling? *The School Counselor, 42,* 5–13.

DeBell, C., & Jones, R. D. (1997). Privileged communication at last? An overview of *Jaffee v. Redmond. Professional Psychology: Research and Practice, 28,* 559–566.

Dickson, D. T. (1995). *Law in the health and human services: A guide for social workers, psychologists, psychiatrists, and related professionals.* New York: Free Press.

Disney, M. J., & Stephens, A. M. (1994). *Legal issues in clinical supervision.* Alexandria, VA: American Counseling Association.

Dye, H. A., & Borders, L. D. (1990). Counseling supervisors: Standards for preparation and practice. *Journal of Counseling and Development, 69,* 30–32.

Eisel v. The Board of Education of Maryland, 597 A.2d 447 (Md. App. Ct. 1991).

Ellis, M. V. (1991). Critical incidents in clinical supervision and in supervisor supervision: Assessing supervisory issues. *Journal of Counseling Psychology, 38,* 342–349.

Ellis, M. V., Ladany, N., Krengel, M., & Schult, D. (1996). Clinical supervision research from 1981 to 1993: A methodological critique. *Journal of Counseling Psychology, 43,* 35–50.

Emory University v. Porubiansky, 282 S.E.2d 903 (Ga. 1981).

Erera, I. P., & Lazar, A. (1994). The administrative and educational functions in supervision: Indications of incompatibility. *The Clinical Supervisor, 12,* 39–55.

Falvey, J. E. (1987). *Handbook of administrative supervision.* Alexandria, VA: American Association for Counseling and Development.

Falvey, J. E., Caldwell, C. F., & Cohen, C. R. (2002). *Documentation in supervision: The Focused Risk Management Supervision System (FoRMSS).* Pacific Grove, CA: Brooks/Cole.

Fischer, L., & Sorenson, G. P. (1996). *School law for counselors, psychologists, and social workers* (2nd ed.). New York: Longman.

Frame, M. W., & Stevens-Smith, P. (1995). Out of harm's way: Enhancing monitoring and dismissal processes in counselor education programs. *Counselor Education and Supervision, 35,* 118–129.

Freeman, B., & McHenry, S. (1996). Clinical supervision of counselors-in-training: A nationwide survey of ideal delivery, goals, and theoretical influences. *Counselor Education and Supervision, 36,* 144–157.

Freeman, E. (1985). The importance of feedback in clinical supervision: Implications for direct practice. *The Clinical Supervisor, 3,* 5–26.

Freeman, S. C. (1993). Structure in counseling supervision. *The Clinical Supervisor, 11,* 245–252.

Frick, D. E., McCartney, C. F., & Lazarus, J. A. (1995). Supervision of sexually exploitative psychiatrists: APA district branch experience. *Psychiatric Annals, 25,* 113–117.

Fukuyama, M. A. (1994). Critical incidents in multicultural counseling supervision: A phenomenological approach to supervision. *Counselor Education and Supervision, 34,* 142–151.

Garner, B. A. (Ed.). (1999). *Black's law dictionary* (8th ed.). St. Paul, MN: West Publishing.

Garrett, K., & Barretta-Herman, A. (1995). Missing links: Professional development in school social work. *Journal of Social Work Education, 17,* 235–243.

Getz, H. G. (1999). Assessment of clinical supervisor competencies. *Journal of Counseling and Development, 77,* 491–497.

Gibelman, M., & Schervish, P. H. (1997). Supervision in social work: Characteristics and trends in a changing environment. *The Clinical Supervisor, 16,* 1–15.

Gilmore v. Board of Psychologist Examiners, 725 P.2d 400 (Or. Ct. App. 1986).

Glaser, R. D., & Thorpe, J. S. (1986). Unethical intimacy: A survey of sexual contact and advances between psychology educators and female graduate students. *American Psychologist, 41,* 43–51.

Glenn, E., & Serovich, J. M. (1994). Documentation of family therapy supervision: A rationale and method. *The American Journal of Family Therapy, 22,* 345–355.

Glosoff, H. L., Herlihy, S. B., Herlihy, B., & Spence, E. B. (1997). Privileged communication in the psychologist–client relationship. *Professional Psychology: Research and Practice, 28,* 573–581.

Goodyear, R. K., & Bernard, J. M. (1999). Clinical supervision: Lessons from the literature. *Counselor Education and Supervision, 38,* 6–21.

Greben, S. E., & Ruskin, R. (Eds.). (1994). *Clinical perspectives on psychotherapy supervision.* Washington, DC: American Psychiatric Press.

Guest, C. L., & Dooley, K. (1999). Supervisor malpractice: Liability to the supervisee in clinical supervision. *Counselor Education and Supervision, 38,* 269–279.

Haas, L. J., & Hall, J. E. (1991). Impaired, unethical or incompetent? Ethical issues for colleagues and ethics committees. *Register Report, 16,* 6–9.

Haas, L. J., & Malouf, J. L. (1995). *Keeping up the good work: A practitioner's guide to mental health ethics* (2nd ed.). Sarasota, FL: Professional Resource Exchange.

Haber, R. (1996). *Dimensions of psychotherapy supervision: Maps and means.* New York: Norton.

Hall, J. (1988a). Protection in supervision. *Register Report, 14,* 3–4.

Hall, J. (1988b). Dual relationships in supervision. *Register Report, 15,* 5–6.

Handelsman, M. M. (1986). Problems with ethics training by "Osmosis." *Professional Psychology: Research and Practice, 17,* 371–372.

Hanna, M. A., & Smith, J. (1998). Using rubrics for documentation of clinical work supervision. *Counselor Education and Supervision, 37,* 269–278.

Hardcastle, D. A. (1991). Toward a model for supervision: A peer supervision pilot project. *The Clinical Supervisor, 9,* 63–76.

Harrar, W. R., VandeCreek, L., & Knapp, S. (1990). Ethical and legal aspects of clinical supervision. *Professional Psychology: Research and Practice, 21,* 37–41.

Hassenfield, I. N. (1987). Ethics and the role of the supervisor of psychotherapy. *Journal of Psychiatric Education, 11,* 73–77.

Hayes, L. L. (1998, December). Supervision of school counselors debated. *Counseling Today,* pp. 1, 19.

Helms, J. E., & Cook, D. A. (1999). Using race and culture in therapy supervision. In J. E. Helms & D. A. Cook (Eds.), *Using race and culture in counseling and psychotherapy: Theory and process.* Boston: Allyn & Bacon.

Henderson, P., & Lampe, R. E. (1992). Clinical supervision of school counselors. *The School Counselor, 39,* 151–157.

Hess, A. K. (1998). Contemporary approaches to the supervision of psychotherapy. *The Clinical Supervisor, 17,* 149–154.

Hewson, J. (1999). Training supervisors to contract in supervision. In E. Holloway & M. Carroll (Eds.), *Training counselling supervisors* (pp. 67–91). Thousand Oaks, CA: Sage.

Hill v. Kokosky, M.D., 463 N.W.2d 265 (Mich. Ct. App. 1990).

Hobbs, B. B., & Collison, B. B. (1995). School-community agency collaboration: Implications for the school counselor. *The School Counselor, 43,* 58–65.

Hobson, S. M., & Kanitz, H. M. (1996). Multicultural counseling: An ethical issue for school counselors. *The School Counselor, 43,* 245–255.

Hoffman, L. W. (1994). The training of psychotherapy supervisors: A barren scape. *Psychotherapy in Private Practice, 13,* 23–42.

Holloway, E. (1999). A framework for supervision training. In E. Holloway & M. Carroll (Eds.), *Training counselling supervisors* (pp. 8–43). Thousand Oaks, CA: Sage.

Holloway, E., & Carroll, M. (Eds.). (1999). *Training counselling supervisors.* Thousand Oaks, CA: Sage.

Holloway, E. L., & Neufeldt, S. A. (1995). Supervision: Its contribution to treatment efficacy. *Journal of Consulting and Clinical Psychology, 63,* 207–213.

Hopkins, B. R., & Anderson, B. S. (1990). *The counselor and the law* (3rd ed.). Alexandria, VA: American Association for Counseling and Development.

Horejsi, C. R., & Garthwait, C. L. (1999). *The social work practicum: A guide and workbook for students.* Boston: Allyn & Bacon.

Huber, C. H. (1994). *Ethical, legal, and professional issues in the practice of marriage and family therapy* (2nd ed.). New York: Merrill.

In re Kozlov, 398 A.2d 882 (N.J. 1979).

In the Matter of C.P., 563 N.E.2d 1275 (Ind. 1990).

Inskipp, F. (1999). Training supervisees to use supervision. In E. Holloway & M. Carroll (Eds.), *Training counselling supervisors* (pp. 184–210). Thousand Oaks, CA: Sage.

Inskipp, F., & Proctor, P. (1989). *Skills for supervising and being supervised* (Principles of Counseling audiotape series). East Sussex, England: Alexia Publishers.

Isaacs, M. L., & Stone, C. (1999). School counselors and confidentiality: Factors affecting professional choices. *Professional School Counseling, 2,* 258–266.

Itzhaky, H., & Itzhaky, T. (1996). The therapy-supervision dialect. *Clinical Social Work Journal, 24,* 77–88.

Jablonski v. United States, 712 F.2d 391 (9th Cir. 1983).

Jacob-Timm, S. (1999). Ethically challenging situations encountered by school psychologists. *Psychology in the Schools, 36,* 205–217.

Jacobs, D., David, P., & Meyer, D. J. (1995). *The supervisory encounter.* New Haven, CT: Yale University Press.

Jaffee v. Redmond, 518 U.S. 1 (1996).

Kadushin, A. (1992). *Supervision in social work* (3rd ed.). New York: Columbia University Press.

Kaiser, T. L. (1997). *Supervisory relationships: Exploring the human element.* Pacific Grove, CA: Brooks/Cole.

Kalenevitch v. Finger, 595 A.2d 1224 (Pa. Super. Ct. 1991).

Kapp, M. B. (1984). Supervising professional trainees: Legal implications for mental health institutions and practitioners. *Hospital and Community Psychiatry, 35,* 143–147.

Kerson, T. S. (1994). Introduction: Field instruction in social work settings: A framework for teaching. *The Clinical Supervisor, 12,* 1–31.

Kinsella v. Kinsella, 696 A.2d 556 (N.J. 1997).

Kleespies, P. M., Smith, M. R., & Becker, B. R. (1990). Psychology interns as patient suicide survivors: Incidence, impact, and recovery. *Professional Psychology: Research and Practice, 21,* 251–263.

Knapp, S., & VandeCreek, L. (1996). Questions and answers about clinical supervision. In L. VandeCreek, S. Knapp, & T. L. Jackson (Eds.), *Innovations in clinical practice: A sourcebook* (Vol. 15, pp. 189–197). Sarasota, FL: Professional Resource Exchange.

Knapp, S., & VandeCreek, L. (1997a). Ethical and legal aspects of clinical supervision. In C. E. Watkins (Ed.), *Handbook of psychotherapy supervision* (pp. 589–602). New York: Wiley.

Knapp, S., & VandeCreek, L. (1997b). *Jaffee v. Redmond*: The Supreme Court recognizes a psychotherapy–patient privilege in federal courts. *Professional Psychology: Research and Practice, 28,* 567–572.

Koocher, G. P., & Keith-Spiegel, P. (1998). *Ethics in psychology: Professional standards and cases* (2nd ed.). New York: Oxford University Press.

Kurpius, D., Gibson, G., Lewis, J., & Corbet, M. (1991). Ethical issues in supervising counseling practitioners. *Counselor Education and Supervision, 31,* 48–57.

Kutcher, J., & Jones, L. (1996). The use of client and counselor feedback forms in the supervision of beginning therapists. In L. VandeCreek, S. Knapp, & T. L. Jackson (Eds.), *Innovations in clinical practice: A sourcebook* (Vol. 15, pp. 255–262). Sarasota, FL: Professional Resource Exchange.

Ladany, N., Hill, C. E., Corbett, M. M., & Nutt, E. A. (1996). Nature, extent, and importance of what psychotherapy trainees do not disclose to their supervisors. *Journal of Counseling Psychology, 43,* 10–24.

Ladany, N., Lehrman-Waterman, D., Molinaro, M., & Wolgast, B. (1999). Psychotherapy supervisor ethical practices. *The Counseling Psychologist, 27,* 443–475.

Lamb, D. H., & Catanzaro, S. J. (1998). Sexual and nonsexual boundary violations involving psychologists, clients, supervisees, and students: Implications for professional practice. *Professional Psychology: Research and Practice, 29,* 498–503.

Lamb, D. H., Cochran, D. J., & Jackson, V. R. (1991). Training and organizational issues associated with identifying and responding to intern impairment. *Professional Psychology: Research and Practice, 22,* 291–296.

Lehner, G. F. J. (1952). Defining psychotherapy. *American Psychologist, 7,* 547.

Leonardelli, C. A., & Gratz, R. R. (1985). Roles and responsibilities in fieldwork experience: A social systems approach. *The Clinical Supervisor, 3*(3), 15–24.

Leong, F. T. L., & Wagner, N. S. (1994). Cross-cultural counseling supervision: What do we know? What do we need to know? *Counselor Education and Supervision, 34,* 117–131.

Lipardi v. Sears, Roebuck & Co., 497 F.Supp. 185 (D. Neb. 1980).

Malley, P. B., & Reilly, E. P. (1999). *Legal and ethical dimensions for mental health professionals.* Philadelphia: Accelerated Development.

McCarthy, M. M., & Sorenson, G. P. (1993). School counselors and consultants: Legal duties and liabilities. *Journal of Counseling and Development, 72,* 159–167.

McCarthy, P., Kulakowski, D., & Kenfield, J. A. (1994). Clinical supervision practices of licensed psychologists. *Professional Psychology: Research and Practice, 25,* 177–181.

McCarthy, P., Sugden, S., Koker, M., Lamendola, F., Maurer, S., & Renninger, S. (1995). A practical guide to informed consent in clinical supervision. *Counselor Education and Supervision, 35,* 130–138.

McConnell, C. R. (Ed.). (1993). *The health care supervisor: Law.* Gaithersburg, MD: Aspen.

Meyer, R. G., Landis, E. R., & Hays, J. R. (1988). *Law for the psychotherapist.* New York: Norton.

Mitchell, R. W. (1991). *Documentation in counseling records.* Alexandria, VA: American Counseling Association.

Moline, M. E., Williams, G. T., & Austin, K. M. (1998). *Documenting psychotherapy.* Thousand Oaks, CA: Sage.

Monahan, J. (1993). Limiting therapist exposure to Tarasoff liability: Guidelines for risk containment. *American Psychologist, 48,* 242–250.

Montgomery, L. M., Cupit, B. E., & Wimberley, T. K. (1999). Complaints, malpractice, and risk management: Professional issues and personal experiences. *Professional Psychology: Research and Practice, 30,* 402–410.

Munson, C. E. (1993). *Clinical social work supervision* (2nd ed.). New York: Haworth.

National Association of Social Workers. (1989). *NASW standards for the practice of clinical social work.* Washington, DC: Author.

National Association of Social Workers. (1994). *Guidelines for clinical social work supervision.* Washington, DC: Author.

National Association of Social Workers. (1997). *Code of ethics.* Washington, DC: Author.

National Board for Certified Counselors. (1997). *Code of ethics.* Greensboro, NC: Author.

National Board for Certified Counselors. (1998). *Standards for the ethical practice of clinical supervision.* Greensboro, NC: Author.

Navin, S., Beamish, P., & Johanson, G. (1995). Ethical practices of field-based mental health counselor supervisors. *Journal of Mental Health Counseling, 17,* 243–253.

Nelson v. Gillette, 571 N.W.2d 332 (N.D. 1997).

Neufeldt, S. A. (1999). *Supervision strategies for the first practicum* (2nd ed.). Alexandria, VA: American Counseling Association.

Norcross, J. C., & Beutler, L. E. (1998). Advances and possibilities in supervising eclectic psychotherapy. *The Clinical Supervisor, 17,* 135–147.

Norcross, J. C., Prochaska, J. O., & Farber, J. (1993). Psychologists conducting psychotherapy: New findings and historical comparisons of the Psychotherapy Division membership. *Psychotherapy, 30,* 692–697.

Osborn, C. J., & Davis, T. E. (1996). The supervision contract: Making it perfectly clear. *The Clinical Supervisor, 14,* 121–134.

Osipow, S., & Fitzgerald, I. (1986). An occupational analysis of counseling psychology: How special is the specialty? *American Psychologist, 41,* 535–545.

Peck v. Counseling Service of Addison County, Inc., 499 A.2d 422 (Vt. 1985).

Perlin, M. L. (1997). The "duty to protect" others from violence. In *The Hatherleigh guide to ethics in therapy* (pp. 127–146). New York: Hatherleigh Press.

Pesce v. J. Sterling Morton High School, District 201, 830 F.2d 789 (7th Cir. 1987).

Pope, K. S., & Bajt, T. R. (1988). When laws and values conflict: A dilemma for psychologists. *American Psychologist, 43,* 828–829.

Pope, K. S., & Vasquez, M. J. (1998). *Ethics in psychotherapy and counseling* (2nd ed.). San Francisco: Jossey-Bass.

Pope, K. S., & Vetter, V. A. (1992). Ethical dilemmas encountered by members of the American Psychological Association: A national survey. *American Psychologist, 47,* 397–411.

Porter v. Nemir, 900 S.W.2d 376 (Tex. App. 1995).

Powell, D. J. (1993). *Clinical supervision in alcohol and drug abuse counseling.* San Francisco: Jossey-Bass.

Pozgar, G. D. (1996). *Legal aspects of health care administration* (6th ed.). Gaithersburg, MD: Aspen.

Prest, L. A., Schindler-Zimmerman, T., & Sporakowski, M. J. (1992). The initial supervision session checklist (ISSC): A guide for the MFT supervision process. *The Clinical Supervisor, 10,* 117–133.

Ray v. County of Delaware, 239 A.D.2d 755 (N.Y. App. Div. 1997).

Reaves, R. P. (1998). *Avoiding liability in mental health practice.* Montgomery, AL: Association of State and Provincial Psychology Boards.

Rich, P. (1993). The form, function, and content of clinical supervision: An integrated model. *The Clinical Supervisor, 11,* 173–178.

Richard, R., & Rodway, M. R. (1992). The peer consultation group: A problem-solving perspective. *The Clinical Supervisor, 10,* 83–100.

Roach, W. H., & Aspen Health Law and Compliance Center. (1998). *Medical records and the law* (3rd ed.). Gaithersburg, MD: Aspen.

Roberts, E. B., & Borders, L. D. (1994). Supervision of school counselors: Administrative, program, and counseling. *The School Counselor, 41,* 149–157.

Robiner, W. N., Fuhrman, M. J., & Bobbitt, B. L. (1990). Supervision in the practice of psychology: Toward the development of a supervisory instrument. *Psychotherapy in Private Practice, 8,* 87–98.

Robiner, W. N., Fuhrman, M. J., & Ristredts, S. (1993). Evaluation difficulties in supervising psychology interns. *Clinical Psychologist, 46,* 3–13.

Robke, D. O. (1993, May-June). Supervisor liability: The buck stops here. *Managed Care News,* 14–15.

Rodenhauser, P. (1995). Experiences and issues in the professional development of psychiatrists for supervising psychotherapy. *The Clinical Supervisor, 13,* 7–22.

Rodenhauser, P. (1996). On the future of psychotherapy supervision and psychiatry. *Academic Psychiatry, 20,* 82–91.

Rodenhauser, P. (1997). Psychotherapy supervision: Prerequisites and problems in the process. In C. E. Watkins (Ed.), *Handbook of psychotherapy supervision* (pp. 527–548). New York: Wiley.

Rodolfa, E. R., Haynes, S., Kaplan, D., Chamberlain, M., Goh, M., Marquis, P., & McBride, L. (1998). Supervisory practices of psychologists—Does time since licensure matter? *The Clinical Supervisor, 17,* 177–183.

Ronnestad, M. H., & Skovholt, T. M. (1993). Supervision of beginning and advanced graduate students of counseling and psychotherapy. *Journal of Counseling and Development, 71,* 396–405.

Rost v. State Board of Psychology, 659 A.2d 626 (Pa. Commw. Ct. 1995).

Rubin, S. S. (1997). Balancing duty to client and therapist in supervision: Clinical, ethical and training issues. *The Clinical Supervisor, 16,* 1–23.

Rubinstein, G. (1992). Supervision and psychotherapy: Toward redefining the differences. *The Clinical Supervisor, 10,* 97–116.

Runyon v. Smith, 730 A.2d 881 (N.J. App. Div. 1999).

Rutter, P. (1989). Sex in the forbidden zone. *Psychology Today, 23,* 34–38.

Sangiuolo v. Leventhal, 505 N.Y.S.2d 507 (Sup. Ct. 1986).

Schindler, N. J., & Talen, M. R. (1996). Supervision 101: The basic elements for teaching beginning supervisors. *The Clinical Supervisor, 14,* 109–120.

Schneider v. Plymouth State College, 1999 WL 1188864 (Dec. 16, 1999, N.H.).

Schroeder, L. O. (1995). *The legal environment of social work* (Rev. ed.). Washington, DC: National Association of Social Workers.

Shanfield, S. B., Matthews, K. L., & Hetherly, V. (1993). What do excellent psychotherapy supervisors do? *American Journal of Psychiatry, 150,* 1081–1084.

Sherry, P. (1991). Ethical issues in the conduct of supervision. *The Counseling Psychologist, 19,* 566–584.

Shulman, L. (1993). *Interactional supervision.* Washington, DC: National Association of Social Workers.

Shuman, D. W., & Weiner, M. S. *The privilege study: An empirical examination of the psychotherapist–patient privilege.* 60 N.C. L. Rev 893, 912 (1982).

Shuster v. Altenberg, 424 N.W.2d 159 (Wis. 1988).

Simmons v. United States, 805 F.2d 1363 (9th Cir. 1986).

Slovenko, R. (1980). Legal issues in psychotherapy supervision. In A. K. Hess (Ed.), *Psychotherapy supervision* (pp. 453–473). New York: Wiley.

Soisson, E. L., VandeCreek, L., & Knapp, S. (1987). Thorough record keeping: A good defense in a litigious era. *Professional Psychology: Research and Practice, 18,* 498–502.

Steckler v. Ohio State Board of Psychology, 613 N.E.2d 1070 (Ohio App. 1992).

Steinman, S. O., Richardson, N. F., & McEnroe, T. (1998). *The ethical decision-making manual for helping professionals.* Pacific Grove, CA: Brooks/Cole.

Stoltenberg, C. D., McNeill, B. W., & Crethar, H. C. (1994). Changes in supervision as counselors and therapists gain experience: A review. *Professional Psychology: Research and Practice, 25,* 416–449.

Stromberg, C. D., Haggerty, D., Mishkin, B. J., Liebenluft, R. F., McMillan, M. H., Rubin, B. L., & Trilling, H. R. (1988). *The psychologist's legal handbook.* Washington, DC: National Register of Health Service Providers in Psychology.

Stromberg, C., & Dellinger, A. (1993). Malpractice and other professional liability. *The Psychologist's Legal Update., 3,* 3–15.

Stromberg, C., Lindberg, D., Mishkin, B., & Baker, M. (1993). Privacy, confidentiality and privilege. *The Psychologist's Legal Update, 1,* 3–16.

Stromberg, C., Schneider, J., & Joondeph, B. (1993). Dealing with potentially dangerous patients. *The Psychologist's Legal Update, 2,* 3–12.

Sumerall, S. W., Barke, C. R., Timmons, P. L., Oehlert, M. E., Lopez, S. J., & Trent, D. D. (1998). The adaptive counseling and therapy model and supervision of mental health care. *The Clinical Supervisor, 17,* 171–176.

Suslovich v. New York State Education Department, 174 A.D.2d 802 (N.Y. App. Div. 1991).

Sutton, J. M., & Page, B. J. (1994). Post-degree clinical supervision of school counselors. *The School Counselor, 42,* 32–39.

Swenson, L. C. (1997). *Psychology and law for the helping professions* (2nd ed.). Pacific Grove, CA: Brooks/Cole.

Szasz, T. (1986). The case against suicide prevention. *American Psychologist, 41,* 806–812.

Taibbi, R. (1995). *Clinical supervision: A four-stage process of growth and discovery.* Milwaukee, WI: Families International, Inc.

Tanenbaum, R. L., & Berman, M. A. (1990). Ethical and legal issues in psychotherapy supervision. *Psychotherapy in Private Practice, 8,* 65–77.

Tarasoff v. Regents of the University of California, 551 P.2d 334 (Cal. 1976).

Tyler, J. M., & Tyler, C. L. (1997). Ethics in supervision: Managing supervisee rights and supervisor responsibilities. In *The Hatherleigh guide to ethics in therapy* (pp. 75–95). New York: Hatherleigh Press.

Vasquez, M. J. T. (1992). Psychologist as clinical supervisor: Promoting ethical practice. *Professional Psychology: Research and Practice, 23,* 196–202.

Vesper, J. H., & Brock, G. W. (1991). *Ethics, legalities, and professional practice issues in marriage and family therapy.* Boston: Allyn & Bacon.

Watkins, C. E. (1995). Psychotherapy supervision in the 1990s: Some observations and reflections. *American Journal of Psychotherapy, 49,* 568–581.

Watkins, C. E. (Ed.) (1997a). *Handbook of psychotherapy supervision.* New York: Wiley.

Watkins, C. E. (1997b). Some concluding thoughts about psychotherapy supervision. In C. E. Watkins (Ed.), *Handbook of psychotherapy supervision* (pp. 603–616). New York: Wiley.

Weiner, B. A., & Wettstein, R. M. (1993). *Legal issues in mental health care.* New York: Plenum.

Welch, B. L. (1998). Walking the documentation tightrope. In *Insight: Safeguarding psychologists against liability risks* (Edition 2). Amityville, NY: American Professional Agency, Inc.

Welch, B. L. (1999). Boundary violations: In the eye of the beholder. In *Insight* (Edition 1). Amityville, NY: American Professional Agency, Inc.

Welfel, E. R. (1998a). Can supervision be ethical if not face-to-face? *ACES Spectrum, 59,* 4–5.

Welfel, E. R. (1998b). *Ethics in counseling and psychotherapy: Standards, research, and emerging issues.* Pacific Grove, CA: Brooks/Cole.

White v. North Carolina State Board of Examiners of Practicing Psychologists, 388 S.E.2d 148 (N.C. Ct. App. 1990).

Whitman, S. M., & Jacobs, E. G. (1998). Responsibilities of the psychotherapy supervisor. *American Journal of Psychotherapy, 52,* 166–175.

Wigmore, 89 Evidence, 2192 at 70, 73 (McNaughton revision, 3rd ed., 1961).

Williams, L. (1994). A tool for training supervisors: Using the supervision feedback form (SFF). *Journal of Marital and Family Therapy, 20,* 311–315.

Younggren, J. N. (1995). Informed consent: Simply a reminder. *Register Report, 21,* 6–7.

Zuckerman, E. L. (1997). *The paper office* (2nd ed.). New York: Guilford Press.

Author Index

Subject Index

Credits

Material for Tables 3.1, 3.2, 4.1, 5.1, 6.1, 6.2, 7.1, 8.1, 8.2, and 8.3 was taken from these sources:

Reprinted from *AAMFT Code of Ethics*. Copyright 1998 American Association for Marriage and Family Therapy. Reprinted with permission.

Reprinted from *AAMFT Supervisor Designation: Standards and Responsibilities Handbook*. Copyright 1999 American Association for Marriage and Family Therapy. Reprinted with permission.

Reprinted from AAPC Code of Ethics, Standards I.F, IV.C, V.A, V.B, V.C, and V.D, and from AAPC supervision standards in *Certification Committee Operational Manual*, 1999. Copyright © 1999 by American Association of Pastoral Counselors. Reprinted by permission.

Reprinted from *ACA Code of Ethics and Standards of Practice*. © ACA. Reprinted with permission. No further reproduction authorized without written permission of the American Counseling Association.

Reprinted from *ACES Standards for Counseling Supervisors* and *ACES Ethical Guidelines for Counseling Supervisors*. © ACA. Reprinted with permission. No further reproduction authorized without written permission of the American Counseling Association.

APA Principles of Medical Ethics with Annotations Especially Applicable to Psychiatry, American Psychiatry Association. Copyright © 1999 by the American Psychiatric Association. Reprinted with permission.

American Psychological Association (1992). Excerpts from the Ethical Principles of Psychologists and Code of Conduct. *American Psychologist, 47,* 1597–1611. Copyright © 1992 by the American Psychological Association. Adapted with permission.

ASPPB Code of Conduct, Rules A.1 and 6.d, Association of State and Provincial Psychology Boards. Copyright © 1991 by the Association of State and Provincial Psychology Boards. Reprinted with permission.

TO THE OWNER OF THIS BOOK:

We hope that you have found *Managing Clinical Supervision: Ethical Practice and Legal Risk Management,* useful. So that this book can be improved in a future edition, would you take the time to complete this sheet and return it? Thank you.

School and address: _____

Department: _____

Instructor's name: _____

1. What I like most about this book is: _____

_____

_____

2. What I like least about this book is: _____

_____

_____

3. My general reaction to this book is: _____

_____

4. The name of the course in which I used this book is: _____

_____

5. Were all of the chapters of the book assigned for you to read? _____

   If not, which ones weren't? _____

6. In the space below, or on a separate sheet of paper, please write specific suggestions for improving this book and anything else you'd care to share about your experience in using the book.

_____

_____

_____

_____

_____

Optional:

Your name: _____ Date: _____

May Brooks/Cole quote you, either in promotion for *Managing Clinical Supervision: Ethical Practice and Legal Risk Management* or in future publishing ventures?

Yes: _____ No: _____

Sincerely,

Janet Elizabeth Falvey

FOLD HERE

FOLD HERE

Brooks/Cole is dedicated to publishing quality books for the helping professions. If you would like to learn more about our publications, please use this mailer to request our catalogue.

Name: ──────────────────────────────

Street Address: ──────────────────────────

City, State, and Zip: ──────────────────────

FOLD HERE

FOLD HERE